2022 年第 1 辑

# 新市場財政學研究

## The Journal of Neo-Public Finance

李俊生 姚东旻 主编

[中英文双语]

02

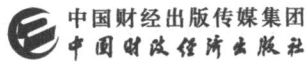

图书在版编目（CIP）数据

新市场财政学研究. 2022年. 第1辑：汉英对照/李俊生，姚东旻主编. --北京：中国财政经济出版社，2022.11

ISBN 978-7-5223-1722-9

Ⅰ.①新… Ⅱ.①李…②姚… Ⅲ.①财政学-研究-汉、英 Ⅳ.①F810

中国版本图书馆CIP数据核字（2022）第196930号

责任编辑：闫　娟
封面设计：陈宇琰

新市场财政学研究

XINSHICHANG CAIZHENGXUE YANJIU

中国财政经济出版社 出版

URL：http：//www.cfeph.cn
E-mail：cfeph@cfeph.cn

（版权所有　翻印必究）

社址：北京市海淀区阜成路甲28号　邮政编码：100142
营销中心电话：010-88191537
北京财经印刷厂印刷　各地新华书店经销
成品尺寸：185mm×260mm　16开　15.5印张　247 000字
2022年11月第1版　2022年11月北京第1次印刷
定价：68.00元
ISBN 978-7-5223-1722-9
（图书出现印装问题，本社负责调换）
本社质量投诉电话：010-88190744
打击盗版举报热线：010-88191661　QQ：2242791300

# 新市场财政学研究
## The Journal of Neo-Public Finance

**主　编**

李俊生　姚东旻

**编辑委员会**（以汉语拼音为序）

| | |
|---|---|
| 樊丽明 | 山东大学 |
| 高培勇 | 中国社会科学院 |
| 耿　曙 | 浙江大学 |
| 郭庆旺 | 中国人民大学 |
| 李俊生 | 中央财经大学 |
| 刘　蓉 | 西南财经大学 |
| 刘尚希 | 中国财政科学研究院 |
| 刘　怡 | 北京大学 |
| 马海涛 | 中央财经大学 |
| 乔宝云 | 中央财经大学 |
| 孙　开 | 东北财经大学 |
| 童锦治 | 厦门大学 |
| 王　乔 | 江西财经大学 |
| 杨灿明 | 中南财经政法大学 |
| 于海峰 | 广东财经大学 |

**编辑部主任**

姚东旻

**主办单位**

中国财政发展协同创新中心
http://ccfd.cufe.edu.cn/
新市场财政学研究所
http://ccfd.cufe.edu.cn/xscxzyjs/index.htm

中国财政发展协同创新中心

# 目录

| | | |
|---|---|---|
| 001 | 建设新时代中国特色社会主义财政学 | 于海峰　朱翠华 |
| 017 | How to Construct Socialist Public Finance with Chinese Characteristics in the New Era | *Yu Haifeng　Zhu Cuihua* |
| 044 | 财政的哲学 | 黎旭东 |
| 068 | The Philosophy of Public Finance | *Li Xudong* |
| 109 | 财政汲取与国家能力：基于文献的考察 | 吕冰洋　胡　深 |
| 121 | Fiscal Extraction and State Capacity: An Investigation Based on Literature | *Lyu Bingyang　Hu Shen* |
| 138 | 中国的古典市场经济理论 | 林光彬 |
| 157 | Chinese Classical Theory of Market Economics | *Lin Guangbin* |
| 195 | 《管子》中的商贸立国方略及其在后世帝国的命运 | 刘守刚 |
| 211 | Strategy of Basing National Development on Trade in *Guanzi* and its Fate in the Empire | *Liu Shougang* |

# 建设新时代中国特色社会主义财政学

于海峰　朱翠华

**摘　要**：中国特色社会主义进入了新时代。财政作为国家治理的基础和重要支柱，在新时代必然呈现新的特征、新的变化、新的目标。为了分析新时代中国特色社会主义财政学建设问题，本文从如何理解财政是国家治理的基础和重要支柱入手，分析了新时代财政职能，在此基础上研究了财政学基本框架的构建问题以及新时代财政学建设重点等几个方面，总结出新时代财政职能包括作为国家治理的物质基础，作为国家治理体系的机制保障以及作为国家治理能力提升有力监督三个方面。财政学在新时代国家治理的视界内在研究目标、研究范围、研究内容、研究工具等方面都将发生新的变化，本文最后对中国特色财政学学科体系构建提出了初步设想。

**关键词**：新时代　国家治理体系　国家治理能力　财政学

[中图分类号] F812　　[文献标志码] A

## 一、引言

"经过长期努力，中国特色社会主义进入了新时代，这是我国发展新的历史方位。"[1]在这个新时代，党中央提出了国家治理体系的构建以及国家治理体系的现代化，并将财政定位为国家治理的基础和重要支柱[2]，将财政提到了一个前所未有的新的战略高度，引起了学者们的广泛关注和讨论。自凯恩斯经济

---

[作者简介]：于海峰，广东财经大学校长，经济学博士、教授，主要研究领域为财政税收与公共经济学。朱翠华，广东财经大学财政税务学院副教授，经济学博士，主要研究领域为财税政策与就业问题研究。

以来，政府干预宏观经济成为政府活动的重要内容，财政收支也以调节经济、稳定经济为根本目标。受"经济帝国主义"①的影响，财政学研究主题主要限定在市场经济条件下市场失灵的调节、公共物品的供给等。许多政治学家、财政学家对此也曾提出质疑。尤其是党的十八届三中全会以来，财政活动上升到了国家治理层面，国家治理除经济领域外，还应包括政治、社会、环境等各个方面。由此掀起了关于财政学学科属性的大讨论，争论的焦点在于财政是属于经济学科还是其他？尽管这一争论至今仍未有定论，但却在争论中发现，财政活动目标不应仅局限于经济领域。李俊生（2017）阐释了如何构建新市场条件下更具解释能力和预测能力的财政理论基础[3]。安体富（2016）重新审视了财政的学科属性和定位[4]。吴俊培（2017）讨论了关于财政理论的三个基本问题[5]。邓力平（2016）构建了中国特色社会主义财税"五大特征"基本框架[6]。高培勇（2017）探讨了国家治理体系中的财政理论建设问题[7]。刘晓路、郭庆旺（2016）梳理了财政学300年来的发展历程[8]。孙正（2017）研究了财政学学科属性及其未来发展[9]。这些研究从不同角度探讨了财政学科发展、财政框架构建、财政学科属性等问题，为财政学发展提供了许多借鉴和启示。党的十九大对我国社会主要矛盾做了新的研判，对社会主义现代化强国特征定义做了新的拓展。我国进入了社会主义新时代，财政将在新时代履行新任务、实现新目标、实施新战略过程中大有所为。新时代条件下财政的职能以及财政框架与市场经济条件下满足公共物品供给的财政也将有新的侧重。新时代条件下财政学的分析和研究具有重要的理论和现实意义。从实践方面来看，这是提升国家治理能力，全面建成小康社会伟大实践的迫切要求。从理论方面来看，这是繁荣发展财政科学自身的内在要求。能指导实践的理论才是伟大的，从实践中来的理论才是正确的。我国经济形势、政府执政理念发生了重大变化，财政理论研究也要有新的发展和变化。本文试图从为什么，是什么以及如何做三个角度分析国家治理体系框架下财政是什么，为什么财政职能发生了变化以及新时代财政框架和未来发展。

本文主要包括以下五个部分：第一部分介绍了建设新时代中国特色社会主义财政学的意义、必要性及本文结构。第二部分分析了如何理解财政是国家治

---

① 经济帝国主义指经济学将其研究领域扩展到传统的非经济学关注的领域，经济学研究范围不断扩张，出现殖民其他学科的趋势。

理的基础和重要支柱，为进一步分析新时代中国特色社会主义财政职能以及财政新框架理清理论基础。第三部分重点分析了财政在国家治理体系现代化以及治理能力提升中所发挥的职能。第四部分初步提出了新时代中国特色社会主义财政学的基本框架，即在理清新时代中国特色社会主义特征的基础上，结合党的十八届三中全会以及十九大提出的建立现代财政制度的目标，初步构建了财政学基本框架。第五部分对如何构建新时代财政学科体系做出了初步设想。

## 二、基于国家治理视角的财政

党的十八届三中全会将财政定位为国家治理的基础和重要支柱，从新的历史地位和高度诠释了何为财政，党的十九大报告中又再次强调了财政在国家治理中的地位。那么，如何理解财政是国家治理的基础和重要支柱呢？为了回答这一问题，应当从何为国家治理以及国家治理体系以及治理能力现代化的要求两个方面来回答。

### （一）国家治理与财政

治理一词本义为"统治"或"管理"，如《汉书·赵广汉传》："壹切治理，威名远闻。"及《孔子家语·贤君》："吾欲使官府治理，为之奈何？"[10]。西方文化中"治理"一词来源于古希腊及古拉丁语，同样具有"统治"和"操纵"之义，并且未与"统治"一词做区分。然而，随着经济社会的不断演化，治理不断地被应用于多种情境，从最初的"治理危机"到后来的"全球治理""经济治理""社会治理"等，治理一词的内涵发生了根本性的转变，治理的理论及其实践导致其含义与最初的"统治""管理"的本义相去甚远，成为从经济、社会等领域扩展到政府以及国家层面的具有现代化色彩的词汇。党的十八届三中全会以来，国家治理现代化成为我国全面深化改革的总目标，在《中共中央关于全面深化改革若干重大问题的决定》中提到"治理"多达二十多次，包括国家治理、依法治理、治理能力等。"治理"与"统治"存在着本质不同，主要表现为：首先，治理与统治的主体不同，统治的主体是以政府主导的国家政治权利，而治理主体并非单一的，而是包括政府、企业组织等。其次，治理有别于统治的强制性，更多体现出合作与协商。再次，治理的权利更多体现平行与协商,有别于统治的自上而下。最后,治理比统治范围更广,以公共领域为边界[11]。综上所述,国家治理要求治理主体以及治理客体的多元化、立体化,治理方式及手段的公开化、透明化以及规范化,治理目标的人本化。

正所谓有政必有财,财为政之资。政治理念的转变、管理理念的变化必然反映到政之资——即财政,财政的各个方面也必将体现国家治理理念所包含的内涵,并且国家治理理念所包含的内涵将反映在政府收支活动中。具体来讲:首先,治理的多元参与的属性决定了治理参与者不再局限于政府,而要包含企业、社会组织等。这一深刻变化必将反映在财政活动的变化中,财政活动参与者不再仅包括政府,还包括企业组织、社会组织乃至居民自治组织。很难想象,财政参与主体仅为政府但国家治理却将企业等社会组织纳入主体范围。其次,政治协商以及治理体系的平行——国家治理的必然要求——必然要求财政民主化建设。财政活动若是政府独立决策,那国家治理就谈不上协商性。最后,国家治理除包括经济、政治范围外,更包含社会、法制等。财政活动也将深入经济、政治以及社会等各个方面。因此,国家治理概念演变出的种种内涵的实现离不开财政活动相应的适应性变化,财政是政府活动的经济体现(尽管财政的学科属性争论激烈,但财政具有经济属性这一特征已是大多数学者的共识,争论的焦点在于财政仅体现政府的经济还是除经济外还有政治、社会等其他内容),有什么样的政府活动就会有什么样的财政,没有哪种国家治理活动内涵的体现可以脱离财政而独自实现的。这恰恰体现了财政是国家治理的基础要义。

## (二)国家治理体系建设以及治理能力现代化与财政

国家治理体系的完善是国家治理能力现代化的基础,国家治理能力现代化离不开治理体系的构建。习近平总书记强调国家治理体系和治理能力是制度及其执行力的集中体现。国家治理体系是党领导下的国家制度体系,包括政治、经济、社会、文化、生态文明、党建等各个领域的体制机制以及法律法规安排。国家治理能力则是在制度的安排下,运用制度管理社会各方面事物的能力,包括:改革发展稳定,治党治国治军等各个方面[12]。同时需要指出的是,治理体系并不是僵化的、一成不变的,而是会随着经济、社会等各方面的变化而变化，治理体系要求适应国家社会发展总体进程。因此，从治理体系上来看，现代化的治理体系要求一系列的法律法规、体制机制的不断建立和完善，并真正成为"将权力关进笼子"的有力抓手。其中财权是众多权力之一，也是最重要的一项权力，财权不进"笼子"一切都是空谈，因此现代财政制度的建设是完善国家治理体系的重要基础，也是实现国家治理能力现代化的重要支柱。

我国目前在国家治理能力现代化建设中可能面临三个领域的潜在风险：一是新常态条件下经济增长方式不可持续的风险；二是国家治理体系现代化能力与经济社会发展融合的挑战；三是一些社会化问题愈发尖锐，如失业率上升、贫富差距拉大等[13]。上述这些问题的解决需要政府强化经济发展能力、整合能力以及改革能力，而这些能力的提升离不开财政的参与。例如，有增有减的结构性减税助力供给侧结构性改革，为经济增长寻求新动力。

总之，财政是连接政府与市场、经济与社会、中央与地方、公平与效率的桥梁，只要政府职能在发挥作用，任何政策的制定和实施均离不开财政的支持——既包括经济方面的支持也包括制度方面的支撑。例如，政府惠民生的政策需要财政转移支付制度的配合；缩小贫富差距的政策需要税收制度的配合；基本公共服务均等化需要政府间财权与事权的规范化。如此种种，均证明财政是国家治理能力现代化的基础和重要支柱。

## 三、新时代财政职能体系再造

### （一）财政是国家治理的物质基础

尽管在不同国家治理理念下，财政形态不一，如刘晓路、郭庆旺（2016）指出了官房学时代的秩序国家、政治经济学时代的法制国家以及经济学时代的民主国家的财政形态分别为：国家财政、市场财政、社会财政，其作用分别为：增加国家能力、维护市场机制以及满足选民偏好。但其背后的财政活动形式均表现为财政的收入、财政的支出等活动。即政府通过征税、发行债券、收费等形式筹集财政资金，又通过转移性支出、购买性支出等形式满足政府实现其职能的需要[8]。按照马克思对国家的定义（阶级统治的工具），国家并不参与直接性的、以收益为目标的生产性活动。但是阶级统治所需的政治权利并非抽象的，它是由警察、监狱、法院、公安以及军队等具体部门来实现的。尤其是随着经济社会发展，财政形态已不仅仅是维持国家权利的存在，更是拓展到经济、社会等各个领域。其职能实现需要一定的物质基础，这一物质基础只能通过财政收入来实现，正如马克思所说：赋税是政府机器的经济基础，而不是其他任何东西[14]。

国家既是政治权力机构又是公共服务机构，在用公共权力提供公共服务的同时需要一定的物质基础作为保证。国家治理体系的建设和治理能力的现代化最终表现为财政过程，财政的收支直接体现政府的政策意图，如累进税制用于调节收入差距，结构性减税用于供给侧结构性改革。党的十九大之后，我国社会主要矛盾发生变化，社会主义现代化强国特征定义发生改变，"五位一体"总体布局、"四个全面"战略布局得到强化，我国财政收支将更加强化统筹、均衡、和谐、民主、可持续以及以人为本的国家治理理念。由此可以看出，社会目标的实现离不开财政作为经济基础的支撑。财政是国家治理能力的财力保障，是其经济基础[4]。财政兴，国家治理才有财力保障，财政衰，各项政策制定和执行将举步维艰，更不用提治理体系的现代化了。

## （二）财政是国家治理体系的机制保障

财政收支涵盖了几乎所有政府活动，包括政治、经济、文化、生态、社会等几个方面，体现了政府与市场、经济与社会、效率与公平、中央与地方的关系，这不仅是经济体制的重要内容，更是国家治理体系中所要包含的重要内容，正确处理财政活动是国家治理能力提升的重要机制。财政活动包括：财政预算，财政支出，财政收入等方面。首先，全面规范、公开透明的财政预算制度是将财权关进笼子最有力的武器，也是公众监督政府治理的有力依托，这在体现国家治理中包含的多元化参与以及民主等内涵具有不可替代的作用。其次，财政收入包括税收、国债以及收费等形式，不仅提供了政府治理活动的物质保障，同时也提供了政府治理的工具。如累进税制在政府解决收入分配差距、自动调节稳定经济方面具有特殊作用。再如税收优惠的安排体现了政府治理中调整经济结构的重要作用。再次，财政支出包括教育、医疗、科技、财政补贴、国防等各个方面，财政是否提供以及财政支出中各部分支出的比重是由公众的意志来决定的。财政支出安排得科学、合理，公共需要得到最大化满足，体现了政府治理边界以及政府治理责任。最后，财政收支的变化也在扩张或紧缩性财政政策中发挥重要作用，是经济稳定与发展的有力工具。因此，在国家治理能力提升、治理体系的现代化过程中，财政活动各个方面都是重要利器，财政是国家治理体系的机制保障。

### （三）财政是国家治理能力提升的有力监督

国家治理能力的提升要求治理体系的现代化，更要求现代化的治理体系得到有力执行，这就需要监督、监管，有效监督也是现代国家治理体系的内在要求。政府职能的履行几乎全部反映在财政收支活动中，因此对财政的监督、预算的透明成为提升国家治理能力的有效武器。其中，对预算的监督可以保证政府活动的范围、方向符合公众的利益，确保政府活动边界的合理。对财政收支的监督在解决可能产生的腐败、寻租等问题上具有重要意义，也是建立廉洁政府的必然要求，更是规范政府权力、合理配置社会资源的重要保障。

综上所述，国家治理能力的提升和现代化，需要财政发挥物质基础、机制保障以及监督机制的作用。建立全面规范、公开透明的财政预算制度，确定合理的财政收支规模，不断完善财政制度，提高财政调控经济，稳定社会等功能，是提升国家治理能力的基础和重要支柱。财政制度安排的规范高效将成为国家治理能力提升的有力抓手，反之，国家治理将缺少物质基础、机制保障以及有效监督，治理体系现代化以及治理能力的提升将成为空谈。

## 四、新时代财政学理论体系框架构建

### （一）财政学研究理论工具：不断引入社会学、政治学、管理学等学科的理论和方法

除经济学的研究方法和理论外，财政学理论研究中应更多地引入政治学、社会学、管理学等学科的思想和方法，不断完善乃至重新构建财政学的研究方法，最终目标是形成有自身的研究与分析范式的、相对的独立研究方法体系。尽管财政活动从形式上表现为财政收支，表现为政府的经济活动，但经济活动的背后隐藏着财政收支决策——政治决策。脱离政治学基础的财政收支活动的

研究意义大幅度降低。吴俊培（2017）提出直接从财政收支分析，会忽视财政体制这一中间环节[5]。到目前为止，财政学主要形成三个阶段：官房学时代、政治经济学时代、经济学时代[8]，形成了三个流派：公共经济学派、新政治经济学派、财政社会学派[9]。其中新政治经济学以公共选择理论为基础，而以詹姆斯·布坎南为代表的公共选择理论将经济学分析方法运用于政治学问题的分析，将财政的经济现象背后隐藏的政治过程内生化，更接近于现实状态。因此财政学具有政治学科的属性。另外，财政作为国家治理的基础和重要支柱，面对特定的社会文化环境，治理目标不仅是经济学中的效率，而是包含公平、正义等各个方面，因此财政学具有社会学科属性。最后，财政活动中的预算管理、国有资产管理、税收管理等互动离不开管理学、会计学等学科的支持。因此财政属于交叉学科，研究的理论基础不应局限于经济学，研究方法应更加包容。马骁、李雪（2017）提出财政学研究一定会突破跨学科的范围，回归更接近现实的本来面貌[15]。

再者，新时代我国社会主要矛盾的变化也决定了财政学研究基础从经济范畴扩展到综合范畴。自凯恩斯经济以来，政府强化宏观管理职能，有效管理和调控经济的发展和运行，财政在这一背景下被视作一个经济范畴。在各类财政学教材中，财政常被定义为政府的收支活动，这一活动之所以必要，是因为政府在解决市场失灵问题时需要资金支撑。这一概念所关注和对接的是政府职能层面的基本问题。但党的十九大报告明确提出"中国特色社会主义进入新时代，我国社会主要矛盾已经转化为人民日益增长的美好生活需要和不平衡不充分的发展之间的矛盾"。社会主要矛盾从"落后的社会生产"到"不平衡不充分的发展"，从"物质文化需要"到"美好生活需要"，矛盾的两极——需求与供给发生了历史性的变革，人们的需求从物质文化扩展到经济、政治、文化、社会、生态等各个方面，社会的供给从对先进生产力的追求扩展到经济、政治、文化、社会、生态各领域的全面协调发展。社会主要矛盾从经济范畴扩展到综合范畴，作为国家治理的基础和重要支柱的财政，仅用经济学理论不足以支撑新时代财政理论体系不断完善的重任。

**（二）财政学研究目标：以不断提高财政学研究的解释和精准预测能力为依托，促进财政解决新时代新问题能力的提升**

财政是国家治理的基础和重要支柱，新时代财政如何担当这一重任以及如何发挥财政在政府治理中的重要作用,需要财政学具有更科学的解释力以及更精准的预测力。如此才能支持财政更加有效地解决新时代现实经济、社会、环境等热点问题。经过长期努力,中国特色社会主义进入了新时代,这是我国发展新的历史方位,意味着近代以来久经磨难的中华民族迎来了从站起来、富起来到强起来的伟大飞跃[1]。然而,伟大成就的取得要靠接续奋斗,伟大事业的推进要靠继往开来。习近平总书记在党的十九大报告对新时代的定位中提出了两个"必须认识到",一是认识到社会主要矛盾的变化,二是认识到我国仍处于并将长期处于社会主义初级阶段的基本国情没有变。为解决社会主要矛盾必须在发展的基础上着力解决不平衡以及不充分的问题,满足人们各方面的需求,推动社会不断发展,人的全面进步。我国处于社会主义初级阶段的国情没有变意味着发展仍是党执政兴国的第一要务[6],因此促发展,而且是更加高质量,更加平衡、充分的发展必然成为财政学研究的主要目标与方向。财政学研究将更加务实,以解决发展过程中可能遇到的各类问题为主要目的。首先,在政府市场关系方面,财政学研究应提供合理界定二者关系的理论基础和指导意见,不断规范政府活动范围,切实保障市场在资源配置中应发挥的主体效应。政府活动边界确定后,各级政府以及各地政府之间才能按照事权与支出责任相适应、与财力相匹配的原则合理确定各地、各级政府的事权与支出责任,共同谋求经济社会发展。其次,我国正处于经济增速放缓以及经济增长动力转型为特征的新常态,加强供给侧结构性改革,促发展动力转换成为这一时期经济发展的关键。财政学研究应以现实经济、社会问题的解决为出发点,不断完善财税政策类研究,如短期减税降费等直接降低企业成本、提高企业竞争力的财税政策,而中长期鼓励企业创新、研发以及人力资本投资等活动等政策,以及财税政策如何推动科技发展战略,构建合理的国民教育发展体系等将对新经济增长动力的形成以及促进更加充分发展起到关键作用[16]。最后,不平衡发展已成为我国社会主要矛盾的重要表现,因此如何促进平衡发展也将成为财政学研究的重要课题。包括城乡之间、区域之间、经济与社会、人与自然、国内发展与对外开放以及财政收支之间的平衡。如何平衡各领域发展也是新时代给财政学研究提出的新课题。同时,财政在发挥其职能作用时,本身的平衡问题也是财政学研究的重要课题之一,如何有效防范潜在风险同时不断创新财政投融资模式,缓解财政在解决各类发展问题时的资金制约也将成为财政学研究的重要问题。财政研究旨在解决不断发生和不断变化的新的经济、社会等问题,与时俱进。为了应对经济社会矛盾发生的新改变,经济形势发生的新变化,财政学研究除了要能够解释财政现象,更应当对未来有一定的预测能力,以适应不断变化的新形势。

### (三)财政学研究对象:多元参与下的政府、企业及社会组织等

国家治理与国家统治的根本区别之一在于:国家治理的多元参与。但在一些财政学教材中,财政常被定义为政府的收支活动,那么这一活动主体无疑是政府,政府将成为财政收支活动的组织者,政府的意志将在很大程度上影响财政收支的安排。但是在国家治理的视界内,财政的活动参与者不是单一的,除了政府,还包括企业组织、社会组织乃至居民自治组织[7]。习近平总书记在党的十九大报告中提出的新时代坚持和发展中国特色社会主义基本方略"十四条"中要求:坚持人民当家作主、坚持以人民为中心。坚持以人民为中心、人民当家作主必然要求人民对财政收支等活动的知情和决策等权利,政府与社会公众将同时作为治理的主体以及被治理的对象。根据公共选择理论,经济学中的"经济人"的基本假设被移植到政治领域,并把经济学的市场交易分析拓展到政治领域,把人们在政治领域的相互作用过程视作"政治上的交易",认为,政治过程和经济过程一样,其基础是交易动机、交易行为,政治的本质是利益的交换[17]。这一理论更加强化了公众作为政府治理参与者的必要性。尽管政府在财政收支活动中仍将必须处于主导性作用,但不再是唯一的参与者,各类企业组织、社会团体也是财政活动的重要参与者。除税收等活动要体现一定的强制性外,财政收支活动应体现出政府与人民之间的协商性,不断优化公共需要的决定机制,不断提高财政透明和公众参与度。这是"财政是国家治理的基础和重要支柱"的应有之义,也是实现党的十八届三中全会提出的现代财政制度中的全面规范、公开透明的现代财政预算制度的有力抓手。

### (四)财政学研究内容:国家治理视野下的现代财政制度的构建

党的十八届三中全会对于全面深化改革的总体目标定义为:完善和发展中国特色社会主义制度、推进国家治理体系和治理能力现代化。党的十九大报告中又再一次强调这一目标,并将其作为新时代如何发展和坚持中国特色社会主

义八个必须明确的问题之一。也就是说，在坚持和发展中国特色社会主义道路过程中不断深化改革、推进国家治理能力现代化将成为当前重要的历史任务。作为国家治理的基础和重要支柱，财税体制改革也将不断推进，以适应不断改革变化了的经济社会环境。《中共中央关于全面深化改革若干重大问题的决定》要求实现"建立现代财政制度"的目标，具体提出了推进预算制度改革、深化税收制度改革、开展事权与支出责任划分改革、不断推进公共服务均等化以及深化财政投融资制度改革等五个方面。目的是建立全面规范、公开透明的现代预算制度，建立有利于科学发展、社会公平、市场统一的税收制度体系，充分发挥税收筹集财政收入、调节分配、促进结构优化的职能作用，建立事权和支出责任相适应的制度等。这些改革手段与改革目标是中国特色社会主义新时代对财政改革提出的新的要求。当经济社会再次发生重大变化时，财政改革将有新的目标和途径，以适应经济社会发展要求。因此，在新时代如何构建现代财政制度将成为财政学研究的重要内容。财政学研究应在借鉴西方财政理论并结合我国现实情况的情况下，不断完善现代财政制度构建的理论基础，以指导我国现代财政制度实践。

### （五）财政学研究范围：多层次、多方面、全方位

党的十九大报告中表明统筹推进"五位一体"总体布局不变，五位一体即经济建设、政治建设、文化建设、社会建设、生态文明建设，着眼于全面建成小康社会、实现社会主义现代化和中华民族伟大复兴[1]，把我国建设成为富强民主文明和谐美丽的社会主义现代化强国。小康社会的奋斗目标包括经济、人民生活、国民素质、生态环境等各方面。社会主义现代化强国的特征除富强、民主、文明、和谐外，党的十九大报告又加入了美丽，肯定了现代化的绿色属性，充分反映了公众对人与自然和谐现代化的诉求。公众的需求在不断地增长变化，并呈现多层次、多方面、全方位等特征。经济社会形势的不断演进也将给政府治理提出新的课题。因此，财政收支等内容也将不断调整，以适应公共需求的不断变化。实际上，在财政支出结构理论中，内生经济增长对财政支出变化的影响早已启示我们：财政支出结构不是一成不变的、僵化的，它将随着经济社会发展的不断变化而变化。这恰恰是由于新的经济形势变化给财政提出了新的要求。一般来讲，随着经济社会的不断发展，人们的需求将有高级化、

广泛化的趋势,财政学研究范围在新时代也将包含更多方面。

### (六)财政职能:由经济职能拓展的经济、政治、社会等各方面职能

高培勇(2017)提出了新的财政职能,优化资源配置、维护市场统一、促进社会公平以及实现国家长治久安[7]。陈共(2015)在再版的财政学教材中关于财政职能的论述,除包含过去的经济稳定与发展、收入分配以及资源配置三大经济职能外,又引入了社会和谐稳定和国家长治久安[18]。越来越多的学者关注除经济职能外的财政其他职能。当财政上升到国家治理层面后,财政职能不应局限于政府活动的某一方面——如经济,而是应包括财政活动的各个方面,诸如社会、政治等方面。财政成为庶政之母,邦国之本,是国家治理的基础和重要支柱,财政职能必然要拓展到经济、政治、社会等各方面,助力国家治理体系现代化以及治理能力的提升。

## 五、构建新时代财政学学科体系的初步设想

### (一)市场经济条件下国家治理的基础和重要支柱将成为财政学理论体系建设的基础

财政是国家治理的基础和重要支柱,财政活动上升到国家治理层面,这给财政学理论体系建设带来深刻变化。在使用多年的财政学教材中,财政学研究的基本理论问题为市场经济条件下的市场失灵问题的解决,如提供公共物品等,与之相对应的是"国家分配论"或"国家本质论"。当然,财政的"国家治理论"并非是对"国家分配论"的全盘否定,而是继承和发展。财政是国家的财政,国家是财政的主体的本质依然不变,这一基本命题是正确、永恒的。把财政上升到国家治理层面是由于在新时代,国家治理现代化已经成为国家不断发展、不断前进的重点,国家财政的侧重点发生了变化,那么财政发挥作用的重点必将体现这一变化,即由国家分配转为国家治理。那么,新时代财政学研究必将以市场经济条件下国家治理的基础和重要支柱为理论基础。

### (二) 跨学科综合性研究方法不断推进财政学研究

作为国家治理的基础和重要支柱，财政学研究将从经济范畴扩展到综合范畴，其研究内容必然要求其从对经济的调节、社会资源的配置的优化到满足不同社会经济主体的公共利益，提供包括满足需求与供给各方面的经济主体公共利益相对应的公共物品与服务。财政学将成为一个可以跨越多个学科、涉及治国理政所有领域的综合性范畴和综合性要素[7]。并且，新时代背景下的新的使命、新的思想、新的方位都将给财政学的综合性范畴和综合性要素带来更加广泛、深刻的影响。财政学研究中不断引入制度经济学、社会学、法学、博弈论、交易成本理论等新的理论方法，不断形成有自身研究与分析范式的、相对独立的学科体系。

### (三) 现代财政制度构建难点突破将成为财政学研究重点

构建现代财政制度，使之成为国家治理的基础和重要支柱。党的十八届三中全会明确指出现代财政制度构建框架包含：现代预算制度、深化税制改革、事权与支出责任的匹配，公共服务均等化以及财政投融资制度几个方面。党的十九大报告再次强调加快这一制度的建立，并强化了事权与支出责任改革重要性。现代财政制度的构建尽管已经有明确的指导框架和改革步骤，但在改革过程中仍面临种种困难和考验。如事权与支出责任改革中各级政府事权的确定，各地区改革进度不一，改革方式多样；又如，部分地区缺少项目库建设经验和技术条件，中期财政规划流于形式；再如，为提高财政资金使用效率而规定的财政支出进度考核，以及为支持特定事业发展的专项资金在一些地区并没有达到预期目的，部分地区为了完成支出进度要求将一些专项资金层层下拨，这非但没有提高资金使用效益，反而增加了财政收支管理困难。以上问题均会影响现代财政制度的顺利构建，为解决这些困难的研究将成为未来财政学的研究重点。

### (四) 能够指导发展着的实践的财政理论创新是财政学学科发展方向

伟大的实践需要科学的理论，科学的理论可以指导伟大的实践。任何一门学科的发展离不开实践，正所谓"实践出真知"，"实践是检验真理的唯一标准"，缺乏实践的理论是没有任何意义的。目前形成的财政学理论体系和理论框架是在实践的基础上不断总结和提炼的，在指导财政实践方面发挥着重要意义，是财政学理论研究者的重大贡献。然而在新时代条件下，构建中国特色社会主义财政还有很多课题需要研究，还有很多问题有待发现，还有许多困难需要解决。新时代下的新任务、新使命、新方向将给政府治理提出新的课题，不断的理论创新将成为必然。习近平总书记指出："实践没有止境，理论创新也没有止境。世界每时每刻都在发生变化，中国也每时每刻都在发生变化，我们必须在理论上跟上时代，不断认识规律，不断推进理论创新、实践创新、制度创新、文化创新以及其他各方面创新。"[1]财政学的理论研究自然不能逃离这一规律。财政学的发展必须跟上时代，不断认识规律，不断进行理论创新，用新的理论指导新的实践，并在新的实践中继续总结新的理论，推进中国特色的财政学理论体系建设，增强财政学理论对中国财政实践的解释能力、预测能力。

### （五）法治原则在财政学研究中将不断强化

中国特色社会主义逐渐强化了依法治国的重要地位。总体来看，社会主义法治在得到不断深化，作为国家治理基础的财政必然少不了法治这一要素，也必然存在内涵不断丰富、理论不断改善、实践不断推进的过程。"依法理财""依法治税""财政法治"将得到不断地丰富、完善和实践。财政的透明、财政的监督、公开透明的预算制度的建设等都离不开财政法治化和民主化建设。因此，如何实现财政法治、财政法治应遵循的原则及其包含的重要内容都将是财政学研究的重要课题。

在党的十八大、十八届三中全会、十八届四中全会、十八届五中全会，十九大等会议精神的引领下，中国特色社会主义建设取得重大成绩，我国已全面建成小康社会，现在比任何一个时期都更接近中华民族伟大复兴这个目标。党的十九大报告指出，中国特色社会主义进入了新时代。新时代中国特色社会主义有了新的历史任务、新的社会矛盾、新的政府治理方法，也给财政学研究带来了新的课题和研究方向。本文在国家治理视界内分析了财政的职能和作用：财政是国家治理的物质基础；财政是国家治理体系的机制保障；财政是国家治理能力提升的有力监督，初步构建了新时代财政学理论体系框架。财政学作为研究财政现象的理论学科，为财政活动提供理论指导。新时代财政学研究必须紧扣国家治理主题，研究基础、研究目标、研究对象、研究内容、研究范围都将有新的变化。主要变化可概括为：更加多元化、更加全方位、更加紧跟时代主题。财政学科体系将以市场经济条件下国家治理的基础和重要支柱为理论基础，以如何破解现代财政制度构建中遇到的困难为研究重点，以跨学科的研究方法为支撑，不断推进财政理论创新，指导财政实践，不断解决财政在担当国家治理的基础和重要支柱这一重任中的困难。总之，中国特色社会主义财政学必须与时俱进，无论在理论方面还是在实践方面，都需紧跟时代主题，把握时代规律，才能最终更好地指导国家治理实践，形成中国特色的财政学理论体系。

**参考文献**

[1] 党的十九大文件汇编［M］．北京：党建读物出版社，2017．

[2] 中国共产党第十八届中央委员会第三次全体会议文件汇编［M］．北京：人民出版社，2013．

[3] 李俊生．新市场财政学：旨在增强财政学解释力的新范式［J］．中央财经大学学报，2017（05）．

[4] 安体富．关于财政的学科属性与定位问题［J］．财贸经济，2016（12）．

[5] 吴俊培．关于财政理论的三个基本问题［C］．第21次全国财政理论研讨会交流论文，2017．

[6] 邓力平．中国特色社会主义财税思考［M］．厦门：厦门大学出版社，2016．

[7] 高培勇．抓住中国特色财政学发展的有利契机［N/OL］．中国共产党新闻网，2017（02）．

[8] 刘晓路，郭庆旺．财政学三百年：基于国家治理视角的分析［J］．财贸经济，2016（03）．

[9] 孙正．对财政学学科属性及其未来跨学科发展趋势的几点探讨［C］．财政学类专业教育教学改革实践论文集，上海：上海财经大学出版社，2017．

[10] 黄薇．康熙字典（现代点校版）［M］．北京：北京燕山出版社，2006．

[11] 徐晓全．西方国家治理理论：内涵与评析［J］．检察风云—社会治理理论专刊，2014（03）．

[12] 罗文东．推进国家治理体系和治理能力现代化［N/OL］．人民网，2017（05）．

[13] 褚松燕. 论中国国家治理能力现代化 [J]. 当代世界, 2015 (05).

[14] 中央编译局. 马克思恩格斯全集 [M]. 北京: 人民出版社, 1963.

[15] 马骁, 李雪. 国家治理现代化语境中财政学的发展方向 [C]. 第 21 次全国财政理论研讨会交流论文, 2017.

[16] 刘伟. 经济新常态与供给侧结构性改革 [J]. 管理世界, 2016 (07).

[17] 阮守武. 公共选择理论的方法与研究框架 [J]. 经济问题探索, 2009 (11).

[18] 陈共. 财政学（第八版）[M]. 北京: 中国人民大学出版社, 2015.

# How to Construct Socialist Public Finance with Chinese Characteristics in the New Era

Yu Haifeng  Zhu Cuihua

Abstract: Socialism with Chinese characteristics has entered a new era. Public finance, as the foundation and important pillar of national governance, is bound to present itself with new features, changes, and goals in the new era. To analyze the construction of socialist public finance with Chinese characteristics in the new era, this study examines the financial function of the new era from the perspective of public finance as the foundation and important pillar of national governance. Accordingly, the research involves the construction of a basic framework of public finance and the key points of the new era of public finance construction. Results show that the financial functions in the new era include three aspects: as the material basis of national governance, as the mechanism guarantee of the national governance system, and as a powerful supervision of the enhancement of national governance ability. The analysis of the financial phenomenon reveals that public finance will change in the new era of national governance in terms of research objectives, research scope, research content, research tools, and other aspects. Finally, this study puts forward a preliminary idea for the construction of a subject system of public finance with Chinese characteristics.

Key words: New era; National governance system; National governance ability; Public finance

CLC number: F812    Document code: A

## I. Introduction

"With decades of hard work, socialism with Chinese characteristics has crossed the threshold into a new era. This is a new historic juncture in China's development."[1] In this new era, the Communist Party of China (CPC) Central Committee proposed the construction and modernization of a national governance system and positioned public finance as the foundation and important pillar of state governance[2]. These actions brought public finance to an unprecedented strategic height, thereby generating scholarly widespread attention and discussion. Since the appearance of the Keynesian economy, government intervention in macroeconomics has become a vital part of government activities. Economic regulation and stability is also the fundamental goal of fiscal revenue and expenditure. Affected by "economic imperialism"①, the theme of research in public finance is mainly limited to the regulation of market failure and the supply of public goods under the conditions of market economy. Many political scientists and public financial scientists have also questioned this condition. Especially since the Third Plenary Session of the 18th CPC Central Committee, fiscal activities have reached the level of national governance, which should include political, social, and environmental aspects apart from the economic one. Such development has triggered a significant discussion about the subject attributes of public finance, with a focus on whether public finance is a branch of the economy or something else. The conclusion on this issue was previously unclear but has been reached in the debate about not limiting the goal of fiscal activity to the economic field. Li Junsheng (2017) explained how to construct a theoretical basis for public finance with more

---

① Economic imperialism refers to the fact that economics extends its research field to the traditional non-economic areas of concern. The scope of economic research has been expanding continuously, and the trend of colonial other disciplines has emerged.

explanatory and predictive capabilities under new market conditions[3]. An Tifu (2016) re-examined the subject attributes and orientation of public finance[4]. Wu Junpei (2017) discussed three basic questions in fiscal theory[5]. Deng Liping (2016) constructed the basic framework of the "five characteristics" of socialist public finance with Chinese characteristics[6]. Gao Peiyong (2017) explored the issues in public finance theory construction in the national governance system[7]. Liu Xiaolu and Guo Qingwang (2016) reviewed the development of public finance in the past 300 years[8]. Sun Zheng (2017) studied the subject attribute of public finance and its future development[9]. These studies discussed issues such as the development of public finance, the construction of the fiscal framework, and the subject attributes of public finance from different perspectives, thereby providing many experiences and inspirations for the development of public finance. A new judgment on the main contradictions of China's society and a new expansion of the definition of the characteristics of a socialist modernization power were extended in the 19th National Congress. China has entered a new era of socialism. Public finance is expected to make a major difference in fulfilling new tasks, achieving novel goals, and implementing original strategies in the new era. New emphasis in financial functions would be present under the conditions of the new era, and public finance would enable the provision of public goods under the financial framework and market economy conditions. The analysis and research of public finance under the new era has important theoretical and practical significance. In terms of practice, such investigation is an urgent requirement for national governance enhancement and the critical practices of building a moderately prosperous society in all respects. From a theoretical perspective, it is an inherent requirement of the prosperity of public finance itself. The theory that can guide practice is important, and the theory that emerges from practice is correct. Public finance theory research must change and develop according to the changes in China's economic situation and the government's governing concept. The current work attempts to analyze what public finance is within the framework of national governance and why fiscal functions have changed. It also explores the financial framework and the future development in the new era from the angles of why, what, and how.

This paper has five main parts. The first part introduces the significance and necessity of building socialistic public finance with Chinese characteristics in the new era and the structure of this study. The second part analyzes how to understand public finance as the foundation and important pillar of national governance and further clarifies the theoretical basis for further analysis of socialistic fiscal functions with Chinese characteristics in the new era and the new fiscal framework. The third part focuses on the functions of public finance in the modernization of the national governance system and the improvement of governance capacity. The fourth part preliminarily proposes the basic framework of socialistic public finance with Chinese characteristics in the new era, that is, the preliminary construction of a public finance framework based on the clarified characteristics of socialism with Chinese characteristics in such era, combined with the goal of establishing the modern financial system proposed in the Third Plenary Session of the 18th CPC Central Committee and the 19th National Congress. The fifth part provides a preliminary idea on how to construct a discipline system of public finance in the new era.

## II. Public finance based on national governance

In the Third Plenary Session of the 18th CPC Central Committee, public finance was positioned as the foundation and important pillar of national governance, which explained what public finance is from the new historical position and height. The 19th National Congress once again emphasized the status of public finance in national governance. Therefore, how does one understand public finance as the foundation and an important pillar of national governance? This question should be answered from two aspects: what national governance is and the requirements of the national governance system and the modernization of governance capacity.

## 1. National governance and public finance

The term "governance" means "ruling" or "management", as in the *Book of Han Biography of Zhao Guanghan*: "Everything is well managed which makes a name for himself"; and in *The School Sayings of Confucius XianJun*: "I want the government to be managed, what should I do?"[10] The term "governance" in Western culture is derived from ancient Greek and Latin. It also means "ruling" and "manipulating" and does not distinguish itself from the word "ruling". However, with the continuous evolution of the economic society, "governance" has been continuously applied to a variety of situations, from the initial "governance crisis" to the later "global governance", "economic governance" and "social governance". The connotation of this word has changed fundamentally. The theory of governance and its practice have made its meaning far different from the original meaning of "ruling" and "management", and it has become a word with modern color involved in the economic and social fields at the governmental and national levels. After the Third Plenary Session of the 18th CPC Central Committee, the modernization of state governance has become the overall goal of China's comprehensively deepening reforms. "Governance" was mentioned as many as 20 times in *The Decision of the Central Committee of the Communist Party of China on Major Issues Concerning Comprehensively Deepening Reforms*, including as state governance, governance by law, and governance capacity. "Governance" and "ruling" are essentially different. The main manifestations are as follows. First, the main subjects of ruling and governance differ. The main subject of the former is the government-dominated political power of state, whereas that of the latter is not singular and includes government and enterprise organizations. Second, governance differs from the coerciveness of rule and reflects more cooperation and negotiation. Third, the right of governance is more parallel and negotiated than the top-down characteristic of ruling. Finally, governance has a broader scope than ruling, with the public sphere as the boundary[11]. In sum, national governance requires the pluralism and three-dimensionality of governance subjects and governance objects; the openness, transparency, and standardization of governance methods and means; and the humanization of governance goals.

Where there is a government, there is public finance, which is the fund for the government. Political fund, which is public finance, manifests the changes in political and management concepts. Every aspect of public finance also reflects the connotation of national governance concepts, and the connotation of national governance concepts is reflected in government revenue and expenditure activities. Specifically: First, the multi-participating nature of governance determines that governance participants are not limited to the government but also include enterprises and social organizations. This profound change is reflected in the changes in fiscal activities. Participants in fiscal activities no longer only include the government but also comprise enterprise organizations, social organizations, and even resident autonomous organizations. Imagining that the main subject of public finance is only the government and that of national governance includes social organizations such as enterprises would be difficult. Second, the parallel relationship of political consultation and the governance system, which is the inevitable requirement of national governance, entails the construction of fiscal democratization. If fiscal activities are determined to be independent of the government, then coordination in national governance will be lacking. Third, in addition to the economic and political spheres, national governance also includes society and the legal system. Financial activities penetrate into economic, political, and social aspects. Therefore, the realization of the various connotations evolving from national governance concepts is inseparable from the corresponding adaptive changes in fiscal activities. Public finance is the economic embodiment of government activities (although the subject attribute of public finance is fiercely debated, most scholars agree that economic attribute is one of the characteristics of public finance. The focus of the debate is whether public finance only reflects the government's economy or other aspects besides the economy, such as politics and society). The kind of government activities determines the kind of public finance. Moreover, no manifestation of connotation of national governance activities can be realized independently from public finance. This situation precisely reflects the fact that public finance is the foundation of national governance.

## 2. The construction of national governance system and the modernization of governance capacity and public finance

The improvement of the national governance system is the basis for the modernization of national governance capacity. Furthermore, the modernization of the national governance capacity is inseparable from the construction of a governance system. General Secretary Xi Jinping emphasized that the national governance system and governance capacity are the concentrated expressions of the system and its executive power. The national governance system is the national institutional system under the leadership of the party, including the institutional mechanisms, as well as the legal and regulatory arrangements in various fields, such as politics, economy, society, culture, ecological civilization, and party building. National governance capacity is the ability to use the system to manage all aspects of society under the arrangement of the system, including reform and development stability, and the governance of the party, the country, the army, and other aspects[12]. At the same time, the governance system is not rigid and static but evolves along with economic and social changes. The governance system must adapt to the overall process of national social development. Therefore, from the perspective of the governance system, the modern governance system requires the continuous establishment and improvement of a series of laws, regulations, and institutional mechanisms and truly becomes a forceful hand for "caging the power". Among them, financial power is the most crucial. Financial power does not enter the "cage", everything would be an empty talk. Therefore, the construction of a modern fiscal system is an essential foundation for improving the national governance system and is a vital pillar in realizing the modernization of national governance capabilities.

China may be confronted with potential risks in the following three areas during the modernization of state governance capacity: (1) the risk of unsustainable economic growth under the new normal conditions, (2) the challenge of integrating the modernization of the national governance system with economic and social development, and (3) the increasing acuity of some socialization problems, such as the rising unemployment and the widening of economic inequality[13]. The resolution of these problems requires the government to strengthen its abilities of economic development, integration, and reform. The improvement of these capabilities is inseparable from financial participation. For example, structural tax reduction with increases and decreases supports supply-side structural reforms and the search for a new impetus for economic growth.

In brief, public finance is a bridge connecting the government and the market, the economy and the society, the central and the local, as well as fairness and efficiency. As long as the government function is playing its role, any policy formulation and implementation cannot be separated from financial support, both economic and institutional. For example, the government's policy of benefiting the people requires the coordination of the fiscal transfer payment system. That is, the policy of narrowing the gap between the rich and the poor requires the synchronization of the tax system, and the equalization of basic public services requires the standardization of intergovernmental fiscal power and responsibilities. All of these examples prove that public finance is a foundation and important pillar of the modernization of national governance capacity.

## III. Reconstruction of public finance functions in the new era

### 1. Public finance as the material foundation for national governance

Different forms of public finance exist with different national governance concepts. Liu Xiaolu and Guo Qingwang (2016) pointed out that the form of public finance of the order state in the cameralism period, the legal state in the political economy period, and the democratic state in the economics period are state finance, market finance, and social finance, respectively, the functions of which are increasing national capacity, protecting market mechanisms, and satisfying voters' preferences, respectively. However, the form of financial activities behind such states is always represented by fiscal revenues and expenditures as well as other activities. That is, the government raises financial funds through taxation, bond issuance, and fees and meets its need to fulfill its functions through transfer payments and purchase expenditures[8]. According to Marx's definition of the state, the tool of class rule, the state does not participate in direct and profit-oriented productive activities. Nevertheless, the political power required for class rule is not abstract but is achieved by specific departments, such as the police, prisons, courts, public security, and the military. Especially with economic and social development, the fiscal form is not only the existence of maintaining state power but also expanded into various fields, including economy and society. The realization of the state's functions requires a certain material foundation, which can only be achieved through fiscal revenue. As Marx said,"Taxes are the economic basis of the government machinery and of nothing else."[14]

The state is both a political power institution and a public service institution, and it needs a certain material basis as a guarantee in the use of public power to provide public services. The construction of a national governance system and the modernization of governance capability are finally manifested as a public financial process. Fiscal revenue and expenditure directly reflect the policy intention of the government, such as the progressive tax system for regulating the income gap and the structural tax reduction for supply-side structural reform. After the 19th CPC National Congress, the main contradiction in our society changed. The definition of the characteristics of a great modern socialist country also changed. The five-sphere integrated plan and four-pronged overall strategy were strengthened, and China's fiscal revenue and expenditure emphasized national governance concepts that are integrated, balanced, harmonious, democratic, sustainable, and people-oriented. Thus, the realization of social goals cannot be separated from public finance as the support of the economic foundation. Public finance is the monetary guarantee and economic basis of national governance capability[4]. Fiscal prosperity brings financial security for national governance, whereas fiscal impotence leads to difficulties in policy formulation and implementation, let alone realizing the modernization of the governance system.

## 2. Public finance as the mechanism guaranteeing national governance system

Fiscal revenue and expenditure covers almost all government activities, including those in terms of politics, economy, culture, ecology, and society. It reflects the relationship between the government and the market, the economy and the society, efficiency and fairness, as well as central and local. This concept is the vital content of not only the economic system but also the national governance system. The correct handling of financial activities is a significant mechanism for the improvement of national governance capabilities. Financial activities involve the budget, fiscal expenditure, and fiscal revenue. First, a roundly normative, open, and transparent fiscal budget system is the most powerful weapon to cage financial power, and it offers powerful support for the public to supervise governance. Such system is irreplaceable in embodying diversified participation and connotation, including democracy in national governance. Second, fiscal revenue includes forms of taxation, government bonds, and fees, which provide not only material security for government governance activities but also tools for governance. For example, the progressive taxation system has special functions in the government for resolving the income gap and automatically adjusting and stabilizing the economy. Another example is the arrangement of tax incentives that embodies the important role of government governance in adjusting the economic structure. Third, fiscal expenditure includes education, health care, science and technology, financial subsidies, and national defense expenditures. Whether public finance provides these elements or not and the proportion of every kind of expenditure are determined by the will of the public. The arrangement of fiscal expenditures is scientific and reasonable, and the public need is maximally satisfied, thereby reflecting the government governance boundary and government governance responsibilities. In addition, changes in fiscal revenue and expenditure play a significant role in expanding or tightening fiscal policies and are powerful tools for economic stability and development. Therefore, in enhancing the national governance capacity and the modernization of the governance system, all aspects of fiscal activities are important tools, and public finance is the mechanism guaranteeing the national governance system.

### 3. Public finance as the potent supervision for enhancing national governance capacity

The improvement of the national governance capability requires the modernization of the governance system and the vigorous implementation of the modernized governance system. These changes require supervision and regulation. Effective supervision is also the inherent requirement of the modern national governance system. The implementation of government functions is almost entirely reflected in fiscal revenue and expenditure activities. Therefore, supervision over public finance and budget transparency have become effective weapons for improving the national governance capability. In particular, supervision over the budget can ensure that the scope and direction of government activities are in line with the interests of the public and guarantees the rationality of the boundaries of government activities. Supervision over fiscal revenue and expenditure is of great significance in solving potential problems, such as corruption and rent-seeking. Moreover, supervision is an inevitable requirement for establishing a clean government and an important guarantee for regulating government power and rationally allocating social resources.

In sum, the improvement and modernization of the national governance capability requires public finance functioning as material foundation, a guaranteeing mechanism, and a supervision mechanism. Public finance is the foundation and important pillar for enhancing the national governance capacity to establish a roundly standardized, open, and transparent fiscal budget system; to determine a reasonable scale of fiscal revenue and expenditure; to continuously perfect the fiscal system; to improve the ability of regulating the economy; and to stabilize society. The standardization and efficiency of fiscal institutional arrangements will become a powerful tool for the improvement of the national governance capability. Conversely, national governance will lack material foundation, a guaranteed mechanism, and effective supervision without public finance, therefore rendering the modernization of the governance system and the improvement of governance capacity as empty talk.

IV. Construction of public finance theory system in the new rea

**1. Theoretical tools of public finance research: The constant introduction of theories and methods of sociology, political science, management science, and other disciplines**

In addition to the research methods and theories in economics, more ideas and methods of political science, sociology, management, and other disciplines should be introduced to the theoretical research of public finance by constantly improving and even reconstructing the research methods of public finance. The ultimate goal is to form a relatively independent research method system with its own research and analysis paradigm. Although fiscal activities are formally embodied by fiscal revenue and expenditure (which are economic activities of the government), hidden financial revenue and expenditure decisions exist as political decisions. The research significance of fiscal revenue and expenditure activities that are separated from a political foundation will be greatly reduced. Wu Junpei (2017) proposed that the public finance system, which is an intermediate link, would be neglected in the direct analysis from the perspective of fiscal revenue and expenditure[5]. For this point, three stages of public finance were formed: the cameralism period, the political economy period, and the economics period[8]. Three schools were also formed: the public economics school, the neo-political economics school, and the financial sociology school[9]. Among them, Neo-political economics is based on the theory of public choice. Public choice theory represented by James Buchanan applies the economic analysis method to the analysis of political issues and internalizes the political process behind the economic phenomenon in public finance, thereby making it close to reality. Therefore, public finance has the attributes of politics. In specific social and cultural environments, the governance goal of public finance, which is the foundation and important pillar of national governance, includes not only efficiency in economics but also aspects such as fairness and justice. Therefore, public finance has the attributes of sociology. Finally, the interaction of budget management, state-owned asset management, and taxation management in financial activities is inseparable from the support of the disciplines of management and accounting. Therefore, public finance is an interdisciplinary subject. The theoretical basis of research should not be limited to economics, and research methods should be inclusive. Ma Xiao and Li Xue (2017) proposed that the study of public finance will definitely break through the interdisciplinary scope and return to the original appearance closer to reality[15].

Furthermore, the transformation of the principal contradictions of Chinese society in the new era determines the expansion of the boundary of fiscal study foundation from an economic to a general category. Fiscal studies are framed in the economic category as the government strengthens the macro-management function to effectively manage and regulate the development and operation of economics based on Keynesian economic theories. In various finance textbooks, finance is often defined as a necessary action for the government, which uses revenue and expenditure to generate financial support when facing marketing failure. This concept only interprets the basic questions of government functions. However, the report of the 19th National Congress of the CPC clearly stated, "As socialism with Chinese characteristics has entered a new era, the principal contradiction facing Chinese society has evolved. What we now face is the contradiction between unbalanced and inadequate development and the people's ever-growing needs for a better life." The principal contradiction has transformed from "backward social production" to "unbalanced and inadequate development" and from "material and cultural needs" to "ever-growing needs for a better life". Thus, a historic change has occurred in the binary side of the contradiction, that is, in demand and supply. People expand their demand area from material and culture to economic, political, cultural, social, and ecological aspects while society expands its supply area from simply chasing advanced productive forces to promoting the comprehensive and coordinated development of society in economic, political, cultural, social, and ecological aspects. As the principal contradictions of Chinese society transform from an economic to a general category, using economic theory to construct an improved theoretical system for finance in the new era is insufficient.

**2. Research objectives of finance: Promoting the capability of finance in solving new problems in the new era, which based on the development of the explanatory power and the accurate predictive power of finance study**

Finance is the foundation and an important pillar of state governance, it takes on this important task and plays a major role in government governance in the new era by improving explanatory power and predictive power. Thus, finance can more effectively solve hot issues in economic, social, and ecological aspects. With decades of hard work, socialism with Chinese characteristics has crossed the threshold into a new era. This period is a new historic juncture in China's development and indicates that the Chinese nation, which has endured so much for so long since modern times, has achieved tremendous transformation from standing up, becoming rich to becoming strong[1]. Realizing our great dream demands great struggle, and developing our great cause calls for inheriting the past and opening up for the future. General Secretary Xi Jinping mentioned two "must recognize" in the 19th National Congress of the CPC when positioning the new era. One is to recognize the transformation of the contradictions of Chinese society, and the other is to recognize that the basic dimension of the Chinese context—that our country is still and will long remain in the primary stage of socialism—has not changed. To solve the principal contradictions of Chinese society, we must focus on the situation of unbalanced and inadequate development and meet people's needs in all aspects to continuously hasten social progress and promote the all-round development of the people. The fact that the basic dimension of the Chinese context has not changed indicates development as the Party's top priority in governance[6]. Such development leads to the notion that promoting a more balanced and adequate development is the main goal and direction of finance study. The result is a pragmatic attitude toward finance to solve all types of questions during the development. First, finance studies are supposed to provide a theoretical principle and guidance to rationally define the relationship between the government and the market, constantly scope the range of governmental activities, and effectively leave the market to play the decisive role in resource allocation. Only when the boundary of governmental activities is confirmed can the government at all levels be able to establish a system whereby the authority of the office matches the responsibility of expenditure. Second, China has entered a new normal in economic development, in which the economy has slowed down and has new drivers of growth. We should further supply-side structural reform and foster new drivers of growth as the main task of this period. Finance studies are supposed to be based on the arbitration of the real economy and social problems that improves public finance and taxation policy, such as directly reducing enterprise cost and improving competitiveness through reduction in taxes and fees in the short term. In the medium and long term, encouraging companies to innovate, R&D and invest in human capital, promoting a technology development strategy, and constructing a sound national education system are essential to foster new drivers of growth and promote more adequate development[16]. Third, finance studies must investigate how to promote a balanced development because an unbalanced development has become an important issue in the principal contradictions of Chinese society, including the balance of binaries, namely, urban and rural, economy and society, human and nature, Chinese domestic development and opening up, and revenue and expenditures. How to balance the development between different fields is also a new mission proposed by the new era for finance studies. At the same time, the balance of finance itself is also one of the important projects of financial research when it plays its functions. Guarding against potential risks effectively while constantly innovating fiscal financing modes and alleviating financial tension in solving various development problems are also important for finance studies. Finance research aims to solve new economic and social problems that are constantly happening and changing, and keep pace with the times. To deal with the changes in the contradictions of Chinese society and the economic situation, finance studies must not only explain financial phenomena but also forecast the future situation, which changes constantly.

## 3. Study subject of public finance: Multi-subject participation of government, firms, and social organizations

An essential difference between national governance and national sovereignty is that the former requires multi-subject participation. However, in some of the literature, finance is always defined as the revenue and expenditure activity of the government, which indicates that as the subject, the government is the organizer of this activity and its will may greatly influence the arrangement of fiscal revenue and expenditure. Nevertheless, from the perspective of national governance, participants of the activity are not single, also include firms, social organizations, and residents' autonomous organizations[7]. General Secretary Xi Jinping mentioned in the 19th National Congress of CPC that the basic policy "Fourteen Points" of addressing the kind of socialism with Chinese characteristics that the new era requires to uphold and develop requires us to see that the people run the country and commit to a people-centered approach. Those two requirements mean that people own rights of decision making and information about revenue and expenditure activities. Moreover, the government and public are subjects and objects of national governance at the same time. According to public choice theory, moving the hypothesis of rational agents and the analysis of market transaction into the political field in economics is regarded as a "political trade-off" because people interact in such field. We also consider that the bases of politics and economics are the same and include trading motive and trading activity. Conversely, the essence of politics is the exchange of interests[17]. This theory strengthened the necessity of the public as a participant of national governance. Although the government still dominates the activities of revenue and expenditure in public finance, it is no longer the only participant, with all kinds of firms and social organizations joining in. Except for compulsory activities like taxation, the activities of revenue and expenditure in public finance should be negotiable between the government and the public, continuously optimize the determination mechanism of public needs, and improve fiscal transparency and public engagement. This notion is what "finance is the foundation and an important pillar of state governance" means and is also a powerful tool for realizing a roundly normative, open, and transparent modern fiscal budget system in the modern fiscal system proposed by the Third Plenary Session of the 18th CPC Central Committee.

## 4. Content of finance studies: The construction of a modern fiscal system from the perspective of national governance

The overall goal of comprehensively deepening the reform mentioned in the Third Plenary Session of the 18th CPC Central Committee is to improve and develop socialism with Chinese characteristics and promote the modernization of the national governance system and capacity. Such goal was emphasized again in the 19th National Congress of the CPC and became one of the eight questions on how to improve and develop socialism with Chinese characteristics in the new era that should be clarified. That is, in the way of insisting and developing socialism with Chinese characteristics, continuously deepening the reform and promoting the modernization of the national governance capacity represent the current important historical task. As the foundation and an important pillar of state governance, the reform of the finance and taxation system has to be put forward to accommodate the constantly changing economic and social society. *The Decision of the Central Committee of the CPC on Several Major Issues Concerning the Comprehensive Deepening of Reform* requires the realization of the goal of the establishment of a modern fiscal system. In this regard, the specific tasks proposed are as follows: improving the budget management system, improving the taxation system, establishing a system whereby the authority of the office matches the responsibility of expenditure, improving the equalization of public services, and furthering the fiscal investment and financing system. The Decision aimed to publish a roundly normative, open, and transparent modern budget system, as well as construct a taxation system that is positive toward scientific development, social equity, and market unification. Moreover, it must make full use of the function of taxation to increase financial revenue, adjust the distribution policy and optimize the structure. It must also establish a system whereby the authority of the office matches the responsibility of expenditure. Those paths and goals to reform proposed by socialism with Chinese characteristics are the new requirements for the reform of the financial system. When major changes occur again in economy and society, fiscal reform will have a new goal to adapt to new requirements. Therefore, establishing a modern fiscal system in the new era plays an important role in finance studies. Such studies should be combined with western finance studies and reality in China and improve the theoretical basis of the modern fiscal system to guide practice.

## 5. Research scope of finance studies: Multilevel, multifaceted, and all-inclusive

The 19th National Congress of the CPC mentioned pursuing coordinated progress in the five-sphere integrated plan, which includes economic construction, political construction, cultural construction, social construction, and ecological civilization construction, on the basis of finishing the building of a moderately prosperous society in all respects to realize socialist modernization, national rejuvenation[1], and bulid our country into modern, powerful socialist country that is prosperous and strong, democratic, civilized, harmonious and beautiful. The objectives of building a moderately prosperous society in all respects include economics, people's livelihood, national quality, and the ecological environment. A modern, powerful socialist country is prosperous and strong, democratic, civilized, and harmonious. The 19th National Congress of the CPC added beauty, which affirms the green attributes of modernization and indicates the public's aspiration for harmony between man and nature, as the public's demand is growing and changing and presents features that are multilevel, multifaceted, and all-inclusive. The constantly change of the economics and society situation will also raise new issues for government governance. Therefore, fiscal revenue and expenditure must adjust in time to fit the public demand. Actually, the impact made by endogenous economic growth on fiscal revenue and expenditure indicates that fiscal expenditure structure is not immutable and frozen and will change by following the step of the development of economics and society. This circumstance is due to the fact that the new economic situation has put forward new requirements for finance. Generally, public demand will be more advanced and broader with the development of economics and society, and finance studies will cover wider aspects in the new era.

**6. Financial functions: From economic functions to all aspects, including economics, politics, and society**

Gao Peiyong (2017) proposed new functions of public finance to optimize resource allocation, maintain market unification, promote social equity and justice, and achieve the lasting stability of the nation[7]. Chen Gong (2015) introduced social harmony and stability and the lasting stability of the nation in the reprinted finance textbook into the expounded notion of finance along with economic stability and development, income distribution, and resource allocation[18]. In fact, an increasing number of scholars are paying attention to other financial functions besides economic functions. When finance rises to the level of national governance, its functions should include every aspect of finance, such as society and politics, instead of being limited to one aspect of government activities, such as economics areas. Finance has become the mother of numerous affairs of the state, the foundation of the state, and the foundation and important pillar of state governance. The functions of finance must expand to all aspects, including economics, politics, and society, to promote the modernization of the state governance system and governance capability.

## V. First step of constructing the discipline system of finance in the new era

**1. The foundation and important pillar of state governance under the market economy condition is becoming the foundation of the construction of the financial theory system**

Finance is called the foundation and important pillar of state governance because fiscal activities have risen to the level of national governance, bringing about profound changes to the construction of the theoretical system of finance. In the finance textbook that has been used for many years, fundamental theoretical issues of finance studies have involved the solution of market failure problems under the market economy condition, such as the provision of public goods. On the contrary, state distribution theory or state essence theory is present. Of course, the theory of state governance is not a total negation of the theory of state distribution. Instead, the former entails the inheritance and development of the latter. The basic proposition that finance is national finance and the state is the subject of finance is correct and eternal. This notion is because the modernization of state governance has become the focus of continuous development and progress of the country in the new era. As the focus of national finance has changed, the focal point of the role of finance will certainly reflect it, that is, from state distribution to state governance. Therefore, the foundation and important pillar of state governance under the market economy is becoming the foundation of the financial theory system in the new era.

**2. Using interdisciplinary and comprehensive research methods to promote financial research**

As the foundation and an important pillar of state governance, finance studies will expand from the economic to a comprehensive category. Hence, its research content will inevitably require change from economic regulation and optimization of the allocation of social resources to meeting the public interests of different socio-economic subjects and providing public goods and services corresponding to the public interests of economic subjects in satisfying demand and supplying various aspects. Finance studies will become a comprehensive category and element that spans multiple disciplines and covers all fields of governance[7]. Moreover, the new mission, new thought, and new orientation under the new era will give finance studies a more extensive and profound influence. Novel theoretical methods, such as institutional economics, sociology, law, game theory, and transaction cost theory, are constantly introduced to finance studies and continuously form a relatively independent disciplinary system with its own research and analysis paradigm.

## 3. Breaking through difficulties of the construction of a modern financial system will become a key to finance studies

Bulid a modern fiscal system and make it the foundation and important pillar of national governance. The Third Plenary Session of the 18th CPC Central Committee clearly pointed out the construction of a framework of a modern financial system by improving the budget management system, improving the taxation system, establishing a system whereby the authority of the office matches the responsibility of the expenditure, equalizing public services, and improving the financial investment and financing system. The 19th National Congress of the CPC hastened the establishment of this system and strengthened the importance of the reform of creating a system whereby the authority of the office matches the responsibility of the expenditure. Although the construction of a modern financial system has already built a clear guiding framework and reform steps, many difficulties must still be faced, and they include the definition of governments at all levels in the establishment of a reformed system whereby the authority of the office matches the responsibility of the expenditure and the progress and patterns of reform varies from region to region. Furthermore, some areas lack experience and technical conditions for project bank construction, leading to the fact that medium-term fiscal planning is a mere formality. Finally, actions for the assessment of the progress of financial expenditure to improve the use efficiency of financial funds and special funds to support the development of specific undertakings fail to reach their goal in some areas. To meet the expenditure schedule, some special funds are allocated at different levels at certain areas. Such action increases the difficulties in the management of fiscal revenue and expenditure instead of improving the efficiency of the use of funds. All these problems will have negative effects on the construction of a modern financial system. How to solve these difficulties will become the key concern of future finance studies.

## 4. The innovation of financial theory can guide practice as the direction of finance studies

Great practice needs scientific theory while scientific theory can guide great practice. Practice is indispensable to the development of any subject. That is, genuine knowledge comes from practice, practice is the only criterion for testing truth, and theory without practice is meaningless. The current financial theoretical system and theoretical framework are continuously summarized and refined on the basis of practice, which play an important role in guiding the practice of finance and are a major contribution of financial theory researchers. However, in the new era, there are still many projects to be studied in building socialist public finance with Chinese characteristics, many problems are waiting to be discovered, and many difficulties must still be solved. New tasks, new missions, and new directions will put forward new subjects for national governance. Continuous theoretical innovation will become inevitable. Xi Jingping pointed out that just as there are no bounds to practice, there is no end to theoretical exploration. The world is changing with every second and moment. China, too, is changing with every second and moment. We must ensure that our theory evolves with the times, deepens our appreciation of objective laws, and advances our theoretical, practical, institutional, cultural, and other explorations[1]. The theoretical study of finance certainly follows that rule. The development of finance studies must follow the new development in the new era, understand the objective laws and carry out theoretical innovation constantly. At the same time, it should guide new practice with original theories and continue to summarize new theories in new practice. Furthermore, such study must promote the construction of a theoretical system of finance with Chinese characteristics and enhance the explanatory and predictive ability of financial theory to financial practice.

### 5. The principle of legality will be strengthened in finance studies

Ruling the country by law has taken an increasingly important role in socialism with Chinese characteristics. Overall, because socialism with the rule of law has deepened, finance as the foundation of national governance, inevitably needs the element of the rule of law. Finance also needs to enrich the connotation, improve the theory, and take advancement of practice continuously. Managing finances according to law, administrating taxes according to law, and ruling the country by law and finance will be enriched, promoted and practiced constantly. Having transparent and supervised finance and constructing an open and transparent budget system cannot be achieved without the legalization of finance and the construction of democratization. Therefore, how to achieve a financial government by law, follow the rules and contain the major contents are the important tasks for finance studies.

Under the guidance of a series of conferences (such as the 18th CPC National Congress, the Third Plenary Session of the 18th CPC Central Committee, the Fourth Plenary Session of the 18th CPC Central Committee, the Fifth Plenary Session of the 18th CPC Central Committee, and the19th CPC National Congress), the construction of socialism with Chinese characteristics has made a great achievement, and our country has built a well-off society in an all-round way. Now, China is closer to the goal of the great rejuvenation of the Chinese nation than in any other period. The 19th National Congress pointed out that socialism with Chinese characteristics has entered a new era. China has entered a new era of socialist modernization, which leads us to a new historical task, social contradictions, national governance methods, and new topics and research orientation to the study of finance. In brief, this work analyzes the functions from the perspective of national governance, that is, finance is the material base of national governance, the mechanism guarantee of a national governance system, and the effective tool for supervision of the improvement of national governance ability. This work constructed a theoretical framework of finance in the new era as the first step. Finance studies are regarded as a theoretical discipline that study fiscal phenomena and provide theoretical guidance for finance activities. Finance studies in the new era must remain close to national governance. Its basis, objectives, objects, contents, and scope of research must follow the step of reform. The main changes can be summarized as follows: more diversified, more comprehensive, and more closely following the theme of the times. A financial discipline system will take the foundation and pillar of national governance under the market economy conditions as a theoretical basis and consider the way to solve problems in the construction of a modern financial system as the research emphasis. Furthermore, such system will be supported by interdisciplinary research methods, promote the innovation of fiscal theory and guide the practice of finance to solve problems in the way of being the foundation and important pillar of national governance. After all, finance with socialism with Chinese characteristics should follow the step of the theme of the times and grasp the law of the times either in theoretical or practical aspects. Accordingly, we can guide the practice of national governance better and form a theoretical system of finance with Chinese characteristics.

**Reference**

[1] *Compilation of the Nineteenth Party Congress Documents*[M]. Beijing: Party Construction Books Publishing House, 2017.

[2] *Compilation of Documents of the Third Plenary Session of the Eighteenth Central Committee of the Communist Party of China*[M]. Beijing: People's Publishing House, 2013.

[3] Li Junsheng. New Market Finance: A New Paradigm for Enhancing the Explanatory Power of Finance [J]. *Journal of Central University of Finance and Economics*, 2017 (5).

[4] An Tifu. on the subject attribute and orientation of finance [J]. *Finance and Trade Economy*, 2016 (12).

[5] Wu Junpei. Three Basic Questions on Fiscal Theory [C]. Exchange Paper of the 21st National Symposium on Fiscal Theory, 2017.

[6] Deng Liping. *Thoughts on Finance and Taxation of Socialism with Chinese Characteristics* [M]. Xiamen: Xiamen University Press, 2016.

[7] Gao Peiyong. Seizing the Favorable Opportunity for the Development of Finance with Chinese Characteristics [N/OL]. CCP News Network, 2017 (2).

[8] Liu Xiaolu and Guo Qingwang. 300 Years of Finance: An Analysis from the Perspective of State Governance [J]. *Finance and Trade Economy*, 2016 (03).

[9] Sun Zheng. Discussions on the Subject Attribute of Finance and Its Future Interdisciplinary Development Trend [C]. Collection of Practical Papers on Education and Teaching Reform of Finance Specialty, Shanghai University of Finance and Economics Press, 2017.

[10] Huang Wei. *Kangxi Lexicon* [M]. Beijing: Beijing Yanshan Press, 2006.

[11] Xu Xiaoquan. Governance Theory of Western Countries: Connotation and Evaluation [J]. *Special Issue of Procuratorial Fengyun-Social Governance Theory*, 2014 (03).

[12] Luo Wendong. Promoting the Modernization of National Governance System and Governance Capability [N/OL]. People's Network, 2017 (05).

[13] Zhu Songyan. On Modernization of China's National Governance Capability [J]. *Contemporary World*, 2015 (05).

[14] Central Compilation Bureau. *Complete Works of Marx and Engels* [M]. Beijing: People's Publishing House of China, 1963.

[15] Ma Xiao and Li Xue. The Development Direction of Finance in the Context of Modernization of National Governance [C]. Exchange papers at the 21st National Symposium on Financial Theory, 2017.

[16] Liu Wei. New Normal Economy and Supply-side Structural Reform [J]. *Managing the World*, 2016 (7).

[17] Ruan Shouwu. Methodology and Research Framework of Public Choice Theory [J]. *Exploration of Economic Issues*, 2009 (11).

[18] Chen Gong. *Finance (8th Edition)* [M]. Beijing: Renmin University Press, 2015.

# 财政的哲学

## 黎旭东

**摘　要：** 人类社会除了社会化的生产、生活和经济的一般关系之外，社会的共同关系将人类更加广泛和紧密地联系在一起，并且围绕实现共同利益为核心而结成共同意志、共有财富、共同事务相统一的关系，共同利益是人类结成共同关系的起因，同时也是共同关系作用的目的，共同意志、共有财富、共同事务相统一的作用是实现共同关系目的的唯一途径。共同体是共同关系组织化的实现形态，共同权力、财政、行政事务对应承接着共同意志、共有财富、共同事务的共同关系要求，因而，财政的性质是共有财富道义和效能的实践工具，财政职能由共有财富在共同关系中的作用所决定，在共同体中发挥着满足共同需要创造共同利益的关键性的作用。所以，财政的本质属于人类社会共同关系的范畴，而不属于社会的经济和生产的一般关系范畴，唯有在共同关系和共同体中才能找到安身立命之所，唯此才会是国家治理的基础和重要支柱。

**关键词：** 共同关系　共同体　共有财富　财政　道义　效能

[中图分类号] F810　　[文献标志码] A

## 财政是共有财富道义和效能的实践工具

　　财政是人类世界当中关系最为复杂也极为重要的社会事物，说其关系复杂，在于财政这一事物关系到人类组织体的政治、经济、社会、文化、生态各个方面，与社会全体成员都有着密切的联系，说其极为重要，在于"财政是国

---

[作者简介]：黎旭东，原广东省财政科研所所长。

家治理的基础和重要支柱"（党的十八届三中全会决议），"不言理财者，决不能平治天下"[1]。从历史的方面来说，财政事物一直都是人类社会关系问题的焦点，社会制度的变迁无不与财政事物密切相关，其本身即是社会制度变迁的内容和标志，"普天之下莫非王土，率土之滨莫非王臣"[2]，财政事物及其本质属性共有财富的归属决定了社会制度的性质。

人类的社会化主要是沿着两条路径发展的，一条路径是生产的社会化，通过专业分工和协同的社会化大生产方式实现的，马克思主义哲学中的政治经济学说得十分明白；一条路径是社会关系的共同体化，通过氏族、部落到国家的组织形态的变化实现的，马克思主义哲学中的科学社会主义说得非常清楚。认识财政事物必须从其本质关系上去把握，必须要有一个基本的定位判断，财政事物究竟是生产社会化中的事物，还是社会共同体中的事物，这是财政事物认识的基本出发点问题，如同会计记账，类款项目记错了科目，会计报表必定平衡不了。如果将财政事物的类别属性搞错了，则对财政事物的认识必定是不得要领，差之毫厘失之千里。

## 财政事物属性

认识财政事物属性的目的，是为了建构财政哲学和财政基本理论，能够正确地反映出财政事物所具有的独立学科属性，独有的运行规律，以此来指导财政事物的工作，而要做到这一点，必须先要完成财政的本质认识的任务。财政本质存在于财政事物属性当中，是财政学科理论体系建立的基点和原点，找到了这个基点才能够构建有着紧密逻辑联系的财政学科体系，才能够形成人们认识财政事物内部构成的定位和标准，才能够科学地指导人们的财政实践活动。财政不是一个简单的事物，更不是一个孤立的事物，任何事物都是在相互关系中确定其独立的存在，认识财政本质离不开这个基本哲学认识方法的运用。

在人类的社会化两条主要路径当中，生产社会化表现为人与物的哲学关系，社会共同体表现为人与人之间的哲学关系，这是人们认识世界的两大基本体系关系，他们之间既有区别也有着密切的联系。财政事物与其他事物相比较更为难以认识一些，就在于财政事物不单纯，既与生产的社会化有关系，也与社会共同体的关系密切，归根结底还是属于社会共同体的范畴，它总是与社会共同关系联系在一起,是社会共同关系中的重要构成,而不是生产社会化中的产物。按照再生产理论,在生产、流通、分配、消费当中,财政不属于再生产四个环节中的任何一个环节,不参与其内部的任何一个方面的活动,仅仅只是以一个再生产的外部影响因素存在着,在马克思的《哥达纲领批判》看来,财政属于再生产外部性的社会必要扣除而存在,而区别于再生产内部的必要扣除。因此,不能将财政的社会必要扣除与再生产当中的简单再生产折旧扣除相混淆,不能将财政分配与再生产的分配视为同一种性质的分配,同样也不能视同为生产关系的分配,财政分配是以与再生产分配、生产关系分配相独立的分配方式存在着,任何将三种分配混为一谈都是学术不精而不得要领。这个道理告诉人们,财政事物虽然与经济密切相关,对经济发挥着十分重要的关系和作用,但终究不属于经济内部因素,而是经济的外部影响变量因素,将财政事物归属于经济学体系的结果,正如荀子所言:"不懂伦类者,不足谓善学",明明是人与人之间的关系问题却错配为人与物之间的关系问题,明知道财政事物的本质认识不应在经济学科,却仍然要缘木求鱼,明知道财政是一个独立的社会事物,却要削足适履,使其理论上失势,非要让其从属于某个学科理论不可,而不能独立存在,使其不能发挥国家治理的重要基础和支柱的作用。

  财政事物总是与氏族、部落、部落联盟、国家这样一些共同体组织联系在一起,是这些共同体组织当中必不可少的有机构成,这些共同体组织的兴衰存亡总是与财政事物状况密切相关,在中国历史中,历朝历代的初期总是会轻徭薄赋、休养生息,中期总是会国库充盈,晚期总是会国库空虚、腐败丛生、横征暴敛、民不聊生、农民起义,又进入一个改朝换代的轮回。中国上古时期的传说中,夏禹计税而崩、诛杀抗税部落首领防风氏,《周礼》中记载的最早的预算:九赋、九算、九贡,杨朱因"拔一毛而利天下不为也"而被孟子骂作"无君无父,禽兽也",周天子"债台高筑"的故事,几千年来,历史上任何一次大的改革和社会变革都以财政问题为主要的内容和手段。无论是马克思还是恩格斯,讨论财政问题都是与社会共同关系相联系的,也就是说财政是命运共同体中的事物,"国家和旧的氏族组织不同的地方,第一点……。第二个不同点,是公共权力的设立,这种公共权力已经不再直接就是自己组织为武装力量的居民了","为了维持这种公共权力,就需要公民缴纳费用——捐税,捐税是以前的氏族社会完全没有的。但是现在我们却十分熟悉它了。随着文明时代的向前进展，甚至捐税也不够了；国家就发行期票、借债，即发行公债"。[3]"物质劳动和精神劳动的最大的一次分工，就是城市和乡村的分离。……随着城市的出现，必然要有行政机关、警察、赋税等，一句话，必然要有公共的政治机构，从而也就必然要有一般政治。"[4]"在亚洲，从远古的时候起一般说来就只有三个政府部门，财政部门，或者说，对内进行掠夺的部门；战争部门，或者说，对外进行掠夺的部门；最后是公共工程部门。……所以亚洲的一切政府都不能不执行一种经济职能，即举办公共工程的职能。"[5]由此可以看到，财政是与公共权力相联系的，而不是与社会化大生产相联系，更不是与市场经济相联系。

公共权力是人类结成社会就已经存在的，无论是氏族、部落、还是部落联盟时代，国家这一组织形态的产生则完全改变了公共权力的形态和性质，亦即是说人类的社会化是以共同体组织为主要载体，而共同体内的共同权利、公共权力是本已存在的，共同体组织形态和性质的改变，取决于公共权力"道义"的问题，亦即是公共权力被谁掌控和"为了谁"的问题。因而，财政事物属性存在于社会共同关系的范畴内，财政本质必须从社会共同关系当中去发现。

世间没有纯粹的政治、经济、财政、管理等事物，人们认识世界却可以将事物当中的某些方面的内容进行分门别类地进行研究，如此即是格物致知、混沌已开，从而产生人类各方面的专门学问。从哲学的方法论上来认识事物，可以划分为人与物之间的关系学问，人与人之间的关系学问，一般说来，自然科学、环境科学、经济学等属于人与物的关系哲学范畴，伦理、道德、法律、政治、管理等属于人与人之间的关系哲学范畴。通过人与物的关系主要是解决认识世界、改变世界、创造财富、服务人类的科学技术和利益生产范围，通过人与人的关系主要是认识人类社会各种关系矛盾，改造社会关系，规范人类关系行为，服务于人类社会的发展。因而，财政事物的本质理应存在于人与人之间的社会共同关系当中，而不是人与物之间的生产和经济的关系当中，如此才能够透过现象看本质，真正找到财政事物的本质所在，否则，以砖磨镜，即使下再大功夫也只会得到南辕北辙的结果，无论是应用经济学、部门经济学、再生产分配说、社会剩余产品说，在这些方面来找财政本质只能是"恰似觅兔角"，是绝对找不到的。

## 共同关系哲学

在上古氏族时代，一个氏族的全体成员是在首领、头人等称谓人士的带领下，表现为一种共同生产、共同居住、共同生活、共享劳动果实的共同生存状态。及至由多个氏族组成部落以后，自然形成氏族首领的"联席会议制"的议事决策机制，从中推选出德高望重的部落酋长作为召集人，主持议事决策，共同议事的结果为各氏族所尊重和遵从，所以就有孔子在《中庸》中高度赞扬"舜之为舜"的"舜好问，好察迩言，抑恶扬善，执其两而用其中之于民"[6]的道理。这种会盟的协商议事决策机制行使着最早的共同权利，从上古时期一直延续到了周朝，发挥着人类组织化的基础性作用，成为维护人类社会共同关系的纽带。考察从古到今人类的各类组织体的内在运行规律，也莫不与社会共同关系的内在元素及其表现形态相关联。从西方理论所认识到的立法权、司法权、行政权，还是公共权力、民主、专制、意志的政治哲学问题，契约论，国家理论等关于国家组织的认识都是建构在社会共同关系之上的。

研究人类社会化的发展必须研究人类的共同关系，人类因共同关系而结成人类社会，或者说，人类社会化的本质即是社会共同关系，亦即是，没有社会共同关系就没有人类的社会共同基础，更加没有人类社会化发展的共同条件，任何对社会共同关系的解构、颠覆都是对社会发展的倒退，任何对社会共同关系的建设、加强、完善都是对社会发展的促进。人类社会的进步都反映在文明、文化的基础上，所谓文明，即是人类的去动物本能化，或者是脱离动物本能驱使的表现，所谓文化，即是人类文明化的过程及其产物，人类的文明、文化都是以人的动物本能为认识基点和起点，人们总是以人类行为与动物本能的差别引以为傲，这是人类认识自我、发展自我的基本坐标原点，除了用火、使用工具、发明文字、劳动分工、价值对于本能的超越等方向之外，人类与动物世界最大的不同在于人类的组织化、社会化，在于人类能够实现由自发到自觉的组织化、社会化的不断超越。社会哲学即是对这种组织化、社会化的深刻理论认识，中国的国学体系本质上即是以社会哲学为主干的中国哲学体系，国学是春秋战国时期思想家们共同以"人、家、国、天下"为主要研究对象，以伦理、道德为主要行为准则和规范，以及在伦理、道德基础上的圣贤哲学、道义哲学，从而共同建立起人类的社会关系哲学。伦理规范的是人与人之间的生命血缘关系行为，道德规范的是人与人之间的利益关系行为，如此就能够认识到孔子的哲学是伦理哲学，主讲"家"的关系，老子、墨子的哲学是道德哲学，管子、老子主讲"国"，墨子主讲"天下"的关系。国学也表现在文学上面，四大文学名著中，《西游记》说的是人的社会化，《红楼梦》说的是家族关系，《水浒》说的是国的问题，《三国演义》说的是天下的概念。在以"人、家、国、天下"为研究对象的国学体系中，包含着一个基本的认知和判断，人类的一切关系都是建立在共同关系之上，家、国、天下都是以人为全部构成，发生于家、国、天下中的事情都是人的共同关系的表现，没有了共同关系也就没有了家、国、天下一切关系发生、存在和发展的任何可能性，也就没有了任何关于社会、组织的发生、存在、发展可能性，也就没有了政治、法律、道德、伦理规范的可能性，也就没有了任何物质财富生产、流通、分配、交换的可能性，任何的文明、文化、哲学、理论、观念、意识也都将不复发生和存在。正是人类区别于动物世界根本不同之处在于人与人之间的共同关系的成立，才制造出不断进化的人类社会，极其多姿多彩的社会关系。

社会哲学包含了一般社会关系哲学，主要是伦理和道德，这两个既不同又有着密切联系的方面，建立起了真正具有普世价值的社会行为规范，是奠定人类社会化基础的哲学，主要创始人为老子、孔子、墨子为代表的春秋战国的思想家们；共同关系哲学，主要是关于人类结成组织以及组织化社会行为的哲学，揭示了人类社会化的内在规律，建立起了人类社会道义与建设的道德与价值关系，明确了人类社会发展的方向，主要创始人是由两大群体构成，一大群体是春秋战国的思想家们，他们倡导了大同社会、天下为公、兼爱的社会共同关系理念，另一大群体是马克思主义者，其代表性的哲学包括历史唯物主义、政治经济学、科学社会主义和毛泽东思想，中国社会主义制度的实践即是共同关系哲学的实践，并且实现了由自发到自觉的共同关系哲学实践的超越。

共同关系主要由共同利益、共同意志、共有财富和共同事务四大要素所构成，共同利益是共同关系的核心，一切都是围绕共同利益展开社会共同关系的，没有共同利益也就没有了社会共同关系，破坏或者背离了共同利益，共同关系就会发生扭曲，也就是打开了潘多拉魔盒，这是人类人为灾难的源头。正是因为有共同利益，国学中才会产生"大同社会""天下为公"的理念，才会产生出"中"的"求同存异"解决对立矛盾问题的方法,正是因为有共同利益,人们才会结成命运共同体和利益共同体,人类才会有组织起来和组织化的发展要求,通过组织起来,人类才会有力量,才能够集中力量办大事,而这又是通过"术业有专攻"以及社会化的分工合作来实现的,而分工合作正是共同利益和共同关系的现实体现。因为有了共同利益才会使人们组织起来,而组织起来的人们需要有共同意志来统一大家的行动,需要有一系列规则来规范和约束各自的行为,才能够发挥出组织化的巨大力量,如果共同意志不能统一到共同利益上来,则必然导致组织成员的离心离德,必然带来组织的分崩离析,舜所采用的就是"执其两而用其中之于民"的求同存异方式来求得组织体内部的统一意志,进而形成共同权利的权威,实现共同利益与共同意志和共同权利的统一。实际上,共产党的政治哲学即是这三者相统一的哲学,资产阶级的政治哲学只讲共同意志与共同权利,封建主义的政治哲学只讲共同权利。共同利益是需要通过完成共同事务来实现的,所以,共同意志、共同权利所要发挥作用的一个方面即是决定和管理好共同事务,通过解决好影响人们生活、生产等方面的问题,通过国家治理和建设来达到实现共同利益的要求,满足人民对安全、对美好生活的向往的要求。要完成共同事务没有财富支撑是行不通的,这就提出了组织体内共同关系中的共有财富的要求,《孙子兵法》开篇即是"兵者,国之大事,死生之地,存亡之道,不可不察也"[7],紧接着第二篇即是讲的国力财用的问题,战争打的就是人、财、物,历来军事界都有一个说法:外行看战略,内行看后勤。由此可见,共有财富的多寡,理财能力的强弱,在相当大程度上决定着战争的胜负。因此,在共同关系中,以共同利益为核心,以共同意志与共同权利相统一,以共同事务与共有财富相匹配,从而使共同意志、共有财富、共同事务形成与共同利益的一致性,这是共同体中的共同关系的内在必然逻辑联系,只有这四个方面高度契合,才可以形成命运共同体和利益共同体两体合一的组织体,否则,产生的是貌合神离没有任何力量的组织。

形而之上谓之道,形而之下谓之器。共同利益、共同意志、共有财富、共同事务四要素构成了共同关系的内核,四要素之间的相互对应的各种关系构成了共同关系的哲学,这就是共同关系形而之上的道。与四要素一一对应的是共同需要、共同权力(政府)、财政、行政服务管理事务,这就是共同关系形而之下的器。共同关系中的"道"和"器"的关系是社会组织体(氏族、部落、部落联盟、国家）具有共性和一直沿革下来的，最早的氏族就是一个完全形态的共同关系体，人们共同生产劳动，共同生活，共同享受劳动成果，共同防御，共同赡养老人养育孩子，组成的是完全形态的命运共同体和利益共同体，这种状态一直延续到部落联盟瓦解，转变为国家形态为止。发生根本性改变的是共同权力的畸变，本来是从属于共同利益和共同意志的共同权力改变为凌驾于共同利益和共同意志之上，不再是服务于共同利益，不再是听从于共同意志，这种共同权力的畸变的目的就是为了将共有财富占为己有，这才形成了"普天之下莫非王土，率土之滨莫非王臣"天下为一己之私利的制度形态，其标志性的事件是夏禹之前共同权力的禅让制改变为之后的世袭制开始的，历史上流传下来的《五子之歌》就很好地反映出了这种改变。这种制度性改变完全破坏了共同关系的统一，使得平等的组织成员关系分化成为统治阶级和被统治阶级，借助共同权力的威权，以税赋的形式强制性地向被统治阶级夺取财富，将这些本应属于共有性质的财富化为统治阶级的私人财富，满足统治阶级穷奢极欲的腐朽生活，这才有"朱门酒肉臭，路有冻死骨"两极分化的社会状态。春秋战国时期思想家们纷纷通过赞扬上古圣人们的品德和才能来研究"人、家、国、天下"的关系问题，期盼着人类能够回归到上古时代的社会共同关系状态上来，"天下为公"、大同社会、兼爱等思想都是对社会共同关系最为基本和朴素的认识。由此也说明，人类的发展史是由天下为公改变为天下为私，但是，只要人类不断地努力，最终还是会回归到天下为公的社会共同关系状态上来，春秋战国时期思想家们这样认为，马克思主义哲学也同样是这样认为的，而且马克思主义还要如此去改变世界。共同关系哲学是对于人类社会化、组织化发展规律认识和进行社会和组织改造的哲学，通过共同关系构成的对立统一规律基础上的矛盾关系可以作为认识人类社会的基本分析方法工具，用于建构社会科学学科体系的理论建设，用于改善社会和组织关系的实践行动。

  在共同关系的诸要素关系当中，共同利益与共同意志及其共同权力之间的关系问题是政治哲学的主要问题，同样的是，共同利益、共同意志、共同事务与共有财富及其财政的关系问题是财政哲学的主要问题，正是因为有了这样的基于相同基本元素的共同关系，财政哲学与政治哲学才有着天然的紧密联系，他们之间许多的原则、思想是相通的，甚至很多的政治哲学的方式方法都要落脚到财政哲学的具体的内容上面才具有可行性。在某种程度上来说，财政哲学与政治哲学之间具有互补的相得益彰的作用关系，离开了财政哲学，政治哲学的实体必然空洞；而离开了政治哲学，财政哲学有失去灵魂之虞，容易落入"技"的作用层次，失去道和器的层次，这就是财政学科理论体系建设至今阙如的内在原因。找不到财政自己的本质，不在于财政没有本质，而在于找错了方向，财政既不属于经济学科属性，也不是政治学科之下的属性，而是拥有自身独立的事物本质，这个本质属性即是社会共同关系中的共有财富，在社会共同关系中，共有财富是一个相对独立的现实存在，与社会中的私人财富更是一个独立的存在，在共同关系中共有财富具有举足轻重的地位和作用，关系到组织体的生死存亡，组织体是强大还是衰弱很大程度上取决于共有财富，可以说，一个没有共有财富的组织体是一个名存实亡的组织体，共有财富之于共同体组织的重要性不言而喻。财政是共有财富的道义和效能的实践工具，一方面，财政必须在共同关系的"道"的哲学层次上与共同利益、共同意志、共同事务相统一；另一方面，财政也必须在共同关系的"器"的层次上与共同需要、共同权力、行政事务相统一。财政唯有在共同关系上的"道"和"器"两个层次上实现统一，方才是正确的财政关系，否则即是错误的、不良的财政关系，在哪一个方面的关系不统一、不正确，就需要去改变这个关系，这就是财政改革、改造、改善、调整等一系列变革问题的内在道理，无论怎样变革，落脚点都是为了落实共有财富的道义和效能的要求。

## 共有财富

共有财富是指社会共同组织体中属于全体成员共同所有产权的财富。共有财富不因个人的能力大小、财富多寡、地位高低贵贱、民族、职业、性别、老幼不同而有所分别，也不与个人发生直接的产权分割界定的关系，也不是一种无主的"公共"存在状态财富性质，可以先到先得，而是具有明确产权属性的财富，是全体成员集体所有的具有法律界定约束效应的财富性质。在共有财富面前，人人都是平等的，具有平等的共有财富贡献责任，具有平等的共有财富产生的利益共享权利，具有平等的话语权，任何的政治权利最终还是要落脚到共有财富的使用和共享上面，任何的社会责任最终也要落脚到共有财富的汇聚、贡献上来，唯有如此，社会共同关系才能够成立，命运共同体、利益共同体的组织才能够成立，平等的社会关系才能够带来社会核心价值观、道德观的实现，带来社会的公平、正义，因此，平等的社会关系是共有财富之于全体成员关系的基本原则，这是社会道义的根本所在，这个道义限定了任何人都无权破坏这个原则，任何人都无权化公为私、侵占、贪污、私分、挪用、占有共有财富，也无权私相授受，礼尚往来，借花献佛，慷共有财富之慨，用于私人之间的等价交换，如果什么人可以破坏这个原则，那么这个人即是这个组织全体成员的公敌。一个组织犹如一条船，所有成员因此而结成为一个命运共同体的关系，结成为同生死共患难的关系，必须同舟共济，共同维护这条船的安危，而那些偷窃、占有共有财富的行为无异于一种凿船底仓行为，是要让全体成员一起葬身海底，因此，对于这种"凿船仓"的行为必须采取零容忍的态度，坚决地制止和防止这种行为的发生，必须高度重视对共有财富的全民监督和管理，全覆盖不留死角地、制度化、规范化地管理好共有财富，既不能让窃国大盗侵占共有财富，也不能让宵小之徒有可乘之机。这是因为共有财富性质是社会制度性质的根本标志，是不同社会制度的根本差异所在，没有任何一个问题能够比共有财富被谁占有、为了谁的问题，更加能够明确无误地告诉世人这个社会制度的性质差异，也没有任何一个问题能够比共有财富被私人占有而形成的对共同关系更加大破坏力，任何政治哲学无论怎样讲得天花乱坠，任何财政理论无论怎样精妙绝伦，任何政治制度无论怎样设计得天衣无缝，但是只要共有财富性质问题不在其中，不讨论共有财富与共同利益的一致性，不能让组织体形成命运共同体和利益共同体，这样的政治哲学、财政理论和政治制度的道义性和科学性都要打上大大的问号。

共有财富来源，一是本有的，如土地、领海及其资源；二是税收和非税收入；三是经营所得（资本、资产、债权债务）；四是其他方式获得和拥有（国家级基础大数据、特许经营权等）。一个国家组织体最大、最基本的共有财富是领土、领海及其蕴含的资源，其领土、领海上出产的主要是人们的生活资料，供养着人们的生存和繁衍，而其下出产的主要是工业的资源原料，供养着整个国家经济的发展。人类几千年的战争史告诉人们，几乎所有的战争都是因为对于土地或者资源的争夺，占据了土地也就表明占有了财富。领土、领海及其资源是组织体全体成员赖以生存繁衍的物质基础，这就决定了领土、领海的共有财富性质，而不能被私人所有占据，任何对土地、领海的私人所有都是对组织的命运共同体的破坏，因为没有土地所有权的人就没有保护拥有土地所有权的人的责任和义务，在土地所有权问题上组织体全体成员之间已经出现了分化，他们已经不是一个命运共同体和利益共同体的关系，这就是一个国家会出现一盘散沙的制度原因。同时，领土、领海是全体成员的共同生存空间，环境保护、江河湖海流域的治理、国土整治，这些方面是全体成员的共同责任，全国性的基础设施建设也都需要保证国土必须是共有财富性质，而如果土地财产权归私人所有，则全体成员的共同利益必然受到损害，很多共同需要的事情就无从谈起。地下资源也是同样道理，必须是属于全体成员共同所有的财富性质，不能是私人所有性质，任何允许私人或公司开采的矿山资源都应当征收资源税，以保证共有财富的利益不受侵害。从历史情况来看，南北宋、清朝晚期、国民党统治时期，屡受外族入侵，屡以破财挡灾，并非武器不先进、并非人口和兵员不众多，但是，屡屡出现外族屠城、全国变焦土的问题，其中最为根本的就是共有财富的私人占有、土地的私有制，才会导致统治阶级与被统治阶级的割裂，不能形成命运共同体的关系，结果就是倾巢之下无完卵。与此相反的是，1950年新中国成立的第一年即发生了抗美援朝的战争，与之前的战争状况和结果不同的是，在没有制空力量，兵器火力弱小的情况下，依然能够战胜挟第二次世界大战主要战胜国之勇的美国及其16国联合国军，靠的就是全国人民同仇敌忾，团结一心，志愿军舍生忘死，不怕牺牲，在这个状况的背后，是由新型的社会主义制度所打造的命运共同体关系所铸就，而恢复土地的共有财富性质是铸就命运共同体的重要措施。与土地的基础性共有财富不同的是从土地资源上通过劳动产生的财富中征纳的税收也是共有财富的性质，税收原本的性质是"聚众人之财，办众人之事，得共同之利"，反映的是共同关系哲学中的共有财富与共同利益之间的正常关系，也是马克思在《哥达纲领批判》中所表述的社会必要扣除，剔除阶级斗争的因素，理论上的表述也就是对社会剩余产品的社会必要扣除，以满足社会共同需要为目的必要扣除。发展经济是扩大税收收入的主要来源，经济规模越大，则税基越大，可以征收到的税收自然就会多，是一个水涨船高的关系。在产生了统治阶级以后，税收的共有财富性质变了，被私人占有了，"为了维持这种公共权力，就需要公民缴纳费用——捐税，捐税是以前的氏族社会完全没有的。但是现在我们却十分熟悉它了。随着文明时代的向前进展，甚至捐税也不够了；国家就发行期票、借债，即发行公债"。[3] 税收的共有财富性质变成了统治阶级可以随意自行支配的私人财富，由满足组织体全体成员共同需要改变为只满足统治阶级少数人的需要，从此共有财富不再与共同利益发生任何关系，统治阶级彻底地走上了与民众敌对的道路，这时的税收收入已经发生所有权的完全改变，不再是共有财富的"聚众人之财"手段，而是抢夺民众财产的手段，故而春秋时期的杨朱提出了"拔一毛而利天下不为也"的代表民众利益的维权声明。税收作为取得共有财富的主要手段，其道义性在于聚集的共有财富能否用来获得共同利益，唯有用到了共同利益上面才是道义的，不能用到共同利益上面就是非道义的，这是判断税收道义性的最为根本的标准。在生产性领域、经济领域、社会基础事业领域和国家管理领域当中，存在着大量的公有产权性质的资产和资本，这些资产、资本也是共有财富的性质，这是国家组织体得以强大的物质基础，有了这些共有财富，国家才可以集中力量办大事，解决单靠个人财富和市场经济力量办不成的事情和问题，如国土整治、基础设施建设、区域协调发展、基础科学和尖端科技发展等方面所需要的分工协同问题，没有强大的国家资本实力、没有完整的产业体系作为基础条件，国家的社会经济全面协调快速发展是难以实现的。共有财富中的资产和资本既是建立利益共同体的需要，也是打造命运共同体的物质基础，有了强大的资本、资产性共有财富，人们所期待的民富国强、共同富裕、民族复兴才会大有希望。

今天的中国已经发展到最接近实现民族复兴梦想的时候，已经发展到了成为世界第二大经济体的阶段，可是想一想，1949年新中国刚刚成立的时候国家被殖民掠夺、被侵略战争直接导致的绝对贫困状态，而之后短短的七十多年时间所发生的翻天覆地的变化，其原因就在于国家组织的政治、军事、经济上的独立自主，自力更生，实现了真正地站起来了，就在于国家共有财富不断积累所形成的支撑力，改革开放前的三十年是以建立命运共同体为目的，才有全国人民勒紧裤腰带，才建立起了独立完整的工业化体系，打下了改革开放的物质基础，如果没有改革开放前共有财富的积累，改革开放就不会存在任何的政治基础、经济基础、社会基础，因此，正确认识新中国成立后两个阶段的价值和意义，必须从共有财富上来认识社会共同关系的作用，不能孤立地、静止地看待改革开放后的成就，中国历来就有"前人栽树后人乘凉"的文化传统，不能数典忘祖，更不能将其承继关系割裂开来，用一个阶段否定另外一个阶段。如果说改革开放前是为了建立命运共同体，解决有难同当的问题，则改革开放后是为了建立利益共同体，解决有福同享的问题。现在共同富裕问题还没有解决，原因就在于命运共同体与利益共同体的统一问题还没有解决，而能够将这两个共同体统一起来解决共同富裕问题的还是在于共有财富如何发挥关键性的作用。

## 财政职能

共有财富反映的是共同关系哲学的问题，在道和器的关系上，共有财富的共同关系哲学是"道"，而财政则是共有财富的"器"，财政是共有财富的道义和效能的实践工具，财政承载着共有财富的道义责任和效能责任，在道义上，财政必须以共同利益和共同需要为依归，共同利益是共同体最大的道义，符合共同利益的要求即是道义的，背离共同利益的即是非道义的，这是最为根本的判断标准，任何有损于共同利益的财政行为都必须通过改革、完善管理来予以制止和修正，必须通过提倡科学、发扬民主、完善法治，明确财政职能，确立制度、政策、体制来建立完整的财政治理体系，有效实现绩效管理、大数据管理，使得财政在财政事物、财政事务、财政实务的"道""器""技"三个层次上实现共同关系哲学思想的一以贯之，从而实现"财政是国家治理的基础和重要支柱"的作用。所谓财政事物层次即是共同关系哲学的道理层次，关于财政这个社会性事物的本源、本质，基本运行规律，事物内外的基本关系，基本原理、基本方法、基本原则、基本属性、基本范畴，系统和体系，在社会共同关系中的作用和地位等问题，有利于人们全面系统辩证发展地认识财政事物以掌握构建社会共同关系的主动权。所谓财政事务层次即是财政的职能和财政制度、财政体制、财政政策以及财政系统的"器具"体系，反映的是财政发挥作用的主要职能、工具、机制方面的规律性、规范性的要求。所谓财政实务层次即是指财政具体的实务性、操作性工作事宜。唯有进行如此"格物"方能"致知"，方能对于现实财政问题进行"伦类"，从而既能够认识清楚财政事物，也能够有效地驾驭财政事物的运行规律，最终能够改革和改善社会共同关系。

财政职能是财政这个共有财富道义和效能的不可替代、不可或缺工具的责任担当，缺少了这些职能作用的发挥，则共同关系内在逻辑链条就会发生断裂，共同关系就不能成立而瓦解。现实中人们没有分清职能与功能的区别，往往将功能与职能混淆使用。功能是一个事物可以发挥作用的方面，而职能则是必须发挥作用的方面，如货币有五项功能，但是只有价值尺度和交换媒介两个方面的功能才是货币的职能，因为只有这两项才具有不可或缺、不可替代性质，而支付手段、价值储藏、世界货币则具有可替代性，因而不是货币的职能。财政职能也是如此，虽然财政与社会方方面面都有着紧密的联系，具有许多的功能，但是就其本身必须承担的责任来说主要是四项职能，聚集、管理、运营、使用共有财富，亦即是"聚财、管财、理财、用财"四个方面。共有财富是为实现共同利益服务的，财政作为共有财富的实现工具，自然要秉承共有财富在共同关系中的内在要求，完成共有财富在共同关系中的任务，上述四个方面构成了财政的基本职能任务，从共有财富的产生，全过程全方位的管理，共有财富存量的运营理财，直到最终一部分共有财富用于日常共同事务以满足共同需要，涵括了共有财富的主要范围和运动方式，从而可以保证共同体组织的健康运转和发展，因此，财政的这四项职能是不可替代也是不可或缺的，而且是缺一不可。

聚财是共有财富的源头活水，是财政的第一项职能。土地共有性质不能直接成为财富，必须通过社会经济领域的劳动和活动才能够生产出财富，国家组织并不直接参与生产和劳动，所以，共有财富的取得主要通过税收和非税收入的方式对社会财富进行必要的社会扣除，从这种意义上来说，税收及非税收入是经济领域中的重要外部变量因素，十分显著地影响着经济的发展数量、质量、结构，除了取得共有财富的职责之外，税收还是一个十分重要的政策杠杆手段，增税、减税，开设新的税种，取消已有税种，调整税率，都会直接或者间接地影响投资和生产经营者的决策，通过鼓励或者限制某种经济行为来影响微观经济活动达到调节宏观经济的目的。正是因为税收具有很大的调节经济关系的作用，税收总量和税种结构与经济总量和经济结构之间有着密切关系，任何的税收制度、政策，甚至财政体制的变动都会影响产业结构、区域经济结构关系的变化，这些反映的是税收对于经济的反向作用。从正向关系上来看，经济的发展是共有财富的主要来源，经济越发展，通过税收手段获取的共有财富就必定会越多，在税收制度不变的情况下，税收与经济的关系必定是一个水涨船高的关系，经济总量决定了共有财富的总量，税收永远都只能是社会财富中的一部分，有多少社会财富才可以从中取得一定比例的共有财富，竭泽而渔是行不通的，取得太多，则经济就会停止或者崩溃，取得太少则不能满足社会共同需要，实现不了社会共同利益，因此在税收和经济之间存在着一个辩证的关系，存在着一个合理的税收比重区间，可以使得经济发展与满足共同利益之间形成一个平衡的关系。聚财的科学合理要求是财政履行共有财富职能的基本要求，反映的是"聚众人之财"的责任任务，是一门大学问，事体重大，关系到经济的协调稳定发展与社会共同关系之间如何才能达成命运共同体和利益共同体的统一问题。

管财是共有财富的道义、效能的重要职责，共有财富的道义安全性、国家治理的有效性的实现，关键就在于如何管好财、管好事情上面。一般说来，财政管理职能应当覆盖财政所有的方面、范围，进行全面的道义、质量、效能、服务管理，管理对象的重点在：一是管理好共有财富，防止共有财富的跑冒滴漏，防止贪污、浪费等犯罪行为的发生，加强管理制度建设；二是在管理好共同事务用好财上，运用法治、科学、民主的手段，全面推行绩效管理，以保障共有财富在使用的过程中规范运行，以实现满足共同利益的目的要求，尽忠职守，保证共有财富的道义要求的实现；三是管理好社会的财务会计事务，过往财政理论对这项管理职能视而不见，没有纳入财政理论和管理范畴的视野当中，现在需要大力加强理论研究和管理建设，尤其是需要尽早推行财税电子票据，将社会经济的交换活动全面实现财税电子票据的全覆盖，利用其财会数据的"源代码"性质，使其成为财务活动的最基础最可靠的原始数据保存下来，以防止财务会计信息的质量和安全问题发生，以此规范全社会的会计诚信，从而达到经济治理的目的。同时，财税电子票据是国家最为重要的社会经济大数据，也是重要的共有财富，电子票据能够提供最为可靠的、精确的统计数据，对其进行挖掘将会产生巨大的社会经济效益，这将有利于国家对于经济方面的治理，公共政策、公共管理也都可以建立在科学的财会电子票据的大数据基础之上。总括起来，财政管财职能需要建立起一套全新的管理体系，在管理方式上，既要重视制度管理，也要重视绩效管理，需要正确处理两者的辩证关系；在管理内容上，需要重点处理好责任管理、行为管理和约束激励的关系；在管理对象上，需要对财政自身、以财行政和共同事务、经济秩序中的财会信息质量和诚信、公共政策和公共管理方面加强管理。管理哲学的核心就是对人或者组织体的行为进行统一协调规范，并能够激发人们合作创新的动能，达到预期的组织状态和成果。财政履行共有财富的责任主要即是管理责任，应当以百分之九十的精力用在抓好管理上面，理顺了管理关系，严格执行了管理的制度，只要约束住了人的不合理、不合法的行为，激励人们自觉遵循规则、自觉地创造性工作，则其他一切事情都好解决。而如果管理上不去，其他的一切工作都会是一团乱麻，共有财富的道义和效能要求必然地都不能得到实现。在共有财富的财政管理当中推行绩效管理的方式是财政的当务之急，因为绩效是哲学方法论最基本的、起点性质的方法，一切方法都建立在绩效的方法之上，所谓绩，指的是业绩，做了什么事情，做得好不好；所谓效，指的是效果，结果有多大；所谓绩效，指的是"值不值"的问题。绩效的方法不仅在财务会计核算上，在投资领域的投入产出上，在一切的领域中都包含了绩效的概念和思维判断方式，一思一想、一言一行、一举一动当中都存在着差之毫厘失之千里的问题，所以绩效管理实质上即是对于人们的思维和行为的管理，绩效发挥作用的道理在于判断、选择、改进等手段上，在四个基本判断上，真伪判断、对错性质判断、价值判断是绩效的基本判断，构成了绩效的一元方程，而道德判断则构成了绩效的二元方程，因此，任何一件事情上面都需要用好绩效的二元方程来计算值不值的问题，有了这些基本的判断以后，人们当然就会选择做真的、对的、有价值的、符合道德要求的正向事情，而不会选择做虚假的、错误的、没有价值甚至有害的、缺德的造成损害的反向事情。人们懂得判断、选择以后，自然在思维和行为上进行必需的改进，选择正确，修正错误，从善如流，如此才能不断提高绩效，事实上，人类社会的一切方面的不断进步即是建立在绩效的观念和方法之上，"如果存在着两个以上矛盾的复杂过程的话，就要用全力找出它的主要矛盾。捉住了这个主要矛盾，一切问题就迎刃而解了"[8]，无论是认识论的方法，还是实践论的方法，还是科学发明、发现都是如此。绩效管理反映的是人们对于自身思维和行为的自觉约束和管理，人的能力即是来自于这种自我约束，能够受到的约束因素、维度越多，则思维越是缜密，行为上犯错误的可能性就越低，成功的可能性和利益所得就越大。人们嘲笑形而上学的孤立、静止、片面看问题思维方式，原因就是对事物的关联性、运动变化性、全面系统性上缺乏认识，少了看问题的维度、因素，反映的是思维的简单化和幼稚，这种情况不因智商、学历、资历改变，唯有通过反复在实践中学习总结而改变。西方哲学如此，在中国古人当中也有这样的问题，守株待兔、刻舟求剑、盲人摸象也同样是孤立、静止、片面地看问题思维方式带来的错误行为。在财政问题上注重绩效管理，重点在于财政自身行为和从事共同事务的组织和个人责任行为上面，保证这些行为的有效性的关键是要保证行为的科学性，所以绩效管理包含了内在的和外部的责任监督落实问题，必须落实法治、科学、民主的原则要求，以纠正形而上学思维带来的错误。所谓科学性也就是正确性，在共有财富的管理问题上，这些有效性、科学性、正确性都是指向共同利益和命运共同体、利益共同体的，受到共同利益、共同意志、共同权力的约束，也受到共有财富多寡的约束，也受到哲学方法论的约束（如问题导向而不是目标导向）。

理财是财政履行共有财富保值增值的重要职能，是全面履行保证共有财富有序有效运营和安全的责任担待，也是实现共同权力战略决策意图的有效政策工具，更是稳固社会主义制度、打造命运共同体和利益共同体的必要手段，其维护共同利益满足共同需要的作用和意义重大。强大的和运营管理有为的共有财富不仅是国家组织的稳固基础，也具有促进社会经济长期加速发展的作用，新中国成立后七十多年的快速发展就是这个道理。与私有财富完全逐利和谋求局部战术性质不同的是，共有财富是谋全局、谋长远的性质，既要谋求短期的战术性质的经营，更要谋求全局、长远战略性布局的策略，以社会长远发展、区域均衡发展的共同利益为目标，服从整体的战略布局要求，在土地共有而没有被私人占有的条件下，一方面可以集中财力办大事，另一方面可以承受得起暂时的利益损失，以改善后发展地区的条件，消除历史、地理、资源禀赋原因带来的贫富差距，从而为区域间的共同发展、共同富裕打下坚实的基础。

实现共有财富的财政理财职能，重点是需要建立政府财务体系：一是将共有财富全部纳入到这个体系中来，分门别类地制定法律和管理制度，明确共有财富的产权属性、管理规则、体制划分、责任界限，清晰界定各类共有财富的作用界限，不能随意混用，同时也是吸取共有财富私有化导致苏联彻底解体，以及时至今日俄罗斯国力难以恢复到冷战时期水平的教训；二是建立共有财富财务管理规则，会计账册，定期全面清产核资，编制年度财务和会计报表，以给最高决策层和全国人民一个清晰的共有财富的状况和家底，以取信于民，让人民放心，从而有利于命运共同体和利益共同体的建设，凝聚人心，而不能把共有财富还是作为"公共"无主状态的财富，采取"肉烂在锅里"的策略；三是建立政府财务发展战略规划和分门类战略发展规划，作为国家战略规划的组成部分；四是建立政府财务风险预警机制和防控机制，防止系统性的国家财务风险发生；五是建立政府财务落实国家经济与产业政策机制，助力国家长远发展大局。

共有财富能够纳入政府财务管理运营的主要是资金（基金）、资产、资本、资源和债权债务等存量性质财富，每年岁入岁出的税收资金使用有《预算法》进行管理约束，而存量的共有财富还缺乏必要的法律制度规范，对其进行管理运营也没有明确法律授权，也没有清晰的责任机制，呈现为一种宏观管理上的无序状态，这个问题理应需要改变，需要进一步理顺管理关系，建立起一套完整的政府财务管理运营体系，清晰权利和责任边界，分门别类地明确各类共有财富的运营边界，尊重各类共有财富的运动变化规律，在此基础上明确各类共有财富的保值或者增值的任务和目标，既要保障有序运营，也要保障主动从容、灵活机动地防范和应对系统性的政府财务风险。用好政府财务的政策性工具，政府促进经济发展的主要政策工具应当逐步转向通过政府财务手段，尊重市场经济的主体地位作用，运用资本运营手段在资本市场上对某些产业方面进入或者退出的双重动作向市场提出明确的鼓励或者不鼓励、限制发展的信号，以配合行政手段，从而能够更加有力地调控经济和产业稳定发展。明确划分税收和政府预算不再对市场和企业进行直接政策出资干预，事实证明用预算资金直接出资鼓励或者奖励企业市场行为、投资行为存在效果差、共有财富流失甚至腐败的问题，也容易导致政府部门争夺分配权而不担负共同事务责任的问题发生。

用财是财政履行共有财富管理分配的重要职能，这个职能体现的是"办众人之事，得共同之利"的共有财富道义和效能要求，直接对应组织体的共同事务，因而必须发挥好以财行政的财政职能作用，通过绩效管理的方式管理好共同事务，通过绩效预算的方式分配好共同事务所需要的资金需求，将宝贵的共有财富真正好钢用在刀刃上，从而达到实现共同利益的目的，一旦实现了这个目的则表明共同关系诸要素是统一的，实现不了这个目的，则表明共同关系诸要素之间是脱节的、背离的，也就意味着共同关系没有了共同性，共同体组织随时都会有解体的革命发生。用财职能关系到组织体生死存亡的大问题，不容小觑等闲视之，必须引起高度重视，在用财的法治、科学、民主原则问题上必须严肃对待，真正落实这个原则的问题是古今中外都没有解决的大问题，也是20 世纪中国社会反复革命的重要原因，皆因为革命所追求的根本目的就是共有财富的归属和支配权问题，所以，欲求组织体的长治久安，带有根本性的重要任务就是必须改变用财职能上没有章法的问题，《预算法》中缺乏实质性内容和程序内容的明确规定，存在着法律空心化的问题，原因就在于人治分配、黑箱操作的问题没有解决，还没有确立起清晰明了的共有财富和共同事务与共同利益的统一关系，也没有清晰明确与共同意志和共同权力相统一的关系，还没有落实法治、科学、民主的原则，没有明确的财政绩效管理和绩效预算的方式方法。

凡事预则立，不预则废。预算，顾名思义即是要落实"凡事预则立"的道理，"预"好事情、确实能够办好事情达到实现共同利益的目的，满足了这个前提条件，才能够再做算钱的事，这是最为基本和浅显的事理。而现实中却并没有这样做，办事的部门单位随便立一个做事的名目就可以来算钱（形同诈骗），要到钱以后就可以长期化，特别是中央和省的部门通过这个方式自行向其系统内进行再分配，行使了财政的分配职能，走了财政的路，让财政无路可走，共有财富的治理没有不乱套之理。要扭转这种错误的分配方式所造成的被动局面，财政用财职能上唯有进行自我革新，紧紧抓住"凡事预则立"道理的运用，将所有的共同事务都要落实到"预"好事情上来，"预"不好事情就没有资格参与分配，即使能够参与到分配也要明确其用钱办事的责任，如此才能够从根本上杜绝不按照法治、科学、民主原则乱要钱、乱花钱，导致中饱私囊、监守自盗预期的问题发生。通过落实绩效管理（事前的预、事后绩效评价和问责）和法治、科学、民主原则的措施之后，所谓绩效预算即是要按照事情的轻重缓急对各部门单位的专项资金申请进行排序（按专家扣分结果排序、按地方民众反对票少的优先和反对理由充分的淘汰结果排序），以落实"大事优先、民生优先、绩效优先"的预算原则来编制预算，从而形成预算科学编制的基本规矩和程序规矩。从纳入预算的事物范围来看，必须是体现共同体的共同利益和共同需要的事项，以此划定预算编制的共同事务边界，不能满足这个根本性要求的必须采取一票否决，命运共同体和利益共同体建设是一个组织体中的最大政治，背离了这个政治的事务就不是共有财富应该承担的责任，这是财政用财职能必须捍卫的底线。唯有如此，《预算法》才能真正落实实体内容和程序内容规范的要求，财政用财职能才能真正做到有法可依。

## 财政工具

工欲善其事，必先利其器。财政作为共有财富的道义和效能的实践工具，是"国家治理的基础和重要支柱"，反映的是共有财富在共同关系中的调节中枢和血脉供给性的重要作用，其与政治、经济、文化、社会、生态环境以及民生的广泛性联系决定了财政工具必须具有通用性、普适性的效能，因应财政职能的不同，财政工具即是处理与各个方面关系以及保障资金血液供应的方式和方法，因应财政与各方面关系的不同、任务不同，财政工具中既具有相对稳定的方式，也有因时因地因对象制宜区别对待灵活变通的方式。无论如何，财政工具都应该贯彻平等、公平、公正的基本原则，都应该以解决现实发展中问题为原则。一般而言，财政的工具库主要是财政制度、财政体制、财政政策三个方面构成，财政制度反映的是维护共有财富道义和效能而需要普遍遵守的基本要求，所有涉财行为上的基础规范，是非对错的基本边界，设定的是财政运行的基本轨道，构成了共有财富在器与技两个层次上的运转基础；财政体制反映的是共同体内部层级之间共有财富的统合与分治的组织关系，因应层级之间、区域之间的共同事务责任的不同、财力适配要求的不同而具有调节配置的功用，从而具有维护共同体内共同关系的重要作用；财政政策是共同体内分类分析、区别对待、协调发展的常规手段，通过共有财富使用上的激励或者限制措施来解决问题、调节关系，反映的是工具运用上的灵活变通要求，"政策和策略是党的生命，各级领导同志务必充分注意，万万不可粗心大意"[9]，制定和运用有效的财政政策是解决现实矛盾问题的法宝。财政工具的制定和运用是共同权利的作用之所在，反映的是共同利益、共同意志与共同权利的政治哲学关系，反映的是如何建设命运共同体和利益共同体的要求，反映的是财政是国家治理的基础和重要支柱的要求，正确和有效地运用财政工具是国家治理效用的基本保障。

财政工具的运用必须遵循解决矛盾问题的方式方法，对于普遍性矛盾必须用普遍性的解决矛盾问题的方法，对于尖锐对立的矛盾必须用求同存异的解决问题方法，这是 2000 多年前孔子在《中庸》告诉我们的方法论。"庸"即是通常、常理，继而产生出无差别的常规，是解决普遍性矛盾问题的方法论。"中"即是对立矛盾问题中的统一性方面，在化解对立矛盾问题上，"中"即是求得共识，达成统一的共同意志，产生出最大公约数，形成统一的制度规范，实现统一的行动，防止共同体的分化、分裂和解体，形成命运共同体和利益共同体的最为基本的方法。对于诸多矛盾当中抓住起决定性作用的主要矛盾，抓住矛盾的主要方面解决问题是最有效的解决问题的办法，对于解决事物之间差异性的矛盾问题，则是需要采取一把钥匙开一把锁的方法，区别对待。财政制度主要遵循的是"庸"的方法论，财政体制主要用到"中"的方法论，财政政策主要用到抓主要矛盾和一把钥匙开一把锁的方法论，如此才能够理解和把握方法论是如何来解决问题的。

财政制度是一套相对不变的规则体系，制定和实施财政制度都必须以实现共同利益为根本，以共同利益标准划定是非对错的行为边界，建立行为规范，其效用在于匡正行为以获得基本绩效，使每一个参与财政事务的人和涉及共有财富关系的行为形成理性预期，从而建立起财政的基本运转秩序，最大限度地减少交易成本和费用。财政制度是依据各项财政职能的要求而建立，不同的财政职能需要有不同的财政制度内容进行限定和约束，财政制度也是依据各项财政工具的要求而建立，不同的财政工具需要有不同的财政制度内容进行规范，财政制度也是依据财政管理的责权利要求而建立，不同的财政管理监督方式需要有不同的财政制度内容进行统一要求，从而使得涉及共有财富的件件事务都有规则可依，种种行为都有规则可循，以避免行为责任人的主观随意性，避免随心所欲对共同关系秩序的破坏，避免共有财富背离共同利益和共同权利的约束、导向。鉴于财政事物所具有的在国家治理中的地位和作用，鉴于财政所具有的共有财富的本质属性和在共同关系哲学中的关键地位和作用，财政制度中代表共同意志和共同权力意志的法律制度必须置于异常重要的位置上，必须高度重视涉及财政职能、财政工具、财政管理方式等方面的立法工作，形成一套较为完整的财政法律和制度规则体系，以确保共有财富不被乱用，共同关系秩序不被破坏。

财政体制是共同体内部层级利益关系的统一规则和制度安排，财政体制内在地必须按照命运共同体和利益共同体的要求来建立、维系和调整,形象地说,财政类似于共同体内"血管"的作用,流动着的是共有财富"血液",而财政体制则像是调节血液流向、流量的总阀门,发挥着维系共同体的组织生命作用。财政体制是组织体内实现共同利益的手段,反映的是共同意志、共同权力对于共有财富去向的选择和决断,因而,财政体制受制于国体和社会制度,受制于共同体内的共同事务的范围、标准和层级分工、区域配置的要求,受制于国家政策的变化,受制于财政收入与财政支出之间的财力规模关系,众多的因素制约和影响着财政体制的设置和变化。现实中看似简单的财政体制,其背后的原理和问题极其复杂,处理不好则必然导致共同体的分化和瓦解,当前社会上要求减税的呼声很高,这是从企业的感受而言的,企业分不清税收和非税收入之间的差别,问题反映在税收方面,根子却在财政体制、财政管理和用财分配上,从财政与行政部门的关系来看,行政部门切割固化财力、代行财政分配的现象十分严重,原因在于每一个部门都想自成独立系统王国,对上僭越政治决策权力,代行共同权力,以此切割财政财力,为本部门系统争取利益,然后由各部门自行向下分配,这就是"跑部钱进"的由来,财政体制中大量的专项转移支付就是这样来的,这种现象意味着在正常的财政体制分配关系之外,另有一套体制分配关系在发生作用。研究财政体制问题,必须研究如何解决部门代行财政分配的问题,这是理顺财政体制关系的首要问题,也是国家治理首要的问题,这个问题不解决,共同关系就会受到严重破坏,不能国家进入到了共和制而财政的运行机制还是郡县制、王爷制的体制,因此,应当杜绝行政部门的财力分配权力和渠道,一个部门独自形成一个血液管网体系实际上是一种分化和分裂利益共同体的现象,肢解了统一的财政的血液管道的功能,造成了不同的部门的命运和利益关系存在巨大差异的局面,带来部门之间严重的苦乐不均。这个问题表明了行政部门不是以达致共同利益的共同事务为导向,而是以自私自利的部门利益要求为导向,背离了共同利益的要求,共同关系没有不乱之理。解决财政体制问题的办法在于依照共同利益、共同意志、共同权力的要求,财政在践行共有财富道义、效能的实践工具作用当中,必须严格对共同事务的管理,将绩效管理、绩效预算、有序的民主参与和监督方式落实到每一个具体的事务项目实施当中,同时共同权力方面施行严格问责,从而打消中饱私囊的预期,只有真正全面落实了法治、科学、民主的原则,全面落实财政管理，财政体制的现实问题才能够得到有效解决。

财政政策是共有财富在解决共同利益问题上因时因地因对象制宜的变通之策，具有区别对待和权宜应对的特征。制度、体制等相对固化的规定往往会在新的情况变化和问题产生时变得失灵，这个时候就需要有应对新情况、新问题的策略，以防止问题的恶化，或者引领新事物的发展。世界上的事物都是在不断地运动和变化着的，没有一成不变的事物，也没有十全十美的制度，事物变化有向好的一面发展的可能性，也有向坏的一面发展的可能性，政策的作用就在于抑制、遏制事物向坏的一面发展，鼓励支持向好的一面发展的可能性，这就要求财政政策的制定必须在坚持共同体的共同利益方向基础上，从维护和巩固命运共同体和利益共同体的目的出发，深入调查研究，摸清情况，实事求是地分清事物变化的状况，发现事物发展变化的脉络与机理，找准问题的根由，分清事物之间的差异，有的放矢，从而有针对性地施以财政政策来解决问题，这就是"政策和策略是党的生命"、实事求是、群策群力的群众路线、《矛盾论》的方法论哲学思想的由来。在研究和制定财政政策的过程中，必须坚持以问题为导向，有什么问题就去研究探讨什么问题，寻找解决这个问题的方法和策略，因为每一个问题都是不同的，因而最需要采取灵活机动的战略战术，而不能从本本教条出发，也不能以目标为导向，不能从经验出发，也不能从本位的部门或者个人的利益出发，在延安整风运动当中，反对主观主义和教条主义以整顿学风、反对党八股以整顿文风、反对官僚主义以整顿作风、反对山头主义以整顿党风，同样在国家财政政策的制定问题上也是需要统一到延安整风精神上来，必须排斥不良学风、文风、作风、政风、党风对财政政策制定的影响，才能够保障共有财富在道义和效能上的具体实践不会走样变形。

财政是这样一个有着极其复杂关系的社会事物，唯有放在社会共同关系哲学当中才能够认识得到财政事物的本来面目。构建财政哲学的目的不仅仅是为了解释财政事物，更加重要的是为了改变和理顺社会共同关系，为了国家治理的实践。

**参考文献**

[1] 李贽. 四书评·大学 [M]. 南京：凤凰出版社，2011.

[2] 诗经·小雅. 北山 [M]. 上海：上海古籍出版社，2013.

[3] 恩格斯. 家庭、私有制和国家的起源 [M]. 北京：人民出版社.

［4］马克思，恩格斯. 马克思恩格斯选集（第1卷），《德意志意识形态》［M］. 北京：人民出版社.

［5］马克思，恩格斯. 马克思恩格斯选集（第1卷），《不列颠在印度的统治》［M］. 北京：人民出版社.

［6］论语·大学. 中庸［M］. 北京：中华书局，2011.

［7］武经七书·孙子兵法［M］. 北京：中华书局，2007.

［8］毛泽东选集（第一卷）［M］. 北京：人民出版社，1991.

［9］毛泽东选集（第四卷）［M］. 北京：人民出版社，1991.

# The Philosophy of Public Finance

Li Xudong

Abstract: In addition to the general relationship between socialized production, life, and economy, the common relationship between human society connects human beings more widely and closely, and achieve common interests as the core and a common will, common wealth, common affairs relations, the unity of common interests is the cause of the human form a mutual relationship is also the purpose of the mutual relationship between function, The unity of common will, common wealth and common affairs is the only way to achieve the purpose of common relations. While community is the instantiation of the organization of common relations, common power, finance, and administrative affairs correspond to the requirements of common relations, which undertake the common will, common wealth and common services. Therefore, the nature of finance can be considered as a practical tool that embodies the morality and efficiency of common wealth. The function of finance, which is determined by the role of common wealth in common relations, plays a key role in the community as it satisfies the common needs and creates common interests. Therefore, the essence of public finance belongs to the category of the common relationship between human society, and not in the category of the general relationship of social economy and production. Only in terms of common relations and communities can finance play a role and become the foundation and an important pillar of state governance.

Keyword: Common relationship; Community; Common wealth; Finance; Morality; Efficiency

CLC number: F810　　Document code: A

## Finance is a practical tool that embodies the morality and efficiency of common wealth

Finance is the most complex and important social concept in the human world. In terms of its complexity, finance is closely related to the political, economic, social, cultural, and ecological aspects of human organizations and all members of society. In terms of its importance, finance is the foundation and an important pillar of state governance (Resolution of the third Plenary Session of the 18th CPC Central Committee). It is impossible for a government official to administer a country if he did not pay attention to finance[1]. Historically speaking, finance has always been the focal point of human social relations and is closely related to the vicissitude of the social system, that is, it is the content and symbol of the vicissitude of the social system. As mentioned in the Classic of Poetry, all over the world, all this territory belongs to the king and all this land, all these people are king's servants[2]. The attribution of common wealth determines the nature of social system.

Human socialization develops along two main paths, one of which is the socialization of production which is realized through professional division of labor and collaborative socialized mass production, as described in political economy in Marxist philosophy. Another path is the communalization of social relations, which is realized through the change of organizational form from clan or tribe to state, as described in scientific socialism in Marxist philosophy. In order to understand financial affairs, we must grasp their essential relations and have a basic orientation to judge whether they are in the socialization of production or the social community, Whether the financial thing is the thing in the socialization of production or the thing in the social community, This is the basic starting point of understanding financial affairs. As in accounting, if a category item is mistakenly recorded, the accounting statements will become imbalanced. If the category attribute of financial affairs is misclassified, the understanding of financial affairs will be incomplete; as the saying goes, a miss is as good as a mile.

## Attributes of financial affairs

The purpose of recognizing the attributes of financial affairs is to construct financial philosophy and basic theory. By correctly reflecting the independent discipline attribute and unique operational law of financial affairs, to guide the work of financial affairs. To achieve this, we must first understand the essence of finance, which exists in the attributes of financial affairs—the basis and origin of the establishment of the theoretical system of finance. Only by finding this basis can we construct a financial discipline system with close logical links, form the orientation and standard of understanding the internal composition of financial affairs, and guide people's financial practice scientifically. Finance is not simple nor isolated. Everything determines its independent existence in a mutual relationship. The essence of finance cannot be understood without the application of this basic philosophical cognitive method.

Among the two main paths of human socialization, the socialization of production shows the philosophical relationship between people and things, and the social community shows the philosophical relationship between human beings. These are the two basic system relationships that people know about in the world, and they are both different and closely related. Financial affairs are more difficult to understand than other affairs because they are not simple. That is, financial affairs are not only related to the socialization of production, but are closely related to the social community. In the final analysis, financial affairs still belong to the category of social community, and are linked to the common relationship of society. In addition, financial affairs are an important component in the common relationship of society, not a product of the socialization of production.

According to reproduction theory, in production, circulation, distribution and consumption, finance does not belong to any of the four links of reproduction and does not participate in any of its internal activities, but only exists as an external factor affecting reproduction. In Marx's *Critique of the Gotha Programme*, finance appears to belong to the social necessary deduction of reproduction externalities, and is different from the necessary deduction within reproduction. Therefore, the social necessary deduction of finance cannot be confused with the simple reproduction depreciation deduction in reproduction. Financial distribution and reproduction cannot be regarded as a distribution of the same nature, nor can it be regarded as the distribution of productive relations. Generally speaking, financial distribution is an independent distribution method with the distribution of reproduction and that of production relations. Any conflation of three kinds of distribution is academic and not to the extent. This fact tells us that, although closely related to the economy, financial affairs play a very important role in the economy. However, they do not belong to the internal factors of the economy, but to its external factors. Just as Xunzi said, "Those who do not understand human relations are not good at learning." The problem of the relationship between man and man is clearly mismatched with that of the relationship between man and object; knowing that the essential understanding of fiscal things should not be in the economic discipline, but still to be classified in it; knowing that finance is an independent social thing, but not having to subordinate it to the theory of a subject rather than enabling it to play its role as an important foundation and pillar of national governance.

Financial affairs are always associated with and are an essential organic component of community organizations such as clans, tribes, tribal coalitions, and the state. Generally speaking, the rise and fall of these community organizations is always closely related to the state of fiscal affairs. In Chinese history, the early dynasties always tended to reduced corvee and taxes, the middle period always filled up the treasury, the late period always emptied treasury, corruption arose and people were destitute, entering a reincarnation of dynasties and generations. According to the legends of Ancient China, Xia Yu collapsed due to taxation and the assassination of Fangfeng, the leader of the anti-tax tribe. The world did not benefit from Yang Zhu pulling out a dime and being scolded by Mencius as a monster. For thousands of years, financial issues have been the main content and means of any major reforms and social changes in history. Whether Marx or Engels discussed financial issues is related to the common relationship of society, that is to say, finance is a matter in the community of destiny. "Where the country is different from the old clan organizations, the first point is…The second difference is the establishment of public power, which is no longer directly organized as a resident of the armed forces." "In order to maintain this public power, citizens are required to pay fees-taxes, which were totally absent from the clan society before. But now we are very familiar with it. With the progress of civilization, even taxation is not enough; the state issues promissory notes and debts, that is, issuing bonds."[3] "The biggest division of labour between material and spiritual work is the separation of the city and the countryside. With the emergence of cities, there must be administrative organs, police, taxation and so on. In a word, there must be public political institutions, so there must be general politics."[4] "In Asia, since ancient times, there have generally been only three government departments, the financial sector, or the internal plundering sector; the war sector, or the external plundering sector; and finally the public works sector. Therefore, all governments in Asia cannot but carry out an economic function, that is, the function of public works."[5] From the above, we can see that finance is related to public power, not to socialized production nor the market economy.

Public power has existed since the formation of human society, whether it is a clan, tribe, or tribal alliance era. The emergence of state as an organizational form has completely changed the form and nature of public power, that is to say, the socialization of human beings is based on organizations as the main carrier, and the common rights and public power in the community had already existed. Changes in the form and nature of community organization depend on the "morality" of public power, that is, the question of who is in control and "for whom" public power is. Therefore, the attributes of financial affairs exists in the category of social common relations, and the essence of finance must also be found in such category.

There is no such thing as pure politics, economics, finance, and management in the world. People know the world by studying the contents of certain aspects of things in different categories, thus producing specialized knowledge of all aspects of human beings. From the perspective of philosophical methodology, things can be divided into two categories, the relationship between people and things and the knowledge of the relationship between people. Generally speaking, natural science, environmental science, economics and so on, belong to the category of the relationship between people and things, while ethics, morality, law, politics, management and so on, belong to the that of the relationship between people. Through the relationship between people and things is mainly to solve the understanding of the world, to change the world, to create wealth, to serve the range of science and technology and interests of human production, through the relationship between people is mainly to understand the contradictions of human society, to transform social relations, to standardize the behavior of human relations, to serve the development of human society. Therefore, the essence of financial things should exist in the common social relations between people, not in the relationship between people's production and economy. Only in this way can we see the essence through the phenomena and really find the essence of financial affairs. Otherwise, we will only get the wrong results even with great effort. Whether it is applied economics, sectoral economics, reproduction and distribution theory, or social surplus product theory, it is absolutely impossible to find the essence of finance from these aspects.

## Common Relationship Philosophy

In the era of the ancient clan, all members of a clan were under the leadership of the leaders, headmen, and other appellations, showing a common living state of co-production, co-residence, common life, and the sharing of the fruits of labor. After the tribes were formed by several clans, the decision-making mechanism of the "joint conference system" of clan leaders naturally came into being, from which the venerable tribal chiefs were selected as convenors to preside over the decision-making process. The results of the joint deliberations were respected and followed by the clans. Therefore, in *The Doctrine of the Mean*, Confucius was full of praise for the truth that "Shun loved to question others, and to study their words, though they might be shallow. He concealed what was bad in them and displayed what was good. He took hold of their two extremes, determined the Mean, and employed it in his government of the people. It was by this that he was Shun. "[6] This consultation and decision-making mechanism of the alliance was an exercise of the earliest common rights, which lasted from the ancient times to the Zhou Dynasty. It played the basic role of human organization and became a link that safeguarded the common relationship of human society. The investigation of the internal rules of various human organizations from ancient to modern times is also closely related to the internal elements of the common social relations and their manifestations. The legislative, judicial, and administrative powers recognized by Western theories; political philosophical issues of public power, democracy, autocracy, and will; or the contract theory, state theory, and other knowledge about state organization, are constructed on social common relations.

To study the development of human socialization, it is necessary to examine the common relations of human beings because they make up the human society. In other words, the essence of human socialization is social common relations. That is to say, without social common relation, there will be no common foundation for human society, and even less common conditions for the development of human socialization. Any deconstruction and subversion of social common relation is a retrogression of social development. On the contrary, any construction, strengthening, and improvement of social common relation is a promotion of social development. The progress of human society is reflected on the basis of civilization and culture. The so-called civilization is the de-animalization of human beings, or the manifestation of driving away from the animal instinct. The so-called culture is the process and product of human civilization. Human civilization and culture are based on human animal instinct. Humans are always proud of the difference between human behavior and animal instinct, which is the basic coordinate origin of human self-knowledge and self-development. In addition to the use of fire and tools, invention of writing, division of labor, and values, among other things, the biggest difference between humans and animals lie in the organization and socialization of human beings. Human beings can continuously surpass the spontaneous state of organization and socialization to achieve the self-conscious state. Social philosophy is the profound theoretical understanding of this kind of organization and socialization.

In essence, the Chinese sinology system is a Chinese philosophy system based on social philosophy. Specifically, Sinology is a sages and deontic philosophy based on ethics and morality, which was jointly established by Chinese thinkers in the Spring and Autumn and Warring States periods, who take "people, family, country and the world" as its main research object, regard ethics and morality as its main code of conduct and norms, and thus evolve into a social philosophy. Ethics regulates the behavior of blood relationships, while morality regulates the behavior of interests between people. Thus, we can realize that Confucius' philosophy is ethical philosophy, which focuses on the family relationship, while Guan Tzu, Lao Tzu and Mozi's philosophy is moral philosophy. Guan Tzu and Lao Tzu mainly focus on the country, and Mozi is more concerned about world relationship. Sinology is also reflected in literature. For example, *Journey to the West*, *Dream of the Red Chamber*, *Water Margins*, *Three Kingdoms* are related to human socialization, family relations, national issues, and the concept of the world, respectively. In the system of sinology studies, there is a basic cognition and judgment that all human relations are based on common relations, and the family, country, and the world are all made up of human beings. What happens in the home, country, and the world, is a manifestation of people's common relationships. Without common relations, there would be possibility of the occurrence, existence, and development of relations between the home, country and the world, nor would these be possible in a society and organization. Thus, it would not be possible to form political, legal, moral, and ethical norms, nor would there be any possibility of production, circulation, distribution, and exchange of material wealth. As a result, any civilization, culture, philosophy, theory, concept, and consciousness will not recur and exist. The existence of common relations among human beings is the fundamental difference between humankind and animals. They create the ever-evolving human society and extremely colorful social relations.

Social philosophy encompasses the philosophy of general social relations (mainly ethics and morality). Ethics and morality differ but are closely connected. They have jointly established social norms of universal value and lay the foundation for human socialization. Their main founders are the Chinese thinkers in the Spring and Autumn and Warring States periods, represented by Laozi, Confucius, and Mozi. Common relation philosophy is mainly about the philosophy of organization formation and organized social behavior. It reveals the inherent laws of human socialization, establishes the moral and value relationship between human social morality and construction, and clarifies the direction of human social development. Its main founders are composed of two groups. The first is the Chinese thinkers from the Spring and Autumn and Warring States periods who advocated the concepts of social common relations in the Great Harmony society, the world as one community, and universal love. The second group is the Marxists, whose representative philosophy includes historical materialism, political economy, scientific socialism, and Mao Zedong Thought. The Chinese socialist system reflects the transcendence of the practice of the philosophy of common relation from spontaneity to self-consciousness.

Common relations mainly contain four elements: common interests, common will, common wealth, and common affairs. Common interests are the core of common relations. Everything in social common relations revolves around common interests. Without common interests, there is no social common relations. If we destroy or deviate from the common interests, the common relations will be distorted. That is to say, Pandora's box, which is the source of man-made disasters, will be opened. It is precisely because of common interests, that the concepts of the "Great Harmony Society" and "the whole world as one community," and the neutral method of "seeking common ground while reserving differences" to solve contradictory problems, arise in Sinology. Only when humankind links together to form a community of destiny and interest will there be organization and the generation of related organizational development requirements. Through organization, humankind will have the power to mobilize resources for big undertakings, which can be achieved through the "specialization of industry" and socialized division of labor and cooperation. Socialized division is the realistic embodiment of common interests and common relations. Common interests will enable people to organize. Organized people need a common will to unify their actions, and a series of rules to regulate and constrain their respective behaviors to enable them to exert the great power of organization. If the common will cannot be unified into the common interests, it will inevitably lead to the alienation of the organizational members and the collapse of the organization.

Shun adopted the method of seeking common ground while reserving differences between the two extremes to obtain the unified will within the organization, thus forming the authority of common rights and realizing the unification of common interests, common will, and common rights. In fact, the political philosophy of the Communist Party is the unity of these three parts. In contrast, the political philosophy of the bourgeoisie only emphasizes common will and common rights, and that of feudalism is only concerned about common rights. Common interests is achieved through the completion of common affairs. Therefore, one aspect of the role of common will and common rights is to determine and manage common affairs, that is, to solve problems that affect people's lives, production, and so on. Through national governance and construction, we can achieve the requirements of realizing common interests and satisfy people's desire for security and a better life. It is impossible to accomplish common affairs without wealth support, which puts forward requirements for common relationships within the organization. The first chapter of *The Art of War* emphasizes that "The art of war is of vital importance to the State. It is a matter of life and death, a road either to safety or to ruin. Hence it is a subject of inquiry which can on no account be neglected". [7] The second chapter is about the use of national resources and finance. The outcome of the war depends on soldiers, wealth, and materials. Historically, there has always been a saying in the military community: outsiders look at military strategy, while experts look at military logistics. It can be seen that the total amount of wealth and the strength of financial management determine the outcome of the war to a considerable extent. Therefore, with common interests at the core of common relations, common will and common rights become unified, and common affairs and common wealth become matched, so that common will, common wealth, and common affairs are formed in accordance with common interests. This is the inherent logical connection of the common relationship in the community. Only when these four aspects are highly compatible can we form an organizational body in which the community of destiny and the community of interests are united. Otherwise, there will be a "seemingly harmonious" organization that has no power at all.

"Hence that which is antecedent to the material form exists, we say, as an ideal method, and that which is subsequent to material form exists, we say, as a defining thing." Common interests, common will, common wealth, and common affairs constitute the core of the common relations. The corresponding relationships among these four elements constitute the common relations philosophy, which is an ideal way for common relations. The one-to-one correspondence with the four elements is common needs, common power (government), finance, and administrative services, which is a defining thing for common relations. The relationship between "an ideal way" and "a defining things" is common to social organizations (clans, tribes, tribal union, countries) and has been evolving over time.

The earliest clan is a complete form of a common relationship. People jointly work, live, defend, enjoy the fruits of labor, support the elderly, and raise their children, forming a complete community of destiny and interest. This state lasted until the tribal union collapsed and the state was formed. What changed fundamentally is the distortion of common power, which, originally belonging to common interests and common will, has been changed to override common interests and common will. No longer serving common interests and obeying the common will, the purpose of the distortion of common power is to take common wealth as private wealth and form a system of self-interest, as depicted by the saying "Under the whole heaven, every spot is the sovereign's ground; To the borders of the land, every individual is the sovereign's minister." Its landmark event is the transformation of the system abdicating common power, before Yu of the Hsia dynasty, into the hereditary system. *The Song of Five Sons* (one chapter of the Book of History) has been passed down from history and reflects this change very well. This institutional change completely destroys the unity of the common relations and divides equal organizational relationship into the exploiting and exploited classes. By its authority of common power, the exploiting class forcibly seizes wealth from the exploited class in the form of taxation. They transformed common wealth into private wealth to satisfy their extremely extravagant and luxurious lives, which leads to the polarized social state of "the poor suffers to die for having nothing while the rich suffers having too much."

Chinese thinkers in the Spring and Autumn and Warring States periods have studied the relationship among "man, family, country and the world" by praising the moral character and talents of ancient saints, hoping that human beings could return to the common social relations in ancient times. Thoughts such as the Great Harmony Society, the World as One Community, and Universal Love are the most basic and simple understanding of social common relations. Form this point, the history of mankind has changed from the world for the public to for the private. However, as long as human beings continue to make great efforts, they will eventually return to the social common relations with the Great Harmony Society. Thinkers in the Spring and Autumn Period and the Warring States Period support this viewpoint, as did Marxist philosophy, which changed the world in this way. Common relations philosophy is a philosophy that recognizes the rule of human socialization and organization and carries out social and organizational transformation. The contradictory relation based on the law of the unity of opposites constituted by common relations can be used as a basic analytical tool to understand human society, design the theoretical construction of the social sciences subject, and improve the social and organizational relations practically.

Among the various elements of common relations, the relationship among common interests, common will, and common power is the main problem in political philosophy. Similarly, the relationship among common interests, common will, common affairs, common wealth, and finance is the main issue in financial philosophy. It is because of such common relations based on the same basic elements that financial philosophy and political philosophy are naturally closely linked. Many principles and ideas between them are interlinked, and a lot of political philosophy methods must be based on financial philosophy content to become feasible. To some extent, fiscal philosophy and political philosophy complement and suit each other. Political philosophy would be vague without financial philosophy; financial philosophy would be at risk of losing its "soul" without political philosophy, easily falling into the "technology" level and losing the ideal method and defining thing aspects. This is an internal reason why there are some doubts about the construction of the financial theoretical system. The essence of finance itself cannot be found not because it does not have any, but that we find the wrong direction. Finance does not have the attributes of economics or politics, but it has its own independent essence, which is the common wealth in common social relations.

In common social relations, common wealth has its own relatively separate reality, especially compared with private wealth in society. Common wealth plays an important role in common relations, which is related to the survival of the organization. In addition, whether the organization is powerful or weak largely depends on common wealth. It can be said that an organization without common wealth has a mere nominal existence. Therefore, the importance of common wealth to community and organizations is self-evident. Finance is a practical tool for the morality and efficiency of common wealth. On the one hand, from an ideal method aspect, finance must be unified with common interests, common will, and common affairs in common relations. On the other hand, from a defining thing aspect, finance must also be unified with common needs, common power, and administrative affairs in common relations. Only when the two levels of "an ideal method" and "a defining thing" in the common relations are unified can the correct financial relationship be achieved. Otherwise, it would be a wrong and unhealthy financial relationship. It is necessary to change the aspect of the relationship that is inconsistent or incorrect. This is the intrinsic rationale of a series of reform issues, such as fiscal reform, transformation, improvement, adjustment and so on. No matter how reforms are formed, the aim is still to fulfill the morality and efficiency requirements of common wealth.

### Common wealth

Common wealth refers to the wealth of the common organization of the society that belongs to all members. Total wealth is not differentiated by the individual's ability, wealth, status, nationality, occupation, gender, and age, nor is it directly related to the delimitation of property rights with the individual. It is also not an ownerless "public" wealth existence, which can be first-come-first-served. Common wealth has clear property rights. It is collectively owned by all members and has legally binding effects. In front of the common wealth, everyone is equal, have equal contribution to the responsibility of wealth, has the equal rights of total of wealth of Shared interests, have equal say, eventually to locate any political rights to the use of common wealth and Shared above, and the social responsibility of any stay to the end to convergence, the contribution of wealth, the only way, Only in this way can common social relations be established, a community of common destiny and a community of shared interests be established, and equal social relations bring about the realization of core social values and morals, as well as social fairness and justice. Therefore, equal social relations are the basic principle of common wealth in the relationship of all members. This is the root of social morality. This morality limits everyone. No one has the right to undermine this principle. No one has the right to publicize, embezzle, privately distribute, misappropriate, and possess common wealth, nor can they give or receive it as private gifts. People cannot be generous with common wealth, nor use it for private exchanges. If anyone violates this principle, then that person will become a public enemy of all members of the organization.

An organization is like a ship where all members form a relationship with a community of common destiny and become a relationship of life and death. The members must work together to safeguard the safety of the ship. Stealing and possessing common wealth are tantamount to chiseling the bottom of the boat, which will bury the members under the seabed. Therefore, a zero-tolerance approach must be adopted for this kind of "chiseling ship" behavior to resolutely prevent and curb the occurrence of such acts. We must attach great importance to the supervision and management of the common wealth, managing it in an institutionalized and standardized manner with no dead ends. Not only the thieves, but the little ones shall also not be given an opportunity to take advantage of the common wealth. This is because the nature of common wealth is the fundamental symbol of the nature of social institutions. It is the fundamental difference between different social systems. There is no problem that can more clearly tell the world about the difference of nature in this social system than the problem of who owns the common wealth and who are responsible for it. No problem can be more destructive for common relations than the private appropriation of common wealth. No matter what the political philosophy is, how delicate the financial theory, or how any political system is designed, as long as the nature of the common wealth is not a problem, the consistency of common wealth and common interests cannot be discussed, and the organization cannot be formed into a community of common destiny and interests. The political and financial theory and the political system will be questioned morally and scientifically.

There are common sources of wealth. First, it can be inherent, such as land, territorial sea, and its resources. Second, it can come from tax and non-tax revenue. Third, it can come from operating income (capital, assets, credits, and debts). Wealth can also be obtained and owned through other means, such as national level basic big data and franchises. The largest and most basic common wealth of a national organization is its territory, territorial sea, and its resources. The main products of its territory and territorial sea serve as the main living materials for the people, which support their survival and reproduction. The production of industrial resources support the development of the entire national economy. Thousands of years of human war history tells people that almost all wars are due to competition for land or resources. Occupying the land also means possessing wealth. Territory, territorial sea, and its resources are the material basis for the survival and reproduction of all members of the organization. This determines the nature of the common wealth of the territory and the territorial sea, which cannot be occupied by private individuals. Any private ownership of the land and territorial sea means destruction for the organization's community of common destiny, because people who do not have land ownership have no responsibility and obligation to protect those who do.

On the issue of land ownership, there has been a division between all members of the organization. They are no longer a community of common destiny and interest, which is the reason why a country will have a loose system. At the same time, the territory and territorial seas serve as the common living space for all members. Environmental protection, the governance of rivers and lakes, and land remediation are the common responsibility of all members. The construction of national infrastructure also needs to ensure that the land must be of the nature of common wealth; if the property rights of the land are privately owned, the common interests of all members will inevitably be damaged, and many things that are commonly needed cannot be discussed. The same applies to underground resources. They must be of the nature of wealth owned by all members and cannot be privately owned. Any resource that allows private or company mining should be subject to a resource tax to ensure that the interests of the common wealth are not infringed upon.

From a historical point of view, during the Northern and Southern Song dynasty, late Qing period, and the period of Kuomintang (KMT) rule, China was frequently invaded and forced to spend a great amount of wealth on preventing disasters. This was not because the weapons were not advanced or the population and troops were small. The fundamental issue was that the private possession of common wealth and the private ownership of the land led to the separation of the ruling and ruled classes and the failure to form a community of common destiny. Contrary to this, in the first year of the founding of the People's Republic of China in 1950, the war against the United States and the aid of the Democratic People's Republic of Korea (DPRK) occurred. Unlike the previous war situation and outcome, China was still able to defeat the United States and its 16-nation United Nations forces in the absence of air power and with the use of weak weapons. Instead, China relied on the people of the whole country to unite as one and fight against the enemy. The volunteers were willing to die and were not afraid of sacrifice. Behind this situation was a community of common destiny, which was created by the new socialist system. The restoration of the common wealth of the land is an important measure to create a community of common destiny. Different from the basic common wealth of land, the tax collected from the wealth generated by labor through land resources is also the nature of common wealth.

The original nature of taxation is "to gather the wealth of all people, to do things for all, to gain common interests," which reflects the normal relationship between common wealth and common interests in the philosophy of common relations. It is also the socially necessary deduction described in Marx's *Critique of the Gotha Programme*. Excluding the factors of class conflict, theoretical expression is the necessary social deduction of social surplus products which is also necessary deduction for the purpose of satisfying social common need. The development of the economy is the main source of expanding tax revenue. The larger the scale of the economy, the larger the tax base, and the more tax can be collected naturally. After the emergence of the ruling class, the nature of the common wealth of taxation changed and became occupied by the private individuals. "In order to maintain this kind of public power, citizens need to pay fees-taxes-which were completely absent in the previous clan society. However, taxes are now something we are very familiar with.

As civilization progressed, the payment of taxes was no longer enough; the state began to issue promissory notes, borrow money, that is, issuing public debt."[3] The common wealth nature of taxation became a private asset that the ruling class can control; its role has changed from satisfying the common needs of all members of the organization to satisfying those of only a few members of the ruling class. Common wealth no longer has any relationship with the common interests, and the ruling class has completely formed a hostile relationship with the people. At this time, the ownership of tax revenue has completely changed; it is no longer a means of "gathering the wealth of all," but rather, is a means of robbing the people's property. Therefore, Yang Zhu put forward a statement defending the interests of the people during the Spring and Autumn Period. Taxation as the main means of obtaining common wealth can only be considered moral when the gathered collective wealth is used to achieve common interests. This is the most fundamental standard on tax morality judgement.

In the fields of production, economy, social basic business, and national management, there are a large number of assets and capital with public property rights. These assets and capital are also the nature of common wealth. They serve as the material basis for the prosperity of state organization. With common wealth, the state can concentrate on solving important issues and problems that cannot be resolved through personal wealth and the market economy alone, such as land consolidation, infrastructure construction, regional coordinated development, basic science, and cutting-edge technology development. Without strong national capital strength and the lack of a complete industrial system as the basic conditions, the country's comprehensive socio-economic coordination and rapid development is difficult to achieve. Assets and capital in the common wealth are necessary for establishing a community of interests, and are also the material bases for building a community of common destiny. With strong capital and asset-based common wealth, the wealth of the people, the common prosperity of the country, and the national rejuvenation people expect will be possible.

Today's China has developed to the point of achieving the dream of national rejuvenation, and is close to becoming the world's second largest economy. When the People's Republic of China was established in 1949, its state of absolute poverty was due to colonization and the war of aggression. However, earth-shaking changes occurred in a short period of over 70 years because of its political, military, and economic independence, self-reliance. The state organization was able to stand up and be supported by the country's accumulated common wealth. The 30 years prior to the reform and opening up was aimed at establishing a community of common destiny. Only when the people of the whole country tightened their belts was an independent and complete industrialization system established and the material foundation for reform and opening up was laid. Without the accumulation of common wealth before the reform and opening up, there will be no political, economic, or social foundation for the reform and opening up. Therefore, to correctly understand the value and significance of the two stages after the founding of the country, we must understand the role of social common relations from the perspective of common wealth.

The achievements after the reform and opening up cannot be viewed in isolation and statically. China has always had the cultural tradition of "One generation plants trees under whose shade another generation rests" We should not forget the tradition, and should not separate inheritance relationship and use another stage to negate another stage. If the purpose of the period before the reform and opening up was to establish a community of common destiny and solve the problem of sharing difficulties, then the period after is meant to establish a community of common interests and solve the problem of sharing happiness. At present, the problem of common prosperity has not yet been resolved. The reason is that the issue of the unity of the community of common destiny and common interests still persists. The ability to unify these two communities to solve the problem of common prosperity lies in how the common wealth plays a key role.

### Financial function

Common wealth reflects the problem of the philosophy of common relations. In the relationship between Tao and instrument, the common philosophy of common wealth is "Tao," while public finance is the "instrument" of common wealth. As a practical tool for the morality and effectiveness of common wealth, public finance bears its moral responsibility and efficiency responsibility. From the perspective of morality, public finance must rely on common interests and common needs. Common interests are the greatest morality of the community. Complying with the requirements of common interests is moral and deviating from them is immoral. This is the most fundamental criterion. Any fiscal behavior that is detrimental to common interests must be stopped and amended through reform and the improvement of management. It is necessary to promote science and democracy, improve the rule of law, clarify the functions of public finance, and develop systems and policies to establish a complete financial governance system, which can effectively realize performance management and big data management. It will make the financial subjects, financial affairs, and financial practice achieve the philosophical thinking of common relations in three levels of "Tao" "instrument" and "skill", realizing the function of "public finance as the role of the foundation and important pillar of country governance". The so-called fiscal level is the principal level of the philosophy of common relationship. Problems about origin and essence, the basic law of operation, basic relationship inside and outside of things, basic principles, basic methods, basic attributes, basic categories, systems, and the role and status in the social common relationship of public finance are conducive to people's comprehensive, systematic, and dialectical understanding of financial affairs that help them grasp the initiative to build social common relations. The so-called fiscal affairs level is the public financial function, fiscal system, fiscal policy, and the "instrument" system of the financial system. It reflects the regularity and normative requirements of the main functions, tools, and mechanisms of the financial function. The so-called fiscal practice level refers to the specific practical and operational work of public finance. Only by analyzing the principles can we acquire knowledge about what it is and identify realistic financial problems. In this way, we not only understand the financial affairs, but also effectively control the operating laws of financial affairs, and ultimately reform and improve the common relationship in society.

The accountable functions of public finance—the irreplaceable and indispensable tools for the fulfillment of the morality and efficiency of common wealth—are responsibilities for public finance to act, without which the internal logic chain of common relationship would break and the relationship would then collapse. In practice, people seldom distinguish between functions and accountable functions, and often confuse them with each other. Functions refer to the fields where one thing can exert its impact, while accountable functions refer to the fields where it must. For instance, currency has five functions, of which only value measurement and exchange medium are its accountable functions, because they are irreplaceable and indispensable. However, its other three functions —payment, value reserve, universal currency are not for they are fungible. The same is true for public finance's functions. Though finance is closely associated to society in every aspect and thus has a number of functions, its accountable functions—its obligatory responsibilities—can be mainly be classified into four aspects, "the accumulation, management, enrichment and good use of common wealth."

Common wealth serves the realization of common interests. As the tool for the fulfillment of common wealth, public finance should uphold the inherent requirements of common wealth and complete its tasks in common relations. Therefore, the four aspects above constitute the basic accountable functions of finance—from the generation of common wealth and its all-around management and the operation of common wealth stock, to its use for daily common affairs to meet common needs—which cover the main scope and movement of common wealth, thus ensuring the healthy operation and development of common organization. For this reason, the four accountable functions of finance are irreplaceable, indispensable, and integral.

The first accountable function of finance—wealth accumulation—is the fountainhead of common wealth. Wealth cannot come directly from the common nature of land, rather it is produced by labor and activities in a socioeconomic field, in which state departments are not involved. As a result, common wealth is mainly acquired through the necessary deduction of social wealth by means of tax and non-tax income. In this sense, tax and non-tax income are important external variables in the economy, which significantly affect the quantity, quality, and structure of economic growth. In addition to the responsibility of acquiring common wealth, tax is also a very important policy lever. Raising or reducing tax, issuing new types of taxes or canceling existing ones, and adjusting tax rates would directly or indirectly influence investment decisions and production agents by encouraging or restricting certain economic behavior to affect microcosmic economic activities for the adjustment of the macro-economy. Because taxation plays a significant role in regulating economic relations, where tax stock and structure are close to those of economy, any change in tax institution, policy, or even fiscal regime would influence industrial and regional economy structure. All these reflect the reverse effect of taxation on the economy. From the view of forward relationship, however, economic growth is the main source of common wealth. The faster the economy grows, the more common wealth is accumulated through taxation. If the tax institution remains invariable, then tax would be to the economy what a rising tide is to a boat—economy stock determines the total amount of common wealth. Taxation will always be a part of social wealth, so the maximum amount of common wealth is restricted by a certain proportion of social wealth. Clearly, draining common wealth from the economy as much as possible is not advised as this could lead to economic stagnation or collapse. However, if too little common wealth is accumulated, the common interests of the community will not be realized. Hence, there exists a dialectical relationship between taxation and the economy, that is, a balanced relationship between economic growth and the acquisition of common wealth can be formed through a reasonable tax proportion range. The scientific and reasonable demand of wealth accumulation is the basic requirement for finance to fulfill the function of common wealth, which reflects the responsibility of "accumulating the wealth of the public." How economic coordination and stable growth and the common relationship of community can work to achieve the unity of community with common future and that with common interests is a serious issue.

Wealth management is significant for the realization of the morality and potency for common wealth. The key to realizing the moral security of common wealth and the effectiveness of state governance lies in managing wealth and affairs. In general, the function of fiscal management should cover all aspects of fiscal administration and conduct comprehensive moral, quality, efficiency, and service management, which focuses on the following. First, it must focus on the management of common wealth to prevent leakage and crimes such as corruption and waste, and strengthen institution construct. Second, in managing common affairs, legal, scientific, and democratic means must be employed for the comprehensive implementation of performance management to assure that the use of common wealth is regulated, the requirements of common interests are being satisfied, and the moral imperative of common wealth is secured. Third, the financial and accounting affairs of the community must be managed. This was ignored in past fiscal theory and was not brought into the fiscal scope. Therefore, it is necessary to vigorously strengthen theoretical research and management, especially for the implementation of digital tax bills. This is to ensure the full coverage of digital fiscal tax bills over all exchange activities in the economy and the use of the "source code" nature of fiscal accounting data as the most basic and reliable raw data for financial activities. This can help regulate the accounting integrity of the community and achieve economic governance in case financial information quality and safety problems occur.

Digital fiscal and tax bills, as the most significant community economy big data in China, are also a source of common wealth. Digital bills provide the most reliable and accurate statistics, which can produce huge social and economic benefits after exploration that can enable the state to better govern the economy. Public policy and management are also built on the big data of scientific accounting digital bills. To sum up, wealth management demands establishing a new management system. This must focus on both institution and performance management and deal with the dialectical relationship between the two. Its content should concern the relationship between responsibility management, behavior management, and restraint and incentives in particular. It must reinforce financial information quality and integrity in finance, fiscal administration, economic order, and public policy and management. The core of management philosophy is to coordinate and standardize the behavior of people or organizations to stimulate cooperation and innovation, and reach the desired status and achievements of the organization. The main task of fulfilling the common wealth is management, in which finance should spend the most resources. Once the management relationships are straightened out and the management institutions are strictly followed, everything else will be easily solved for irrational and illegal behaviors will be restrained when people consciously follow the rules and do the creative work. However, if management fails, all other work would be a mess, making it impossible to realize the moral and efficiency requirements of common wealth.

It is imperative for finance to implement performance management in the financial management of common wealth, as performance is the most basic point of philosophical methodology, which is the basis of all other methods. Performance has two different senses of meaning: one refers to achievements at work—for example, what has been done and whether it has been done well; the other refers to the extent of the result of the work. In one word, performance presents the question "Is it worthwhile or not?" The method of performance is reflected not only in financial accounting, but also in the input and output of investment. Something can easily go wrong in every word, action, thought, and action, so performance management is essentially the management of people's thinking and behavior. The ways performance work lie in the means of judgement, selection, and improvement. There are four natural judgments: authenticity judgment, right-or-wrong judgement, value judgment, and moral judgment. The first three judgments are basic for performance, which constitutes its monadic equation, while the last one constitutes the binary equation. Therefore, it is necessary to make good use of the binary equation to evaluate its worth.

With these basic judgments, people would choose to do what is true, right, and valuable and has a positive influence that meets moral requirements, rather than the opposite, which is false, wrong, worthless or even harmful and has a negative influence. People would make necessary improvements in their thinking and behavior after they learn to judge and choose. Only by way of correctly choosing, amending mistakes, and following the road to kindness can performance continuously be improved. In fact, the continuous progress of all aspects in human society is based on the conception and methodology of performance. "If there exist two or more contradictory complex process, it's necessary to find out its principal contradiction with all efforts. Once the principal contradiction is caught, all other problems would be readily solved."[8] This is true of epistemological methods, practical methods, and scientific inventions or discoveries.

Performance management reflects the conscious restraint and management of people's thinking and behavior. The more constraints one has, the more thoughtful he/she is, the less mistakes he/she will make, and the more likely he/she will succeed and benefit. The reason why people scoff at the isolated, static, and one-sided ways of metaphysical thinking lies in their inability to understand the relevance, movement, and variability. They lack a comprehensive, systematic, and dimensional way of thinking, which reflects their simplicity and naivety. This can only be changed with repeated learning and summarization in practice, but not with IQ or academic qualifications. This is true of Western philosophy and such issue also exists among the ancient Chinese. Those who wait for windfalls, take measures without attention to the changes or take a part for the whole are also blinded by this wrong way of thinking. Performance management in financial issues focuses on the behavior of finance itself, the engagement of the organization in common affairs, and individual responsibility behavior. The key to realizing these behaviors is to ensure the scientific nature of these behaviors. Thus, performance management involves both internal and external responsibility in monitoring and implementation. It is necessary to implement the spirit of law, science, and democracy in order to correct the mistakes caused by metaphysical thinking. The so-called scientificity means correctness. In terms of management of common wealth, the nature of effectiveness, scientificity, and correctness all lead to shared interests, as well as a community of common destiny and interests, which are constrained by common interests, common will, shared power, and the scale of common wealth or philosophical methodology (e. g. , problem-oriented rather than goal-oriented).

Wealth enrichment refers to the function of finance in maintaining and increasing the value of common wealth. It is not only meant to fully ensure the order and effective operation and security of common wealth, but is also an effective policy tool for realizing the strategic decision-making intention of common power. Most importantly, in the sense of safeguarding common interests and meeting common needs, it serves as a necessary means to stabilize the socialist system and build a community of shared future and interests. Strong operation and management, along with promising common wealth, not only serve as a solid foundation for state organizations, but also promote the long-term acceleration of social and economic development. This is true of China, which achieved rapid development in the past 70 years.

Unlike private wealth, which is entirely profit-seeking and locally tactical in nature, common wealth is naturally holistic and long-term. It requires short-term tactical operations and long-term, overall strategic layouts, the latter of which takes the common interests within social long-term development and regional balanced development as the goal, thus obeying the requirements of overall strategic layouts. Under the condition that the land is common and not within private possession, common wealth, on one hand, makes it possible to pool resources for great things. On the other hand, it could afford the temporary loss of interests in order to improve the conditions of developing areas and eliminate the wealth gap caused by the historical, geographical, and resource endowment, thereby laying a solid foundation for common development and common prosperity among different regions.

The key to realizing the wealth enrichment function is to establish a government financial system. First, all the common wealth must be incorporated into the system, laws and management institutions must be classified into different categories, and the equity attribute, management norm, institution category, and responsibility boundary of common wealth must be clearly defined. The aforementioned stresses not only the clear demarcation on the effective range of different types of common wealth, which must not be mixed at will, but also lessons from the Soviet Union—it is the privatization of common wealth that led to the Soviet Union's complete collapse, as well as Russia's inability to restore its strength to the level it was in before the Cold War. Second, financial rules for common wealth must be established, which include accounting books, periodic comprehensive liquidation and verification of assets, and annual financial and accounting statements, so the top decision-makers and the public would be provided with a clear picture of the common wealth and national finance. Only in this way can the government win the trust of the people, then build a community of shared future and interests with the people's support. The view that common wealth is "ownerless" wealth must be avoided or the "letting meat spoil in pot" strategy must be adopted. Third, program planning for government financial development strategy must be done and strategic development must be classified as national strategic planning. Fourth, a risk warning mechanism and prevention-control mechanism for government finance must be established in order to prevent systemic financial risks of a national scale. Fifth, a mechanism for government finance must be established to implement the country's economic and industrial policies, which can help promote the country's long-term development.

The common wealth that can be incorporated into the government's financial management and operation mainly includes capital (fund), assets, capital resources, debt, and other stock property wealth. While the annual use of tax funds is subject to management constraints by the Budget Law, there is no necessary legal norms to constrain the stock of common wealth, nor is there clear legal authorization or a clear responsibility mechanism for its management and operation. This kind of macro-management disorder is supposed to be solved. It is necessary to further straighten out the management relationship, establish a complete set of management and operations system for government finance, clarify the boundaries of rights and responsibilities, and classify the operational boundaries of various types of common wealth. With respect to the changeable pattern of all kinds of common wealth, the government should clarify the tasks and goals for maintaining or increasing the value of common wealth, which include measures to ensure orderly operation as well as proactive, deliberate, and flexible mechanisms for prevention and response to systemic risks of government finance. The use of financial policy tools must be maximized. The government should gradually consider the financial tool as the main policy means to promote economic development, that is, to respect the principal position of the market economy and use tools of capital operation in to send a clear signal of encouragement or discouragement to the market through the dual action of entering or exiting certain industries. With cooperation from administrative means, this can ensure the economy is under effective regulation and control, and steady industry development is achieved. Meanwhile, the government should make it clear that taxes and government budgets no longer directly fund and intervene in the market or businesses. It has been proved that the direct investment from budget funds to encourage or reward enterprises' market behaviors has poor effects, and can even lead to problems, such as the loss of common wealth and corruption. It would also be easy for different departments to compete for the distribution right without fulfilling the responsibility of common affairs.

Wealth use is the distribution function for the government to perform on common wealth, which reflects the morality and efficiency requirement that can be expressed as "all for one, one for all." It directly corresponds to the common affairs of the organizations. Therefore, it is necessary to fully explore the administrative effect of finance, that is, the management of common affairs by means of performance management, allocation of the capital needed by common affairs by means of performance budget, and maximization of common wealth to achieve the goal of common interests. The elements of common relationship are unified if this goal is achieved; failure to achieve this goal indicates that the elements are disjointed and deviated, which means the common relationship has no commonality, and the community organization can disintegrate at any time.

Wealth use is related to the survival of the organization, so it cannot be ignored. The principles of law, science, and democracy in financial use must be taken seriously. The implementation of these principles is a severe problem that has not yet been solved, which was also the reason for the repeated revolutions in Chinese society in the 20th century. The fundamental goal of these revolutions was to gain ownership and control of common wealth. Therefore, the essential task for the long-term peace and stability of the organization is to solve the problem of disorder in wealth use. The reason why the Budget Law lacks substantive content and explicit stipulation about procedure lies in its failure to solve the problems of distribution by man and black-box operation. It has not established a clear and unified relationship between common wealth, common affairs, and common interests, nor has it established the similar relationship between common will and common power. With the principles of law, science, and democracy unimplemented, there is also no clear method for establishing financial performance management and performance budget.

In all things, success lies in previous preparations, without which, there will be failures. Budget, as the name implies, is to implement the principle of "success lies in previous preparations in all things." Preparing things well can result in the achievement of the purpose of common interests. Only when this precondition is satisfied, can money be counted, which is the most basic and simple logic. However, things are quite different in reality, department units that handle affairs can calculate money by erecting a job casually and namely (just like a fraud). They can then keep the money long term after acquiring it, especially the central departments and provincial departments. The redistribution of money in this way within the system is an exercise of financial allocation, taking the place of public finance, making public finance nowhere to go, there is no reason that the management of common wealth is not chaotic and disordered. The passive situation caused by the wrong allocation can only be reversed if public finance leads to self-innovation in terms of fiscal function, grasps the application of the principle that "success lies in previous preparations in all things," underscores "prepare well" in all the common affairs, and deprive them of eligible rights to participate in the distribution if they cannot prepare well. Despite the ability to participate in the distribution, their responsibility of using money must be clarified. This way, problems of self-enrichment and self-theft that resulted from them casually asking for and spending money that is not in accordance with the principle of laws, science, and democracy can be resolved fundamentally.

Through the implementation of performance management (the advance forecast before the performance and evaluation, and asking for accountability after the performance) and the principles of laws, science, and democracy, the performance budget ranks the special fund application of each department and unit according to priorities (rank according to the point deduction results by expert, rank according the priority of less dissenting votes, and the elimination results of sound dissenting reason by local citizens). This is to draw up a budget prepared according to the principle of "big event first, improving people's livelihood first, performance first," forming the basic rules and procedure rules of scientific budget establishment. From the perspective of the scope of issues that can be included in the budget, the issues must reflect the common interests and common demand of the community to delineate the common service boundaries for budgeting. Those that cannot meet the fundamental requirements should be vetoed. The construction of a community of common destiny and common interests is the biggest political issue in an organization. Common wealth should not bear the responsibility of anything that deviates from political affairs, which is the bottom line that public finance should defend using fiscal functions. Only in this way can the *Budget Law* truly implement the requirements of the specification of entity content and procedure content, and the fiscal functions of public finance can truly be legally abided by.

### Financial tools

Good tools are prerequisite to the successful execution of a job. As the practical tool for the morality and efficacy of common wealth, public finance "is the basis and important pillar for governance." Public finance plays an important role in regulating the center and blood supply common in the mutual relationship, which has extensive links with the political, economic, cultural, social, ecological environment. People's livelihood determines that fiscal tools must have effectiveness of generality and universality. Due to differences in fiscal functions, financial tools are the ways and methods to deal with various relationships and safeguard the blood supply of funds. On one hand, the use of fiscal tools is a relatively stable method because of the various relationships of public finance with other aspects and its different tasks, as well as the flexible ways it can handle issues differently depending on the circumstances and conditions. In any case, fiscal instruments should follow the basic principles of equality, fairness, and justice, and take solving problems in developmental reality as the principle.

In general, the pool of fiscal tools is constituted from three aspects: fiscal system, fiscal institutional system, and fiscal policy. Fiscal system reflects the general rudimentary requirements for maintain the morality and efficacy of common wealth, basic norms pertaining to fiscal behaviors, basic boundaries distinguishing right from wrong, setting the basic trajectory of fiscal operation, and constructing the operating foundation of common wealth from two aspects—the issue and the technology. The financial institutional system reflects the organizational relationship of the unity and division of common wealth among the levels within the community. It has the function of regulating and allocating due to the different responsibilities of common affairs between levels and regions and the different requirements of fiscal resources. Therefore, it plays a significant role in maintaining the common relationship within the community. Fiscal policy is a conventional method of classification analysis, differential treatment, and harmonious development for solving problems and regulating relations on the usage of common wealth through incentives or restrictions, reflecting the flexible requirements of tool implementation, "Policy and tactics are the life of the Party; leading comrades at all levels must give them full attention and must never on any account be negligent". [9] Formulating and applying effective fiscal policy is a magic weapon for solving realistic contradictions. The formulation and operation of financial tools is the function of mutual rights, which reflects the political philosophy relationship among common interests, common will, and common rights; the requirements for building a community of common destiny and common interests; and public finance as the basis and important pillar for governance. The correct and effective use of fiscal tools is the basic guarantee for national governance effectiveness.

　　The use of fiscal instruments must follow the ways and means of resolving contradictions. For solving universal contradictions, the universal method must be used. For sharp contradictions, the method of seeking common ground while reserving differences must be used. This is the methodology taught by Confucius in *The Doctrine of the Mean* more than 2000 years ago. "Doctrine" refers to generality and general rules, and produces an undifferentiated routine, which is the methodology for solving the universal contradiction problem. "Mean" is the unity of opposition and contradiction problems. On the issue of resolving contradictions, "mean" is the most basic method for seeking consensus; achieving a unified common will; producing the greatest common divisor; forming a unified system and norms; realizing unified action; preventing the division, splitting, and disintegration of the community; and constituting a community of common destiny and common interests. The most effective way to solve the problem is to grasp the main decisive contradiction, and to grasp the main aspects of the contradiction and to solve the contradiction of differences between things. It is necessary to adopt the method that opens different locks with different keys. The fiscal system mainly follows the methodology of "doctrine," and the fiscal structure mainly follows the methodology of "mean", and the fiscal policy mainly follows the methodology of grasping the main contradiction and opening different locks with different keys. Only in this way can we understand and grasp how the methodology solves the problem.

A fiscal system is a set of relatively unchanged rules. Formulating and implementing a fiscal system must be based on realizing the common interests, delineating the boundary of right and wrong based on the standard of common interest, and establishing norms of conduct. This rectifies actions to achieve basic performance, forming one's expectations of the kind of rational behavior involved in fiscal affairs and common wealth. This establishes the basic operation order of public finance and minimizes transaction costs and fees.

A fiscal system is established upon the requirements of various fiscal functions; therefore, different fiscal functions need various fiscal system content to limit and constrain. A fiscal system is also established upon the requirements of various fiscal tools, which need different fiscal system content to be standardized. Besides the fiscal system is built up according to the responsibilities, rights, and benefits requirements of fiscal management. Different modes of fiscal management and supervision need various fiscal system contents to unify the requirements, so that rules can be imposed on all matters involving common wealth. All kinds of behavior correspond to rules that need to be obeyed to prevent the subjective arbitrariness of the person responsible for the behavior. The destruction of the order of common relations arbitrarily, and the deviation of common wealth from the guides and constraints of common interests and common rights. Given public finance's position in national governance, and the inherent nature of common wealth and its key position and role in the philosophy of mutual relations, the legal system that represents common will must be placed in an extremely important position. Great importance should be attached to legislation involving fiscal functions, fiscal tools, and fiscal management method. A relatively complete fiscal legal system and institutional system must be forced to ensure that the common wealth is not disorderly spent, and that mutual order relationship will not be destroyed.

A fiscal system is the unified rule and institutional arrangement of interest relations at different levels within the community. Intrinsically, the fiscal system must be established, maintained, and adjusted in accordance with the requirements of the community of destiny and interests. Figuratively speaking, the role of public finance is similar to that of "blood vessels" in the community. What flows is the "blood" of common wealth, and the fiscal system, actioned as the total valve regulating the direction and flow of blood, plays the role of maintaining the community's organizational life. A fiscal institutional system is a means of realizing common interests within an organization, reflecting the choice and decision of common will and common power on the direction of common wealth. Therefore, a financial system is subject to the state system and social system, the requirements of the scope, standards, hierarchical division and regional allocation of labor within the community, changes in national policies, and the fiscal amount relationship between fiscal revenue and fiscal revenue.

Many factors restrict and influence the establishment of and changes in a fiscal institutional system. Behind the seemingly simple fiscal institutional system are complex principle and problems, which can lead to the divisions and collapse of the community if improperly handled. In the current society, demand for tax cuts is high. This is based on the feeling of the enterprise, which is unable distinguish the difference between tax and non-tax revenue. Problems are reflected in the aspect of taxes, but are rooted in the fiscal institutional system, fiscal management, and wealth distribution. From the perspective of the relationship between the public finance department and other administrative departments, the phenomenon of administrative departments cutting the solidifying financial resources and acting on behalf of financial distribution is very serious. The reason lies in that each department wants to become an independent system. This way, they overstep the power of political decision-making and act on behalf of common power to cut financial resources, fight for the interests of their own department's system, and distribute them downwards per department. This is where the phenomenon "the more you beg administrative departments, the more money you will get" originates and how numerous special transfer payments in the fiscal system are done. This phenomenon means that in addition to the normal distribution relations in the fiscal institutional system, there is another set of fiscal institutional distribution relations at work. To study the problem of fiscal institutional systems, we must analyze how to solve the problem of financial distribution among administrative departments acting on behalf of the government. This is the primary problem with straightening out the relationship between fiscal institutional systems and national governance. If this problem cannot be solved, the common relationship will be seriously damaged, and the country cannot enter the republican system while the operating mechanism of finance still follows the system of county and monarchy. Therefore, we should end the distribution power and channels of administrative departments allocating financial resources. The formation of a blood network system by a department alone is actually a phenomenon of division and disruption of the community of interests. It dismembers the unified function of the fiscal blood pipeline, resulting in huge differences and serious disparities in the fate and interests of different departments. This problem shows that the administrative departments are not guided by the common affairs to achieve common interests, but by selfish and egoistic interest, which is a deviation from the requirements of common interests, and there is no reason that the common relations are not disordered. The solution to the problem of fiscal institutional system lies in the role of public finance in serving as practice tools for the morality and efficiency function of common wealth. Public finance must strictly manage common affairs, implement performance management, performance budgeting, and conduct orderly democratic participation and supervision for the implementation of each specific affairs project in accordance with the requirements of common interests, common will and common power. At the same time, it must implement strict accountability in the area of common power to eliminate self-serving expectations. Only when the principles of rule of law, science, and democracy, and financial management are fully implemented can the practical problems of fiscal institutional system be effectively solved.

Fiscal policy is a flexible strategy for common wealth to solve the problem of common interests according to time, place, and object. It has the characteristics of discrimination and appropriate response. Relatively fixed provisions such as institutions and systems tend to fail when new situations change and problems arise. At this time, we need strategies to deal with new situations and problems in order to prevent the deterioration of problems or accelerate new developments.

Everything in the world is constantly moving and changing. There is no unchangeable thing or perfect system. There is a possibility that things will change for better or for worse. The function of policy is to restrain and contain negative developments and encourage and promote the possibility positive ones. This requires the formulation of fiscal policy to be based on the direction of the common interests of the community. to maintain and consolidate the destiny community and interest community, in-depth investigation and research must be conducted to examine the situation. Moreover, changes in the situation of must be practically and correctly identified, as well as the context and mechanism of these developments and changes. The root cause of the problem must also be identified, and the differences between things must be distinguished and treated differently. Implementing fiscal policy can purposefully solve the problem. This is the origin of the "policy and strategy are the life of the party," seeking truth from facts, the mass line of working and pulling together, and methodological philosophical thought of *On Contradiction*. In the process of researching and formulating fiscal policies, we must adhere to the "problem-oriented" approach. If there are any problems, we should study and discuss them and find out the methods and strategies to solve them. Because each problem is different, we need to adopt flexible strategies and tactics. We cannot proceed from the doctrine, the goal-oriented approach, experience, nor from the interests of our own departments or individuals. In the spirit of the Yan'an Rectification Movement, we should oppose subjectivism and dogmatism in order to rectify the style of studying, oppose eight-part opposition parties to rectify the style of writing, oppose bureaucracy to rectify the style of working, and oppose mountain-top doctrine to rectify the style of the party. Similarly, it is necessary to unify in the spirit of the Yan'an rectification for the formulation of national fiscal policy. We must reject the influence of bad styles of studying, writing, and working. Only the influence of governance and the style of the Party on the formulation of fiscal policy must be considered to ensure that the concrete practice of common wealth in morality and efficiency will not be distorted.

Public finance is such a social thing with extremely complex relations. Only by putting it in the context of the philosophy of social common relations can we understand the true face of fiscal affairs. The purpose of constructing financial philosophy is not only to explain financial affairs, but also to change and straighten out the common relationship in society and practice state governance.

### Reference

[1] Li Zhi. *Comments on four books: the great learning* [M]. Nanjing: Phoenix Press, 2011.

[2] *Classic of Poetry, Xiaoya, Beishan* [M]. Shanghai: Shanghai Classics Publishing House, 2013.

[3] Friedrich Engels. *The Origin of Family, Private Ownership and State* [M]. Beijing: People's Publishing House.

[4] Karl Marx, Friedrich Engels. *German Ideology, from Selected Works of Marx and Engels, Vol. 1* [M]. Beijing: People's Publishing House.

[5] Karl Marx, Friedrich Engels. *The Rule of Britain in India, from Selected Works of Marx and Engels, Vol. 1* [M]. Beijing: People's Publishing House.

[6] *The Analects of Confucius, The Great Learning, and The Doctrine of Mean* [M]. Beijing: Zhonghua Book Company, 2011.

[7] *Seven Military Classics of Ancient China and The Art of War* [M]. Beijing: Zhonghua Book Company, 2007.

[8] *On Contradiction, from Selected Works of Mao Zedong Vol. 1* [M]. Beijing: People's Publishing House, 1991.

[9] *Briefing on the Situation, from Selected Works of Mao Zedong Vol. 4* [M]. Beijing: People's Publishing House, 1991.

# 财政汲取与国家能力：基于文献的考察*

吕冰洋 胡深

**摘 要**：财政汲取能力是国家能力的基础，本文通过文献梳理，总结三种代表性国家起源理论，即契约论、阶级论以及暴力论中关于财政汲取能力的分析，进而总结在历史视角、利益集团视角、制度和经济视角下影响财政汲取能力的因素，以及影响财政汲取能力的方式与发展过程。通过文献考察，有助于思考财政汲取在国家能力建设中的作用，以及思考如何提升我国财政汲取能力这一容易被忽视的问题。

**关键词**：财政汲取能力 国家能力 国家起源

[中图分类号] F810.2 [文献标志码] A

## 一、财政汲取与国家能力的关系

随着 20 世纪末期制度经济学的蓬勃发展，国家在经济发展中所起到的作用和地位得到了广泛的重视，国家能力也被纳入经济学的研究范围之内。国家能力（state capacity）的概念最早出现在社会学家和政治学家的研究之中（Tilly，1975，1990；斯考克波，1984；Mann，1986），对国家能力一词的精确含义，不同学者有不同的见解。如斯考克波（1984）认为，国家能力是国家实

---

\* 基金项目：国家社会科学基金重大项目，"现代治理框架中的中国财税体制研究"（项目编号：16ZDA027）。

[作者简介]：吕冰洋，中国人民大学财政金融学院，教授。胡深，对外经济贸易大学国际经济贸易学院，讲师。

现一些并非仅仅是反映社会团体或阶级的利益的能力①。米格代尔（1988）将领导人的意志作为国家意志的代表，认为"国家能力是国家领导人运用国家机构让人民去做领导人希望它们做的事情的能力"，并且将国家能力详细分为"……渗入社会的能力、调节社会关系、提取资源，以及以特定方式配置或运用资源四大能力"。王绍光和胡鞍钢（1993）则认为"国家能力是指国家将自己的意志、目标转化为现实的能力"，并将国家能力分为汲取能力（extractive capacity）、调控能力（steering capacity）、合法化能力（legitimation capacity）、强制能力（coercive capacity）四种②。

无论是在政治学领域还是经济学领域，财政汲取能力都无疑是国家能力的重要基础和组成部分。"财政汲取能力……是国家能力的核心，是国家实现其他能力的基础"（王绍光、胡鞍钢，1993）。"任何对国家能力的研究需要选择的基本要素，都涉及国家财政收入的来源和数量，以及国家聚集并调度这些财源的可能的弹性程度"（斯考克波，1984）。相比政治学者，经济学者笔下的国家能力进一步强调其与经济问题的关联性。经济学领域中提及的国家能力一词所涵盖的范围更多地集中在财政收入汲取和法律实施等方面的能力，而较少讨论国家能力中诸如社会渗透、调节等与经济直接联系较弱的能力。国家能力被刻画为国家征税、实施法律、稳定秩序、提供公共物品的能力，概括地说包含财政能力（fiscal capacity）和法律能力（legal capacity）两大能力（Besley & Persson, 2009; Johnson & Koyama, 2016）。根据情况的不同，财政汲取能力也经常作为国家能力的代名词使用。

财政汲取能力决定着政府活动的规模和强度。这一能力不只决定了当前支出的上限，同时基于支出增加的要求所引致的财政收入需要，也必须建立在汲取能力可以达到的可能性上。长时间以来，理论研究都存在着一个缺陷，即想当然地认为国家具备完全的征税能力。在这样的假定下，国家不止可以对任意对象征税、自由决定税率，征管系统的构建和维护也近乎无成本。这种假定用在发达国家上时仍可接受，但对于广大发展中国家，在默认其具有强大的财政汲取能力基础上所提出的政策建议往往经不起推敲。因此，国家能力研究的一

---

① 斯考克波还认为对国家遭遇强势社会集团的现实或潜在的反对，或者是面临不利的社会经济环境时的情况进行考察，是研究国家能力的重点。
② 沃尔德（1995）也使用了同样的分类与定义。

个重要方面便是解释国家的财政汲取能力的决定因素、影响方式与发展过程。本文也将主要关注这一研究方向。

## 二、从国家起源理论看财政汲取能力的形成

国家是财政汲取的主体，了解国家起源过程和理论，有助于了解决定汲取能力大小的根本因素。当前对于国家起源的理论有许多，广泛为人们所了解的主要有契约论、阶级论以及暴力论。

### （一）契约论

国家起源契约论的主要代表人物为霍布斯、洛克、孟德斯鸠和卢梭。契约论为我们虚构了一种国家财政汲取能力的极限状态。契约论假定，在国家存在之前的时期，以及那些无国家的地方，是一种松散的遍布危机同时又绝对自由的社会状态，这一状态下每人都要为保护自身财产付出极大努力。个体联合与今后的主权者订立契约并成立了国家，由国家来保护国民的安全，并由主权者作为国家的代理人。但从世界史看，可以由契约论解释的国家很少。奥尔森（1965）指出，这种完全自发自愿的行动，即便直接来看总收益大于成本，在人数增加的前提下，其沟通谈判、缔结契约所需的成本也会迅速地扩大，因而这种契约的想法只能是一种设想，或者是为了解释已经存在的国家而进行的合理化解释罢了。

由于这种关于国家起源的假说是一种思想上的假定，国家获取收入的方式并没有被详细论述，但其中的分析仍有其参考价值。霍布斯与卢梭分别在著作《利维坦》和《社会契约论》中涉及了国家的财政汲取能力。霍布斯在《利维坦》一书中认为，签订契约时个人自愿将其权利与财产（主要是土地）全部交付于国家，因而国家也按照整体的意愿，在合乎公道或公共利益的方式下将所有财产（土地）分配给每人一份，使其成为私人所有。不过，尽管"……臣民的土地私有权是排斥所有其他臣民使用他的土地的一种权利，但却不能排斥主权者，不论是议会还是君主都一样"（霍布斯，1651）；"诚然，一个主权君主或主权会议中的大部分人可能违反自己的良知，因追求私欲而下令做许多事情，这是破坏臣民对他的托付和自然法的，但这却不足以使任何臣民有权对他

开展或控诉他的不义，或是对主权者发出任何怨恨；因为他们已经承认他的一切行为，而且在授予主权时就已经使这些行为成为自己的行为了"（霍布斯，1651）。从这些表述可以看出，在霍布斯的假设下，国家可以根据其自身意愿，任意地支配其国民的所有财富，也即是说，在契约论所虚构的国家中，国家具有完全的财政汲取能力。

卢梭与霍布斯的观点不同。卢梭（1762）在《社会契约论》中说到："我要指出，通过社会协约每一个个体只是放弃了部分必需的权力、财产和自由，因为由社区对之进行控制至关重要；还必须说明的是，主权者是决定此种重要性的唯一评判。""只要公民力所能及，一旦主权者需要，为国出力就是他的责任。但是主权者不能对臣民强加上无用于社区的任何限制。""把我们和社会实体联结的责任不过是一种我们要自觉履行的义务，因为它是彼此双赢互惠的，在本质上，履行这些责任的个体在为他人服务的同时也在为自己服务。"显然，卢梭认为国家或主权者所能调动的资源来自于个人的主动让与，在需要时这种让与不但是必然发生的，而且只要在公民承受能力范围内，那么也一定会是足额的。

尽管霍布斯与卢梭两人对由契约构成的国家的财政汲取方式描述上有差异，但无论是财政收入可以任意支配还是总能足额获取，都意味着国家的汲取能力在这种契约建立的国家中达到了上限。在这样的状态下，不存在能使国家汲取能力增大的任何可能性，因为当统治者能够获得国民的所有权力或者国民基于信任乐意贡献出其所有财富时，国家的财政汲取能力达到最大。

## （二）阶级论

在卢梭逝世40年后，两位伟大的思想家马克思与恩格斯相继诞生。马克思和恩格斯关于国家起源的论述强调经济上的统治者对暴力的掌控，及依靠暴力实现的对资源的汲取。马克思与恩格斯的《家庭、私有制与国家起源》一书是关于国家起源观点的综合。书中详细分析了易洛魁人氏族、罗马氏族、克尔特人和德意志人氏族的社会状况，以及之后在此基础上形成雅典、罗马、德意志三个国家的具体过程。在三个氏族社会中，都存在着人民大会、氏族酋长议事会和企图获得真正主权的军事首长（这是在氏族制度下一般所能达到的最发达的制度）。并且"只要社会一越出这一制度所适用的界限，氏族制度的末日就到来了；它就被炸毁，由国家来代替了"（恩格斯，1884）。

根据马克思与恩格斯的观点，国家并不是从来就有的。曾经有过不需要国家而且根本不知国家和国家权力为何物的社会。而国家产生的必要，出现在"在经济发展到一定阶段而必然使社会分裂为阶级时"（恩格斯，1884）。在原始社会后期，由于社会分工的发展社会内部出现了私有制。私有制使人类社会分裂为主人与奴隶、富人与穷人，分化为利益相互冲突对立的阶级，并演变为两大对立的阶级——剥削阶级与被剥削阶级。两大阶级之间的斗争使人类陷入生存的困境，为了控制阶级斗争，或把阶级斗争控制在社会所允许的范围内，在经济上占统治地位的阶级便建立了国家。因此，"……国家是社会在一定发展阶段上的产物；国家是表示：这个社会陷入了不可解决的自我矛盾，分裂为不可调和的对立面而又无力摆脱这些对立面。而为了使这些对立面，这些经济利益相互冲突的阶级，不致在无谓的争斗中把自己和社会消灭，就需要有一种表面上凌驾于社会之上的力量，这种力量应当缓和冲突，把冲突保持在'秩序'的范围之内；这种从社会中产生但又自居于社会之上并且日益同社会脱离的力量，就是国家。"（恩格斯，1884）

在谈到国家的统治者和统治者汲取收入的手段时，马克思和恩格斯认为"由于国家是从控制阶级对立的需要中产生的，同时又是在这些阶级的冲突中产生的，所以，它照例是最强大的、在经济上占统治地位的阶级的国家，这个阶级借助国家而在政治上也成为占统治地位的阶级，因而获得了镇压和剥削被压迫阶级的新手段。"（恩格斯，1884）这种新手段就是指公共权力，因为"国家的本质特征，是和人民大众分离的公共权力"（恩格斯，1884）。同时，"为了维持这种公共权力，就需要公共公民缴纳费用——捐税，捐税是以前氏族社会完全没有的。"（恩格斯，1884）因而在马克思和恩格斯的观点中，国家汲取收入的行为是在经济上占据优势的统治阶级对被统治阶级的暴力掠夺行为，这种暴力的压迫是国家维持汲取能力的根源。

### （三）暴力论

与马克思和恩格斯关于暴力的看法颇为相似，奥尔森也提出了其自己对于国家起源的看法，即暴力论，又称"匪帮"理论。这一理论认为暴力能力对国家汲取能力非常重要。

根据该理论，原始的个体要想生存下去就必须获得足够的资源，而获取资源主要有三种途径：第一种是生产性劳动，如采集与捕猎；第二种是自愿交换；第三种则是直接通过暴力从他人那里掠夺资源。由于每种方式都有一定的成本，对于理性自利的个人来说，选择何种方式取决于它们之间的成本收益比。不同的个体有不同的自身优势，对于暴力资源丰富的个体而言，显然抢夺他人的成果是最为直接和方便的。"如果一个人拥有比他人多得多的权力，他也许更可能通过武力威胁或使用武力，而不是自愿交换来实现自己的利益"（奥尔森，2000）。由于使用权力进行劫掠能够带来巨大的收益，可以想象出一个由单个强盗发展成众多流窜匪帮的社会。在这种社会中，各流窜匪帮会尽可能地进行劫掠活动，将某地的资源掠夺殆尽后再转到下一地点。不过这种仅为自身私利，而不顾社会长期发展的、无止境的掠夺状态，会很快因过度消耗资源面临困境，因而每次能够获取的资源与流窜的成本的比值迅速降低。最终匪帮面临着无资源可抢的危机，在这时一些匪帮为了生存便必须要改变策略，这一策略便是不再流窜转而定居在某地，这个地方最好还要资源丰富并且易守难攻，从而有利于阻止其他匪帮的入侵。此时根据生产与消耗的速度，不止其他在其定居范围内的个体需要每年缴纳一些财物（或者更普遍以类似税收的形式缴纳其年收入的某个比例如十分之一的年收入），一部分底层的匪徒可能也会在匪帮首领的暴力威胁下从事劳动。

由于个体已经在暴力威胁下固定上缴收入，因而匪帮不再有动力、也没有必要再次掠夺本地区。为了保证其能每年固定获得这笔收入，匪帮转而保护本地的个体不受其他匪帮的侵扰。在进行了收益（保有部分收入、免受其他匪徒侵扰）和成本（缴纳保护费）的衡量后，其他地方的个体也会部分向此地靠拢，而有了稳定收入的匪帮也可以继续扩张其领地，直至达到能力的边界。此时的匪帮在经历一段时间后，由于对本地个体的掠夺活动的消失（在其辖地的居民看来，对其领地外个体和其他匪帮的掠夺并不能称之为掠夺），匪帮也更名换姓成为国王和官吏，国家便由此诞生并可以通过正名后的"保护费"即税收来汲取收入，尽管这一切的背后仍是暴力在起作用。这样的国家今后在兴修水利、保护产权等方面的投资，也仍然遵循的是暴力决定的原则。奥尔森的理论指出，汲取能力的大小取决于相对暴力能力的强弱，国家暴力能力与国民对比越大，那么其从国民中取得的收入比例就越高。

由于战争也是暴力的一种，对于暴力作为国家起源的看法可以根据实证来获得支持。如梯利（1984）对欧洲数个世纪的经验研究后，归纳了欧洲缔造国家的一般顺序，并以此指出战争、国家建立和汲取能力建设的内在关系。Dincecco 和 Prado（2012）发现历史上战争越多的地区，国家征税能力越强，当下的经济发展水平越高。Besley 和 Persson（2008）研究了内战与国家间战争对财政汲取能力的不同影响，认为在外部战争威胁会加强国家的财政汲取能力，而内战则起到削弱汲取能力的作用。

## 三、影响汲取能力的各种因素

国家形成之后，在几千年的国家历程中，财政汲取能力发生了纷繁复杂的变化，各个国家的形成与财政发展给研究提供了丰富的材料。此外，诸如集权国家统治集团的利益分配、民主国家的政府合法性、产权制度健全程度、社会发展过程中形成的风俗习惯等都被证实与国家的汲取能力关系密切。这些研究多数较为分散，少部分较为集中的文献关注腐败与寻租（Svensson，2005；Treisman，2000）或掠夺（Azam et al.，2009；Dixit，2006；Grossman and Kim，1995），但在观点上也经常有所冲突，以下分三个角度进行介绍和分析。

### （一）历史视角的分析

对各个国家发展历史的考察表明，国家所处的地理位置和地缘形势、社会发展过程中的文化、宗教信仰和政治体制，一起影响着国家财政汲取能力。英国作为强国家能力的代表，其国家的财政汲取能力的成型与发展的历程极具参考价值。不过对于决定英国财政汲取能力的核心要素，当前学术界并没有得到完全统一的结论。学界广泛认同光荣革命与联合法案后的英国财政汲取能力迅速增长，但对于造成该现象的更深层次原因则有不同看法。有学者（North 和 Weingast，1989）认为宪法的引入以及法治对皇室权利的约束是保证英国能够顺利且大规模地征税与借贷的重要条件。Johnson（2006）将法国大革命之后财政汲取能力得以持续增长的原因也归结于此。Stasavage（2010）指出英国征税能力的提升得益于英国紧凑的地理结构所带来的国家管理成本的降低。Prest（1998）则认为是英国各民族间的高相似性促使了英国比其他国家更具高的内聚性，高内聚性则促使之后英国财政和法律系统的迅速统一。Johnson 和 Koyama（2014）进一步指出这种内聚性是英国比法国等欧洲国家更早结束包税制，转向更具汲取能力的直接征税方式的主要原因。

### （二）利益集团视角的分析

掌握国家权力的各集团之间的利益目标、利益分配关系影响着国家汲取能力大小。当利益目标不一致时，各方为追逐自身私利难免会采取不利于整体的策略，进而导致国家汲取能力下降，下降程度取决于集团间的力量对比；当利益目标一致时，朝着相同目标的努力不但不会相互削弱，反而会相互促进增强国家的财政汲取能力。奥尔森（1993）在《国家兴衰探源：经济增长、滞涨与社会僵化》一书中提出了"狭隘利益"（narrow interest）和"共容利益"（encompassing interests）① 两个概念来解释这一问题。奥尔森认为如果统治集团的利益关系能达到协调，就能通过更大地权力、权威来镇压民众对资源掠取的反抗，也能稳固提升诸如产权等制度的建设，那么财政汲取能力就能得到提升。Acemoglu 等（2004）对一些非洲发展中国家的研究表示，在一个由少数精英统治的不稳定的弱国家，当权者会收买反对势力达成合作协议以实现继续统治。当精英之间利益关系不协调时，发生的内斗会对其控制暴力的水平产生影响，使精英无论是在压制民众暴乱方面还是长期制度建设方面都力不从心，财政汲取能力也会对应下滑。Acemoglu 等（2005）通过对南北韩和欧洲殖民地的研究发现，拥有强大政治权力的精英们如地主、部落首领会对一些能提高工人生产率但降低精英政治权力的制度进行抵制。Galor 等（2009）也在研究中发现由于地主的干预导致了较低的税率和教育投资的不足。

### （三）制度与经济视角的分析

产权制度、经济结构与国家汲取能力强弱有很高的相关性。North（1990）、North 和 Thomas（1973）强调了产权保护在西欧历史发展中的重要作用，North 和 Weingast（1989）将导致建立产权保护制度的光荣革命视为英国历史的重要

---

① "狭隘利益"指该利益集团认为自身利益与社会繁荣的相关性不大，而存在强烈的以损害社会利益达到增进该利益集团的企图；"共容利益"指该利益集团认为，其自身利益与社会繁荣密切相关，因而它们在寻求自身利益和社会收入再分配时，比较有节制并尽可能减少对社会的损害。

部分。Besley 和 Persson（2009，2010）构造的动态博弈模型将征税能力作为汲取能力的代表，并将产权保护作为另一种重要能力——法律能力的代表进行了互动，指出在稳定存在的国家中，产权保护程度与汲取能力能够相互促进。Acemoglu（2005）的模型认为国家汲取能力强弱存在最适水平，过强和过弱都对经济发展不利。坦茨（2011）指出对资源税、原材料出口较为依赖的国家其在征税能力建设和公共产品提供上较为落后。Acemoglu 等（2004）、Besley 和 Persson（2010）发现国际援助对第三世界国家在国家能力建设方面有负面影响。

## 四、对我国的启示

通过以上文献分析，可以发现大量一流思想家将财政汲取能力视作国家能力的重要组成部分，并进而分析影响财政汲取能力的因素。这对我们的启示有三：

第一，在中华民族面临伟大复兴的重要历史节点，应重视对国家能力的研究和国家能力的建设。毫无疑问，民族复兴需要国家能力支撑，但是目前学术界对国家能力的内涵的分析并不多，也远远没达成共识。通过产权保护来促进自由和市场发展，通过社会保护来避免个体受到剧烈市场冲击，这两者大概没有争议地是国家能力的组成部分，但是，为实现长远目标、为应对随时出现的危机，是否应将组织动员能力作为国家能力的重要组成部分呢？如果是这样，财政汲取就是一个非常重要的能力建设。

第二，不应该污名化"财政汲取能力"这一词语，应重视对财政汲取能力的研究。在当前中国，有大量声音抨击政府收入规模过大和税收负担过重，不论是舆论还是学者研究，倾向性的声音是要求政府减税，而闭口不谈减税之后财政支出结构如何调整和如何保障问题。但是，曾几何时，中国财政收入占GDP比重，中央财政收入占国家财政收入比重，连续十多年大幅下降，引发了广为关注的"两个比重下降"问题，朝野对此充满了危机感。从世界各国看，强大国家一定是强大政府和强大财政（Acemoglu，2005），我们应重视对中国特殊国情背景下的财政汲取能力的研究，包括对国有企业作用的研究、政府资源垄断问题的研究。

第三，从财政汲取能力这一角度出发，重新审视财政本质和财政职能问题。传统财政学研究中，财政活动的出发点是弥补市场失灵和提供公共物品，但是如果同意"财政是国家治理的基础"这一重要判断，那么财政汲取无疑是国家能力建设的重要组成部分。由此要重新思考财政的本质（吕冰洋，2018）：是提供公共物品还是增进公共秩序？思考财政的职能：是经济职能还是国家治理职能？思考财政制度的建设方向：在经济治理之外，如何促进社会和政治治理？

## 参考文献

[1] 查尔斯·梯利. 发动战争和缔造国家与有组织的犯罪之间的相似性》见：彼得·埃文斯、迪特里希·鲁施迈耶、西达·斯考克波. 找回国家 [M]. 北京：三联书店，1984.

[2] 弗里德里希·恩格斯. 家庭、私有制和国家起源 [M]. 北京：人民出版社，1972.

[3] 吕冰洋. 国家治理财政论：从公共物品到公共秩序 [EB/OL]. 2018.

[4] 曼瑟尔·奥尔森. 集体行动的逻辑 [M]. 上海：上海人民出版社，2005.

[5] 曼瑟尔·奥尔森. 权力与繁荣 [M]. 上海：上海人民出版社，2005.

[6] 乔尔·S. 米格代尔. 强社会与弱国家 [M]. 南京：江苏人民出版社，1988.

[7] 让·雅克·卢梭. 社会契约论 [M]. 1762.

[8] 托马斯·霍布斯. 利维坦 [M]. 黎思复，黎廷弼译，北京：商务印书馆，1651.

[9] 王绍光，胡鞍钢. 中国国家能力报告 [M]. 沈阳：辽宁人民出版社，1993.

[10] 维托·坦茨. 政府与市场：变革中的政府 [M]. 北京：商务印书馆，2011.

[11] 西达·斯考克波. 找回国家 [M]. 北京：三联书店，1984.

[12] Acemoglu D. Politics and Economics in Weak and Strong States [J]. *Journal of Monetary Economics*，2005.

[13] Acemoglu D., J. A. Robinson, and T. Verdier. Alfred Marshall Lecture：Kleptocracy and Divide-and-rule：A Model of Personal Rule [J]. *Journal of the European Economic Association*，2004.

[14] Acemoglu D., S. Johnson, and J. A. Robinson. *Institution as a Fundamental Cause of Long-run Growth in P. Aghion and S. N. Durlauf* [M]. *Handbook of Economic Growth*，2005.

[15] Azam Jean-Paul, Robert H. Bates, and Biais Bruno. Political Predation and Economic Development [J]. *Economics and Politics*，2009.

[16] Besley T. and T. Persson. The Origins of State Capacity：Property Rights，Taxation，

and Politics [J]. *American Economic Review*, 2009.

[17] Besley T. and T. Persson. Wars and State Capacity [J]. *Journal of the European Economic Association*, 2008.

[18] Besley T. and T. Persson. *Pillars of Prosperity: The Political Economics of Development Clusters* [M]. Princeton: Princeton University Press, 2010.

[19] Dincecco M. and M. Prado. Warfare, Fiscal Capacity, and Performance [J]. *Journal of Economic Growth*, 2012.

[20] Dixit A. Predatory States and Failing States: An Agency Perspective [R]. CEPS Working Paper, 2006, No. 131.

[21] Galor O., Moav O. and D. Vollrath. Inequality in Land Ownership, the Emergence of Human Capital Promoting Institutions, and the Great Divergence [J]. *Review of Economic Studies*, 2009.

[22] Grossman Herschel I. and Minseong Kim. Swords or Plowshares? A Theory of the Security of Claims to Property [J]. *Journal of Political Economy*, 1995.

[23] Johnson Noel D. Banking on the king: the evolution of the royal revenue farms in old regime France [J]. *Journal of Economics History*, 2006.

[24] Johnson Noel D. and Mark Koyama. Taxes, Lawyers, and The Decline of Witchcraft Trials in France [J]. *Journal of Law & Economics*, 2014.

[25] Johnson Noel D. and Mark Koyama. States and economic growth: Capacity and constraints [J]. *Explorations in Economic History*, 2016.

[26] North Douglass C. *Institutions, Institutional Change and Economic Performance* [M]. Cambridge: Cambridge University Press, 1990.

[27] North D. C. and B. R. Weingast. Constitutions and Commitment: The Evolution of Institutional Governing Public Choice in Seventeenth-Century England [J]. *Journal of Economic History*, 1989.

[28] North Douglass C. and Robert Paul Thomas. *The Rise of the Western World: A New Economic History* [M]. New York: Cambridge University Press, 1973.

[29] Prest Wilfrid. *Albion Ascendant* [M]. Oxford: Oxford University Press, 1998.

[30] Stasavage David. When Distance Mattered: Geographic Scale and the Development of European Representative Assemblies [J]. *American Political Science Review*, 2010.

[31] Svensson Jakob. Eight Questions about Corruption [J]. *Journal of Economic Perspectives*, 2005.

[32] Tilly Charles. *Reflections on the history of European state-making*. In: Tilly, C. (Ed.),

The Formation of Nation States in Western Europe [M]. Princeton University Press, Princeton, New Jersey, 1975.

[33] Tilly Charles. *Coercion, Capital, and European States, AD 990 - 1990* [M]. Blackwell, Oxford, 1990.

[34] Treisman Daniel. The Causes of Corruption: A Cross-National Study [J]. *Journal of Public Economics*, 2000.

[35] Walder Andrew G. *The Waning of the Communist State—Economic Origins of Political Decline in China and Hungary* [M]. University of California Press, 1995.

# Fiscal Extraction and State Capacity: An Investigation Based on Literature

Lyu Bingyang  Hu Shen

**Abstract:** Fiscal extraction is a basic facet of state capacity. Based on previous studies, this work summarizes the analysis of fiscal extractive capacity in three representative theories of the Origin of the State, namely, contract theory, class theory, and violence theory. The factors affecting fiscal extractive capacity from the historical, interest group, institutional, and economic perspectives, as well as the influence mode and development process of fiscal extractive capacity, are discussed. A comprehensive survey of the literature provides insights into the role of fiscal extraction in state capacity building and the ways to improve China's fiscal extractive capacity, which could be easily neglected.

**Key words:** Extractive Capacity; State Capacity; Origin of State

CLC number: F810.2   Document code: A

## I. Relationship between fiscal extraction and state capacity

With the flourishing development of institutional economics in the late 20th century, the role and status of the state in economic growth have aroused extensive attention. The concept of state capacity has also been incorporated into economic research, first appearing in the study of sociologists and politicians (e.g., Tilly, 1975, 1990; Skocpol, 1984; Mann, 1986). Nevertheless, scholars hold different opinions about the exact meaning of this term. Skocpol (1984) describes state capacity as the ability of the state to achieve something that is not merely a reflection of the interests of social groups or classes[①]. Migdale (1988) illustrates the will of leaders as representative of state will, and states that "the ability of state leaders to use the agencies of state to get people in society to do what they want them to do" (:prologue), and divides state capacity into "the capacities to penetrate society, regulate social relationships, extract resources, and appropriate or use resources in determined ways" (:4). Wang and Hu (1993) acknowledge that "state capacity refers to the ability of the state to transfer its will and goals into reality" and that it could be categorized into four dimensions: extractive, steering, legitimation, and coercive capacities[②].

In politics and economics, fiscal extractive capacity is undoubtedly a critical foundation and component of a state's power. "Fiscal extractive capacity… is the core of the state capacities and the basis for implementing other capacities" (Wang and Hu, 1993). "Basic sets of facts to sort out in any study of state capacities involve the sources and amounts of state revenues and the degree of flexibility possible in their collection and deployment" (Skocpol 1984:prologue). Compared with political scholars, economists describe state capacity with further emphasis on its relevance to economic issues. The term "state capacity" in economics focuses on the capacity of fiscal revenue extraction and law enforcement, whereas a few studies discussed weak capacity in direct relation to economy, such as social penetration and regulation. State capacity is portrayed as state taxation, law enforcement, order maintenance, and public goods provision. In sum, it encompasses two types of capacities: fiscal and legal capacities (Besley & Persson, 2009; Johnson & Koyama, 2016). According to different

---

① Skocpol (1984) also argues that the focus of state capacity research is to investigate the situation when the country encounters real or potential opposition from powerful social groups, or when it faces adverse socio-economic environment.

② Andrew G. Walder (1995) also uses the same classification and definition.

situations, fiscal extractive capacity is often used as a proxy for state capacity.

The extractive capacity of the state determines the current scale and strength of government activities. This capacity determines not only the upper limit for expenditure but also the need for fiscal revenues caused by an increase in expenditure requirement that must be based on the possibility that extractive capacity could be achieved. For a long time, a flaw existed in theoretical research in that it took for granted the fact that the state has sufficient capacity to tax. Under such supposition, the state is granted autonomy in levying tax on arbitrary objects and freely deciding the tax rate, and it incurs almost no cost in the construction and maintenance of the tax imposing system. This presupposition is still acceptable in developed countries, but for most developing countries, policy proposals based on the acquiescence of a strong fiscal extractive capacity cannot withstand scrutiny. Hence, an important aspect of state capacity research is to explain the determinants, influence mechanisms, and development processes of state capacity. The current work will also focus on this research direction.

## II. Formation of fiscal extractive capacity from state origin theory perspective

The state is the mainstay for fiscal extraction. Understanding the process and theory of state origin will shed some light on the fundamental factors influencing the extractive capacity. At present, there are many theories about the origin of the state, and the most well-known ones are contract theory, class theory and violence theory.

### 1. Contract theory

The main representatives of the contract theory of state origin are

Hobbes, Locke, Montesquieu, and Rousseau. Contract theory sets a limit on state extractive capacity. The period prior to the establishment of the government and during the absence of a country is assumed to indicate a loose social state full of crisis and absolute liberty, in which all men must exert great efforts to protect their own property. The individual coalition enters into a social contract with future sovereigns and then forms a state, which protects and preserves the safety of its citizens. Hence, sovereigns act as agents of the state. However, from the perspective of world history, contract theory can't explain the origin of most states. Olson(1965) states that even if the total revenue outweighs the cost, the cost related to communication, negotiation, and contract-making for this completely voluntary action will increase rapidly with the premise of a rise in population. Therefore, the idea of such contract theory can only be a hypothetical construction or a reasonable interpretation for the purpose of explaining existing countries.

As this hypothesis about state origin is an ideological assumption, the way in which the state obtains income has not been discussed in detail while the analysis therein still has its reference value. Hobbes (1651) and Rousseau (1762) explained fiscal extractive capacity in *Leviathan* and *Du Contract Social*, respectively. *Leviathan* by Hobbes (1651) illustrates that individuals voluntarily surrender all their rights and property (mainly land) to an authority under the contract. Hence, the state would distribute all property (land) to everyone fairly and with consideration of public interest based on general will so that it becomes private ownership. However, although "the propriety which a subject hath in his lands, consisteth in a right to exclude all other subjects from the use of them; and not to exclude their sovereign, be it an assembly, or a monarch" (Hobbes 1651:140). "It is true, that a sovereign monarch, or the greater part of a sovereign assembly, may ordain the doing of many things in pursuit of their passions, contrary to their own consciences, which is a breach of trust, and of the law of nature; but this is not enough to authorize any subject, either to make war upon, or so much as to accuse of injustice, or any way to speak evil of their sovereign; because they have authorized all his actions, and in bestowing the sovereign power, made them their own. " ( :140). According to these statements, as a result of this contract, the state can arbitrarily control all the wealth from its citizens in accordance with its own will per Hobbes's assumption. In other words, the state fabricated by contract theory has complete fiscal extractive capacity.

Rousseau's theory of Social Contract is different from that of Hobbes. Rousseau ( 1762 ) states that in his work *Du Contract Social* and Discourse: "Each man alienates, I admit, by the social compact, only such part of his powers, goods and liberty as it is important for the community to control; but it must also be granted that the Sovereign is sole judge of what is important" ( :54) ; "Every service a citizen can render the State he ought to render as soon as the Sovereign demands it; but the Sovereign, for its part, cannot impose upon its subjects any fetters that are useless to the community" ( :54) ; "The undertakings which bind us to the social body are obligatory only because they are mutual; and their nature is such that in fulfilling them we cannot work for others without working for ourselves" ( :54). Obviously, Rousseau asserts that the resources which the state or sovereign could mobilize come from the individual's voluntary concession, which not only inevitably occurs when needed, but also will be sufficient as long as it is within the affordability of citizens.

Despite the variations of the descriptions of the fiscal extractive method from the viewpoints of Hobbes and Rousseau, the fiscal revenue can be arbitrarily controlled or fully obtained, that is, the national extractive capacity has reached the upper limit in the state established by the contract. In such a situation, increasing the state's extractive ability is impossible. This assumption is expressed in another way, that is, when the sovereign or monarch can acquire all the power from the nation or when citizens are willing to contribute all their property because of trust, maximum state fiscal extractive capacity is reached.

## 2. Class theory

Forty years after Rousseau's death, two great philosophers, Marx and Engels, were born in succession. Marx and Engels' expositions on the origin of the state emphasize the economic ruler's control over violence and the extraction of resources through violence. *The Origin of the Family, Private Property and the State* by Marx and Engels provides a synthesis of the viewpoints on the origin of the state. It analyzes in detail the social conditions of Iroquois, Roman, Celtic, and German people and discusses the concrete process of forming three states (Athens, Rome, and Germany) on the basis of the analysis. There exists the assembly of the people, the council of chiefs of the genets, and military leaders who are striving for real monarchic power (the highest form of constitution that the gentile order could achieve) in the three gentile societies. And "if society passed beyond the limits within which this constitution was adequate, that meant the end of the gentile order; it was broken up and the state took its place" (Engels 1884:89).

According to Marx and Engels, the state has not always existed. Societies that do not need the state and lack any notion of state and state power do exist. The necessity of the state arises "At a definite stage of economic development, which necessarily involved the cleavage of society into classes" (Engels 1884:107). In the later stage of the primitive society, private ownership appeared in society due to the development of the social division of labor. Private ownership causes the cleavage of society by dividing it into classes with conflicting interests (such as master and slave and rich and poor), hence the emergence of two opposing classes—exploiting and exploited classes. The struggle between the two classes has put humanity in a great living predicament. To control the class struggle or keep it within the limits allowed by society, the economically dominant class established the state. As a result, "... Rather, it is a product of society at a particular stage of development; it is the admission that this society has involved itself in insoluble self-contradiction and is cleft into irreconcilable antagonisms which it is powerless to exorcise. But in order that these antagonisms, classes with conflicting economic interests, shall not consume themselves and society in fruitless struggle, a power, apparently standing above society, has become necessary to moderate the conflict and keep it within the bounds of 'order'; and this power, arisen out of society, but placing itself above it and increasingly alienating itself from it, is the state." (Engels 1884:104)

As for the ruler of the state and the means by which the ruler generates revenue, Marx and Engels believe that "As the state arose from the need to keep class antagonisms in check, but also arose in the thick of the fight between the classes, it is normally the state of the most powerful, economically ruling class, which by its means becomes also the politically ruling class, and so acquires new means of holding down and exploiting the oppressed class." (Engels 1884:105) This new definition refers to public power because "an essential characteristic of the state is the existence of a public force differentiated from the mass of the people" (:74). At the same time, "In order to maintain this public power, contributions from the state citizens are necessary—taxes. These were completely unknown to gentile society." (:105) Thus, in the views of Marx and Engels, the state's income-extracting behavior is the violent seizure by the economically dominant ruling class against the ruled class, which is the root of the state in maintaining its revenue-generating abilities.

### 3. Violence theory

Similar to Marx and Engels' views on violence, Olsen's own version of the origin of the state, that is, the theory of violence, which is also known as bandit theory, suggests that a violent capacity plays an important role in a state's revenue extraction.

According to violence theory, primitive individuals mainly have three ways to acquire sufficient resources to support their survival: (1) productive labor, such as collection and hunting; (2) voluntary exchange; and (3) direct plunder of resources from other people through violence. As each method has a certain cost, the choice of method for rational self-interested individuals depends on the cost-benefit ratio between them. Moreover, different individuals have their own advantages, and thus, the most direct and convenient way for individuals with abundant resources of violence is to seize the supply of others. "When an individual has much power than another, he may be better able to serve his interests by threatening to use-or by using-force than by voluntary exchange" (Olsen 2000:60). Utilizing power to plunder could bring enormous benefits, and imagining a society that evolves from an individual bandit into a multitude of bandits is possible. Under this situation, roving bandits would carry out predatory activities as much as possible and then move to another location after plundering the resources of one place. However, this endless predatory state for its own self-interests regardless of the long-term development of society will soon be confronted with difficulties due to the excessive consumption of resources. It will cause the ratio of resources available to mobility costs to decrease rapidly. Ultimately, bandits will face a crisis of having no resources to plunder. At this time, some bandits must change their tactics with the purpose of survival, shifting from moving around into settling down in the best defensive place with abundant resources, with the latter being conducive to the prevention of invasion by outsiders. As a result, depending on the speed of production and consumption, individuals in a territory controlled by bandit leaders need to pay a portion of their property annually (or generally pay a percentage of the annual income in forms of tax, such as one-tenth of the annual income), and some bandits at the bottom of society may work for them under the threat of violence.

As individuals have already paid a fixed income under the threat of violence, no incentive and need exists for bandits to plunder the region again. Conversely, stationary bandits turn to protect the local population against competing bandits to ensure their regular annual income. After comparing the benefits (keeping part of the income from other bandits) and costs (protection fee payments), individuals elsewhere will also partially move toward this place, and then bandits with stable incomes could continue to expand their territory until they reach the limits of their capabilities. After some time, stationary bandits would transform themselves into kings and officials in a sense because of the disappearance of the predatory activities of local individuals (in the view of the inhabitants of their jurisdiction, plunder by individuals outside their territory and by other bandits could not be called plunder). Hence, the state is formed and could generate revenue through protection fees with sensible reasons, namely, tax, although violence still plays a role in this development. Moreover, such state continues to follow the principles of violent dominance in their future investments in water conservancy projects and protection of property rights. Olson's theory indicates that extractive capacity depends on the strength of relative violence. The greater the national violence ability is compared with nationals, the higher the proportion of income it receives from nationals.

Wars are also a form of violence, and many empirical studies provide support for this version of violence as the origin of the state. After studying centuries of experience in Europe, Tilly (1984) summarizes the general order of European state formation and indicates the inherent relationship between war, state building, and capacity building. Dincecco and Prado (2012) found that national taxation capacity and current economic development level in regions, which with more wars in history, are significantly stronger than orther regions. Besley and Persson (2008) examine the different impacts of civil war and external war on fiscal extractive capacity and suggest that external war threats tend to strengthen the state's fiscal capacity, whereas civil wars play the opposite role.

## III. Factors affecting extractive capacity

In the course of several thousand years of national history, a state's ability to generate revenue has undergone numerous and complicated changes. The formation and fiscal development in each country provide abundant materials for research. In addition, many factors, including the distribution of interests among the ruling hierarchy in centralized states, the legitimacy of the government in democratic states, property rights institution, and the customs and habits formed during social development have been proven to be closely related to the state's extractive capacity. Most of these studies are relatively scattered, and we find that extant research focuses on corruption and rent-seeking (Treisman, 2000; Svensson, 2005) or predation (Grossman and Kim, 1995; Dixit, 2006; Azam et al., 2009) and that the conclusions are contradictory. The following section is introduced and analyzed from three perspectives: the historical, interest group, and institutional and economic perspectives.

### 1. Historical perspective

The investigation on the historical development of states shows that the geographical locations and situations of a country, together with its culture, religion, and political institutions during social development, may jointly influence the state's extractive capacity. As a representative of strong state capacity, Britain offers significant reference about the formation and development of its fiscal capacity. However, no consensus is found with regard to the central factors that determine Britain's fiscal capacity. As widely accepted by academia, Britain's extractive capacity developed rapidly after the Glorious Revolution and the Act of the Union; by contrast, the views on the underlying causes of this phenomenon differ. Some scholars (North and Weingast, 1989) argue that the introduction of the constitution and the rule of law limiting the Crown's power are essential conditions to ensure massive taxation and borrowing in Britain. Johnson (2006) also attributes the sustained growth of fiscal extractive capacity after the French Revolution to this fact. Stasavage (2010) explains that the reduction in state administrative costs brought about by the compact geographical structure benefits the improvement of British taxation capacity. Prest (1998) believes that the high similarity among different nationalities in Britain has led to a higher level of cohesion compared with that in other countries, thereby facilitating the rapid unification of fiscal and legal systems. Johnson and Koyama (2014) further point out that this cohesion is the main reason why Britain ended its tax farming earlier than the other European countries (such as France) did and subsequently shifted to a direct tax collection with high extractive capacity.

## 2. Interest group perspective

Interest goals and the interest distribution relationship among groups that are in power affect the state's fiscal capacity. When confronted with a conflict of interests, groups will inevitably tend to adopt a strategy that is not conducive to the whole in pursuit of their own interests. This action will lead to a decrease in fiscal capacity. The extent of the decrease depends on the power struggle among interest groups. By contrast, when confronted with the same interest objectives, groups working toward the same goal will exhibit efforts that reciprocally promote and then increase fiscal extractive capacity instead of weakening each other. Olson (1993) proposes two concepts of narrow interest and encompassing interests in his work *The Rise and Decline of Nations: Economic Growth, Stagflation, and Social Rigidities* to explain this issue①. Olson argues that if the interests among ruling groups could be coordinated, then such groups will be able to acquire great power and authority to suppress the population's effect on resisting resource plunder and strengthen institution building, including property rights, so that the state's fiscal capacity could be improved. Acemoglu et al. (2004) examine developing African countries and show that authorities will buy off opponents to keep the ruler in power in weakly institutionalized polities ruled by a minority of elites. When ruling elites have unharmonious relations with various interests, the infighting among ruling groups will influence their violence control ability, making elites unable to suppress the civic unrest or the long-term institutional construction; fiscal capacity will decline accordingly. By studying North and South Korea and the European colonies, Acemoglu et al. (2005) find that elites with great political power (such as landlords and clan leaders) would resist institutions that could increase worker productivity while reducing their political rights. Galor et al. (2009) also conclude that the intervention of landlords will result in low tax rates and insufficient investment in education.

### 3. Institutional and economic perspective

Property rights institutions and economic structure are highly correlated with the state's extractive capacity levels. North (1990) and North and Thomas (1973) emphasize that property rights protection plays a central role in the historical development of Western Europe. North and Weingast (1989) regard the Glorious Revolution as the cause of the establishment of property rights protection institutions as an important part of British histo-

---

① Narrow interest refers to interest groups believe their own interests are not closely related to social prosperity, and they have strong attempts to reach their narrow interest at the expense of social public interest; Encompassing interests refers to interest groups believe their own interests are closely related to social prosperity, so they act with restraint and minimize social damages as much as possible when pursuing their own interests and redistributing public income.

ry. Furthermore, Besley and Persson (2009, 2010) construct a dynamic game model employing taxation as a proxy for the level of fiscal capacity and interacting with property rights protection as another important capability, namely, legal capacity, thereby indicating that property rights protection levels and fiscal capacity could mutually promote political stable countries. The model of Acemoglu (2005) shows that fiscal extractive capacity should be maintained at the optimal level because weak and strong states are detrimental to economic development. Tanzi (2011) points out that countries that relied heavily on resource taxes and raw material exports have comparatively backward tax capacity building and public goods provision. Acemoglu et al. (2004) and Besley and Persson (2010) find that international assistance has a negative impact on national state capacity building in third-world countries.

## Ⅳ. Implications for China

Given the above literature analysis, we find that numerous world-class ideologists regard fiscal extractive capacity as an important component of state capacity and analyze the factors influencing fiscal extractive capacity. This situation prompts us to reflect on three aspects.

First, we should attach great importance to the study of state capacity and its building in the face of the important historical node to achieve the great renewal of the Chinese nation. National renewal undoubtedly needs the support of state capacity, but only a few studies analyze the connotation of state capacity at present, and no consensus has been reached. Promoting the development of freedom and market through property rights protection, as well as protecting individuals from sharp market shocks through social protection, partly represents state capabilities. However, should organizational mobilization capability be an important component of state capacity to achieve long-term goals and respond to crises at any time?

If such is the case, then fiscal extraction is a prominent part of capacity building.

Second, we should prioritize the study of fiscal extractive capacity instead of stigmatizing this term. In contemporary China, many voices oppose the oversized scale of government revenue and heavy burden of taxes. Regardless of public opinion and academic research, the propensity is to call on the government to reduce taxes without consideration of how to adjust the structure of government expenditures and how to protect it after the tax cut. However, the proportion of China's fiscal revenue in GDP and the central government revenue in state revenue have declined significantly for more than a decade, thereby triggering a widespread concern about the "two proportions decline" issues and the considerable sense of crisis of political parties. Various countries indicate that a strong state must have a powerful government and solid public finance (Acemoglu, 2005). We should prioritize the research on fiscal extractive capacity in the Chinese context, including investigations into the function of state-owned enterprises and the government's resource monopoly issues.

Finally, we should reconceive fiscal essence and fiscal function in view of fiscal extractive capacity. In traditional finance research, the starting point of fiscal activities is to remedy market failures and provide public goods. However, if we agree with the important thesis that "finance is the foundation of state governance," then fiscal extraction is undoubtedly a key component of state capacity building. The consequence involves rethinking the essence of finance (Lv, 2018): provide public goods or promote public order? We should also ponder on fiscal function: is it an economic function or a state governance function? Finally, we must examine the direction of finance system building: how should social and political governance be promoted outside economic governance?

## References

[1] Tilly Charles. *War Making and State Making as Organized Crime.* In: Evans P. B., Rueschemeyer D. & Skocpol T. (Eds.). (1985). Bringing the State Back In[M]. Cambridge University Press, 1984.

[2] Engels F. & Morgan, L. H. *The Origin of the Family, Private Property and the State*[M]. Moscow: Foreign Languages Publishing House, 1978.

[3] Lv B. Y. Fiscal Theory of State Governance: From Public Goods to Public Order[EB/OL]. Working paper, 2018.

[4] Olson M. *Logic of Collective Action: Public Goods and the Theory of Group*[M]. Harvard University Press, 1965.

[5] Olson M. *Power and prosperity: Outgrowing Communist and Capitalist Dictatorships*[M]. Basic Books Press, 2000.

[6] Migdal J. S. *Strong Societies and Weak States: State-Society Relations and State Capabilities in the Third World*[M]. Princeton University Press, 1988.

[7] Rousseau J. J. *The Social Contract or Principles of Political Right*[M]. 1762.

[8] Hobbes T. *Leviathan*[M]. Penguin Classics, London, 1651.

[9] Wang S. G, Hu A. G. *State Capacity Report in China*[M]. Liaoning People's Publishing House Press (In Chinese), 1993.

[10] Tanzi V. *Government versus markets: The changing economic role of the state*[M]. Cambridge University Press, 2011.

[11] Skocpol Theda. *Bringing the State Back In*[M]. Cambridge University Press, 1984.

[12] Acemoglu D. Politics and Economics in Weak and Strong States[J]. *Journal of Monetary Economics*, 2005.

[13] Acemoglu D., J. A. Robinson, and T. Verdier. Alfred Marshall Lecture: Kleptocracy and Divide-and-rule: A Model of Personal Rule[J]. *Journal of the European Economic Association*, 2004.

[14] Acemoglu D., S. Johnson, and J. A. Robinson. Institution as a Fundamental Cause of Long-run Growth in P. Aghion and S. N. Durlauf[M]. *Handbook of Economic Growth*, 2005.

[15] Azam Jean-Paul, Robert H. Bates, and Biais Bruno. Political Predation and Economic Development[J]. *Economics and Politics*, 2009.

[16] Besley T. and T. Persson. The Origins of State Capacity: Property Rights, Taxation, and Politics[J]. *American Economic Review*, 2009.

[17] Besley T. and T. Persson. Wars and State Capacity[J]. *Journal of the European Eco-*

nomic Association, 2008.

[18] Besley T. and T. Persson. *Pillars of Prosperity: The Political Economics of Development Clusters*[M]. Princeton: Princeton University Press, 2010.

[19] Dincecco M. and M. Prado. Warfare, Fiscal Capacity, and Performance[J]. *Journal of Economic Growth*, 2012.

[20] Dixit A. Predatory States and Failing States: An Agency Perspective[R]. CEPS Working Paper, 2006, No. 131.

[21] Galor O. , Moav O. and D. Vollrath. Inequality in Land Ownership, the Emergence of Human Capital Promoting Institutions, and the Great Divergence[J]. *Review of Economic Studies*, 2009.

[22] Grossman Herschel I. and Minseong Kim. Swords or Plowshares? A Theory of the Security of Claims to Property[J]. *Journal of Political Economy*, 1995.

[23] Johnson Noel D. Banking on the king: the evolution of the royal revenue farms in old regime France[J]. *Journal of Economics History*, 2006.

[24] Johnson Noel D. and Mark Koyama. Taxes, Lawyers, and The Decline of Witchcraft Trials in France[J]. *Journal of Law & Economics*, 2014.

[25] Johnson Noel D. and Mark Koyama. States and economic growth: Capacity and constraints[J]. *Explorations in Economic History*, 2016.

[26] North Douglass C. *Institutions, Institutional Change and Economic Performance*[M]. Cambridge: Cambridge University Press, 1990.

[27] North D. C. and B. R. Weingast. Constitutions and Commitment: The Evolution of Institutional Governing Public Choice in Seventeenth-Century England[J]. *Journal of Economic History*, 1989.

[28] North Douglass C. and Robert Paul Thomas. *The Rise of the Western World: A New Economic History*[M]. New York: Cambridge University Press, 1973.

[29] Prest Wilfrid. *Albion Ascendant*[M]. Oxford: Oxford University Press, 1998.

[30] Stasavage David. When Distance Mattered: Geographic Scale and the Development of European Representative Assemblies[J]. *American Political Science Review*, 2010.

[31] Svensson Jakob. Eight Questions about Corruption[J]. *Journal of Economic Perspectives*, 2005.

[32] Tilly Charles. *Reflections on the history of European state-making*. In: Tilly, C. (Ed.), The Formation of Nation States in Western Europe[M]. Princeton University Press, Princeton, New Jersey, 1975.

[33] Tilly Charles. *Coercion, Capital, and European States, AD 990 – 1990*[M]. Blackwell, Oxford, 1990.

[34] Treisman Daniel. The Causes of Corruption: A Cross-National Study[J]. *Journal of Public Economics*, 2000.

[35] Walder Andrew G. *The Waning of the Communist State—Economic Origins of Political Decline in China and Hungary*[M]. University of California Press, 1995.

# 中国的古典市场经济理论*

### 林光彬

**摘　要：** 17世纪以前的中国，一直是世界市场经济的一个重要领航者，对市场的认识也处于领先的地位，有关市场经济的理论非常丰富。本文对中国古典市场经济理论做了一点寻根探源的研究，以期发现一些中国人原创的市场经济理论认识，说明存在不同于当前中国流行的两种关于市场经济的认识倾向。本文仅就中国古代的"政府引导市场理论"和"古典市场经济理论"做一些文献梳理，以揭示今天中国政府发展市场经济的理论和历史演进渊源。通过梳理后本文认为，我国古典市场经济理论随着经济发展阶段的不同都有与时俱进的创新学术成果和理论发展；没有完美的市场和市场经济，只有合意的适合发展阶段和约束条件的市场与市场经济；关于"看不见的手"的经济理论最早出现在《管子》一书中；从"谷贱伤农，谷贵伤民"到"谷贱伤农，谷贵亦伤农"，反映了我国古典经济学家对市场经济的深刻认识，这个认识应该说目前现代微观经济学中还没有看见。

**关键词：** 市场经济　古典理论　中国认识　现代价值

[中图分类号] F123.9　　[文献标志码] A

## 引言：关于市场的两种现代认识倾向

如何认识市场是当今中国最主要的话题。新市场财政学如何体现出不同于以

---

\* 基金项目：国家社科基金重大招标项目（19ZDA057），中央财经大学重大研究与持计划"中国特色社会主义政治经济学研究"（2022）。

[作者简介]：林光彬，中央财经大学财经研究院院长，教授，博士生导师，主要研究领域为中国特色社会主义政治经济学、国家理论与市场理论、中国经济、高等教育等。

往的财政学，关键是对市场和财政有了新的认识。这种新的认识是在对传统认识批判的基础上，观察中国和世界的市场与财政关系的实践演进中逐渐形成的。

我国从社会主义计划经济到有计划的商品经济再到社会主义市场经济，从计划为主、市场为辅，国家引导市场、市场引导企业到市场在资源配置中起基础性作用再到市场在资源配置中起决定性作用。这反映了我国学术界、政界、舆论界对市场经济的认识不断深入，但也存在两种需要讨论的认识倾向。一种认识把市场虚拟化，认为市场可以解决好一切，搞定所有经济问题，认为政府是经济问题的根源，主张回到亚当·斯密"守夜人"政府的学术主张。还有一种认为中国古代没有市场经济，市场经济是改革开放后的话语体系。这两种认识被当今的中国经济学精英所秉持、所传播，现在几乎成为一种宗教宣言，笼罩在今天中国学术界的上空，尤其需要反思、思辨，甄别其中的有益与有害成分。因此，重新理解中国市场经济又成为一个时代焦点问题，甚至关涉到我国的改革与发展道路，关系到全体中国人民的切身利益。

关于市场和市场经济的主流认识，主要由西方社会科学二分法研究所主导。这种方法论认为政府与市场是对立的，公平与效率是对立的，个体与整体是对立的。在经济学上具体表现为三种观点，转引如下：第一种观点认为政府多一点，市场就会少一点，并且提出政府的经济作用是弥补市场失灵，用"看得见的手"辅助"看不见的手"减少经济运行中的过度波动和造成的伤害，使经济社会能够可持续发展。这是新古典经济学派、凯恩斯学派等所持有的基本观点。第二种观点是把政府排斥在市场之外，认为企业是市场的主体，支配一切，在资源配置中起决定性作用。这种观点多见于盎格鲁-撒克逊学派（尤其是芝加哥学派）、奥地利学派等新老自由主义的经济学当中，他们认为市场是医治一切经济问题的良方。《新帕尔格雷夫经济学辞典》中，市场这一概念意味着"由独立工商企业（国营的、私营的和其他的）的决策来决定生产和分配"，即把政府排斥在市场的生产和分配的决策之外。这个明显与历史发展事实不符。第三种观点是提出按照理想的市场经济体系设想推进中国改革，提出"中国下一步推进深层次市场化改革，也要有一个基准点或参照系说起"，认为"现代经济理论以理想经济环境为基准点，以自由竞争市场为参照系，严格给出了市场导致有效配置从而成为好的市场经济的前提，而这些前提条件正好指明了改革的长远方向，从而起到明道、指明方向的前瞻性指导作用，通过理论指导改革、变革及创新来促进现实经济运行不断向理想状态逼近。"这种认识对市场经济从所谓的公理假设出发进行演绎，而不是从历史演进真实出发，好像有点刻舟求剑的味道！这种空想自由市场经济理论就是一个乌托邦，用这个理论给中国描绘蓝图和路线图明显存在误导性。这种理论完全不顾20世纪30年代后，世界市场结构依次进入垄断竞争阶段—寡头垄断阶段—国家垄断阶段—国际垄断阶段。在现实经济世界，完全竞争的市场几乎不存在；而且大企业之间竞争的目标往往也是垄断或寡头合谋。因此，这种主张明显脱离现实、脱离历史演进的基本常识。我们在西方现实世界看到的是，政府做的是一套，主流理论界和对外意识形态说的又是一套。最典型的就是2008年以来的各国政府政策与主流的经济理论界、意识形态的背离。

总之，上述三种认识和观点存在混淆分析范畴的问题，存在分析主体与客体错位的现象。因为，市场不管理解为最初的交易场所、交易平台，还是理解为一种机制，都与作为组织的政府，不是一对对应的分析范畴。我们知道，国家、社会、市场等都是集约性的整体人造概念，都是由身在其间的个人以及个人之上的家庭、企业、政府等行为主体组成，并由这些主体所驱动和运行。在分析范畴与层次上，政府与企业、家庭是对应关系，市场与社会、国家才是对应关系。市场以交易利益为核心运转，目的是实现货通；社会以伦理道德秩序为核心运转，目的是实现内部和谐相处；国家以法律秩序为中心运转，目的是通过有强制力为后盾的组织化行为实现法定的秩序。这构成了人类社会演进的基本样态。

中国五千年的经济史和中国特色社会主义市场经济的实践证明，西方社会科学这种二分研究方法和路径，至少不适合中国的发展实践和发展目标，需要扬弃。本文不打算对西方关于市场研究的二分法展开深入细致的分析，仅对中国古典市场经济理论做了一点寻根探源的研究，以期发现一些不同于上述两种主流认识的中国市场经济理论演进，发现一些中国人原创的市场经济理论认识。这是因为，17世纪以前的中国，一直是世界市场经济的一个重要领航者，对市场的认识也处于领先的地位。

我国关于市场经济的理论非常丰富，有整有零散见于众多古典文献之中，可谓汗牛充栋，本文仅就"政府引导市场理论"和"古典市场经济理论"做一些文献梳理，以揭示今天中国发展市场经济中的理论和历史演进渊源。

## 一、政府引导市场理论

我国经典《周易·系辞下传》说，神农氏不仅发明创造了犁地的耒，而且还"日中为市，致天下之民，聚天下之货，交易而退，各得其所，盖取诸《噬嗑》。"这段话说明，上古的市场，至少一种重要的形式是当时的领袖神农氏创设的，市场的主要作用是交易货通。

我国《尚书·洪范》中提出国家治理的八政中第一政是食，第二政是货。《汉书·食货志》进一步指出国实民富只需食足货通而已。"洪范八政，一曰食，二曰货。食谓农殖嘉谷可食之物，货谓布帛可衣，及金刀龟贝，所以分财布利通有无者也。二者，生民之本，兴自神农之世。'斫木为耜，煣木为耒，耒之利以教天下'，而食足；'日中为市，致天下之民，聚天下之货，交易而退，各得其所'，而货通。食足货通，然后国实民富，而教化成。"由此可见，两部经典都提出，我国最早的市场是上古的"部族国家"领袖神农氏创设的，并把生产和市场流通作为民富国实的核心。

根据古典文献，到周代，我国已经是一个很有秩序的政府主导的市场经济国家，市场是城市的一个有机的必需部分。根据《周礼》记载，周代的交易市场主要由政府在城郭之内设立。《周礼·天官冢宰第一》："惟王建国，辨方正位，体经野，设官分职，以为民极（准则）。"这里的"体国"是指国都城中南北向和东西向分别用九条道路来纵横交叉划分，并把宗庙置于左边，社稷置于右边，把政府机关之处放在前面，集市放在后面。又说"凡建国，佐后立市，设其次，置其叙，正其肆，陈其货贿，出其度、量、淳、制，祭之以阴礼。"即建立国都后，内宰要辅佐王后建立集市，设立管理市场官员的办公室，在市场门口也要设立办公室，规整市场中售卖货物的摊位，让商人的金玉和布帛陈列出来，并按照标准的度量衡进行交易。

根据《周礼·地官司徒第二》的记述，周朝出现了专门管理市场事务的官员——司市，手下有164人。现代的物价局、税务局、质监局、工商局等市场管理机构不仅周代已经存在，而且分工明确。其中：质人掌管评定市场上的货物价格，负责平抑物价及买卖契约。廛人掌管征收市场的店铺房屋税、货物税、质剂税、罚款、市宅税，而将税款交入泉府。胥师负责工商质检。贾师负责对商品进行分类分等，确定价格，下令市场开始交易。司暴和司稽负责市场的秩序维护。泉府掌管利用所征收来的市场税款，收购市场上的滞销货物，调节货物供求，确定市场上赊贷的基准利息。司门负责在国门征收货物税。司关负责查验进出口货物的关税凭证，惩治走私货物。肆长负责征收本市场上的货物税，并对市场上的货物和价格进行监控。

《周礼·地官》"司市"中还记载了当时的市场管理原则，即"凡治市之货贿、六畜、珍异，亡（无）者使有，利者使阜，使亡，靡者使微"。即政府管理市场商品流通的原则是：使短缺商品恢复供应，使质量好且于民有利的货品更加丰富，使有害的货品不能出售，使侈靡的货品需求减少。这样的市场管理原则，在今天建设社会主义市场经济体制中仍然应该是基本原则。

到东周的春秋战国时期，政府引导市场的理论获得极大的发展，集中体现在《管子》中集合形成的市场理论。在《管子》中，政府通过运用"物多则贱、寡则贵、散则轻、聚则重"的市场供求规律，实行"敛轻散重"的市场经济政策，以达到"无籍而赡国"，即"不益赋而天下用饶"的财政目的。《管子》中提出的"轻重论"认为：政府可利用对货币和粮食的垄断地位，通过权衡货币、粮食、百物的供求和贵贱，在谷价过低时，政府采取收购措施，使其价格回升；当谷价过高时，政府抛售谷物，使其价格回归正常水平；高抛低收、贱买贵卖，从价格波动中套利，既稳定粮价又增加政府收入。《管子·山国轨》中提出根据事物与经济运行的规律，制定货币和物价的调控政策，即"币重而万物轻，敛万物应之以币。币在下，万物皆在上。万物重十倍，府官以市櫎万物，隆而止。国轨布于未形，据其已成，乘令而进退，无求于民，谓之国轨。"《管子·国蓄》说："五谷食米，民之司命也；黄金刀币，民之通施也。故善者执其通施以御其司命，故民力可得而尽也。……故善者委始于民之所不足，操事于民之所有余。夫民有余则轻之，古人君敛之于轻；民不足则重之，古人君散之以重。敛积之以轻，散行之以重。故君必有什倍之利，而才之櫎可得而平也。凡轻重之大利，以重射轻，以贱泄平，万物之满虚，随财准平而不变，衡绝则重见。人君知其然，故守之以准平。"《管子·山至数》提出："人君操谷、币、金衡，而天下可定也。"《管子》认为，如果政府不掌握调控轻重的权利，则会被大商贾掌控，这会形成贫富差距，社会失衡。在《管子·七臣七主》中指出："彼时有春秋，岁有败凶，政有急缓。政有急缓故物有轻重；岁有败凶故民有义不足；时有春秋故谷有贵贱。而上不调淫，故游商得以什伯（百）其本也。百姓之不田，贫富之不訾，皆用此作。"《管子·治国》中分析了形成这种结果的原因是政府没有调控轻重均衡的结果，即"今也仓廪虚而民无积，农夫以鬻子者，上无术以均之也。"

"轻重论"中已经发现了供求决定价格和价格影响供求的原理，并发现货币与商品、货币与粮食以及粮食与其他商品之间的比价变化的原理，提出了国家调控市场价格政策的初步框架，即通过政府垄断货币与粮食，驾驭市场供求与物价变化，实行双向调控，稳定物价，兼取套利，充裕国家财政收入。"轻重论"将粮食价格和粮食产量与货币发行量的多少相关联，包含了"货币数量论"的基本思想。赵靖教授认为："轻重的主要内容包括三个部分：一是研究轻重问题并实施轻重政策的目的，即所谓轻重之势或轻重之权。二是关于实施轻重政策的手段和方法，也即轻重之术。三是关于轻重问题的一些基本的学理，也即轻重之学或轻重之数。……轻重之学包括商品价格和供求关系的原理和货币、粮食以及其他商品之间的比价变化的原理，是轻重之势和轻重之术的理论依据。"也就是说，轻重论涵盖了经济规律、经济制度和经济管理三个层次的学术成果，这在经济学说体系上具有奠基性的开创意义。

管子之后，范蠡和李悝又根据经济发展的实践，对国家引导和调控市场的理论进行了创造性发展。

范蠡（前536—前448年）是中国春秋末期政治家和经济学家。范蠡继承其师计然的"农业周期论"，提出了基于供求市场的农产品价格区间管理理论——"平粜论"。《史记·货值列传》记载："决万物不过三岁而发矣。……天下六岁一穰，六岁一康，凡十二岁一饥。""农业周期论"认为农业产出的波动同木星的运行相关，通过研究木星运转对应的气候规律可以发现农业的周期规律，从而产生3年、6年、12年的短、中、长期农业经济周期理论。这里3年为小循环、6年为中循环、12年为大循环。这就产生了宏观经济的思维方法，将社会经济现象作为统一体来分析。范蠡因此提出应依据天气、战争变化来储存物资，从而控制物资。胡寄窗先生认为，范蠡从生产本身发现了社会经济变化具有规律性的原因，从上游的生产环节来分析下游的流通环节，非常了不起。农业的周期性波动决定了农产品供应和价格的波动；歉收时农业减产造成价格上涨，丰收时农业增产导致价格下降。"平粜论"认为："夫粜，二十病农，九十病末，末病则财不出，农病则草不辟矣。上不过八十，下不过三十，则农末俱利。平粜齐物，关市不乏，治国之道也。""平粜论"认为把粮食价格变动的弹性区间稳定在每石三十至八十钱之间，对农业和商业都有利，能够确保粮食市场供应充足。"平粜论"认识到了价值规律支配下的价格波动现象，不仅提出基于市场供求的粮食价格区间管理理论，而且第一次提出"谷贵伤民"和"谷贱伤农"理论，包含了微观市场价格管理实践中的限制和扶持政策。这在世界经济学发展史上是一个杰出的贡献。

范蠡之后，魏国改革家和理财专家李悝（前445—前395年）提出"尽地力之教"的理论框架，建立了农业经济再生产理论，把范蠡的"平粜论"发展到"平籴论"。李悝重视所有制、分配制度和劳动生产率的作用，分析了价格对生产与消费的作用原理，粮食价格过高和过低的不良后果，即"籴甚贵伤民，甚贱伤农。民伤则离散，农伤则国贫。"据此提出了"平籴论"，即实行价格限制政策、价格扶持政策和弹性税制，使"使民适足，贾平则止""虽遇饥馑水旱，籴不贵而民不散""民无伤而农益劝"。

平籴论和平粜论的差异在于，范蠡的着眼点是农商俱利，重点是使商人有利可图；而李悝的着眼点是"民无伤而农益劝"，不是商，甚至还有抑商的性质。这是因为李悝所在的魏国是以农业为主的国家。

政府引导市场的理论在汉代又有了与时俱进的发展。《管子》的轻重论在汉代被实践、发展、改进、创新，其中桑弘羊的"平准法"和王莽的市平政策是我国市场价格管理制度的又一个与时俱进的制度创新。到西汉市场经济大发展后，豪强官吏操纵市场，使物价波动很大，为了稳定市场、增加政府收入，汉武帝时政府又发明创立均输制度、平准制度和盐铁专营制度。

公元前110年，西汉正式实行均输制度，设置均输官。将政府原来要自商贾手中购买的货物改作贡赋缴纳，由工官制造运输工具将贡物输送到京师；对中央政府不需要的货物，由均输官运到卖价高的地方出售，将钱交回国库，如此，中央政府收入增加，商人牟利机会减少。后又设立平准制度，专管从全国各地运到京师的货物，在市场价贱时买入，贵时卖出。如此，理论上，政府不仅可平抑物价，而且可增加收入，防止商人垄断市场。上述政策背景为汉武帝征伐匈奴耗费巨大，而富商巨贾又不愿踊跃捐输，不得不开源，实行均输平准、盐铁专卖，增加政府收入。据《史记·平准书》记载："置平准于京师，都受天下委输。召工官治车诸器,皆仰给大农。大农之诸官尽笼天下之货物,贵即卖之,贱则买之",从而"抑天下物,名曰平准"。该法与均输法配合使用,取得了平抑物价的效果。《汉书·食货志》第四下说:"中央政府一年因均输而获得帛500万匹,人民虽不加赋税,但国家富庶异常"。桑弘羊创造的均输制度、平准制度、盐铁专营政策有效地解决了政府财政收入、边境军队粮食供给和物价问题,因此被以后的历代政府所继承和创新。尤其是桑弘羊和当时贤良文学关于"盐铁专营"制度的理论和政策系列辩论,被桓宽整理形成《盐铁论》,成为世界经济学学术史上第一本专题性的经典文献。

公元前54年,汉宣帝时期的理财专家和科学家耿寿昌,根据平粜论和平准论,发明创造了"常平仓制度"。耿寿昌建议政府在边郡设置谷仓,"以谷贱时增其贾而籴以利农,谷贵时减贵而粜,名曰常平仓"。常平仓制度有效地解决了军队的供给和粮食价格的波动问题,有益于政府和民众,因此皇帝封耿寿昌为关内侯。常平仓制度被以后的历代政府所继承与创新,一直沿用到现在。

公元一世纪,王莽在常平仓制度的基础上又创立"市平"价格管理制度。根据《汉书·食货志》记载,王莽的"市平"政策规定:各大城市应以一年四季的中月(即阴历二、五、八、十一月)的价格为基础,按照五谷及丝帛的质量,根据市场实际情况,定为上、中、下三种价格,即"市平"价格。五谷市场价格在高于"市平"10%的限度内自由涨跌;如超过10%,则由政府按"市平"价格抛售该种商品;如跌到成本价以下,则由政府按其成本价收购。这样既稳定了物价,又保护生产者的积极性。王莽创立的"市平"政策,是世界经济史上最早的成体系的市场价格调控制度,被我国历代政府所继承和发展。比如:"唐玄宗统治时期(公元742—754年),以每斗粮加市价三钱购买;唐宪宗诏令,加市价十钱;在宋真宗统治时期(公元1006年),确定的粮价调控方案是:政府收购粮食时,在市场价上加三五文;在出售粮食时,从市场价中扣除三五文。扣除额不低于最初收购粮食的价格。金朝(公元1161—1189年)的法律规定,政府收购粮食增市价十分之二,政府出手减市价十分之一。公元1190年,政府出售价格减至市场价的三分之一。公元1757年,本朝(清朝)的高宗规定,一石粮食的售出价减市价银三钱。"

到唐朝,刘晏(公元715—780年)创造性地把轻重论推广到"万物"价格的调控,同时把商人作为推行轻重政策的助手,而不是对立面,实行官商结合举措，政府统购、批发，商人运送、零售，在救灾、漕运、政府盐铁专营等取得成功。他发明的"榷盐法"和"漕运法"，将市场机制引入政府专营领域，将盐的国家专卖权让渡给商人，将漕运开放给商人经营，进一步扩大商业税的税基，使国家能以最小付出，获得最大的商业利益。刘晏还建立了全国价格信息网和信息报告制度，用于市场物价的调控，解决信息不对称和滞后问题，提高政府政策的有效性。《管子·山国轨》已经有国轨，即政府统计土地、人口、粮价等信息作为制定政策的基本依据。从唐朝开始，政府把谷物价格的报告与常平仓的运营联系起来。在制度上，刘晏创设知院官，即在各地设置监视粮食价格变化的情报网，按旬（十天）和月上报各地气候、农业生产、物价等信息，歉收时低于市价出售粮食，丰收时高于市价收购粮食。"刘晏在诸道设置地方巡院，在所有巡院设立无数的驿站，并以高价招募那里善走的人，于是四方物价及其余的详细情况，乃至在极遥远偏僻的地方，不到四五日，其情形全在刘晏的掌握之中。"据记载"公元763年，刘晏利用帝国邮驿建立了一个快速的价格报告系统。三个世纪后，北宋的沈括任三司使（公元1075—1077）时使用了同样的方法，并且写道，刘晏方法的关键是，使用以十年期价格波动之事先分析为基础而建立的报告所指示的干预限度。这使地方官员在价格变化之前，就可以进行买卖（《梦溪笔谈》192条）。帝国晚期，报告价格已成为一种惯例。"明朝的邱俊（公元1420—1495年）在《大学衍义补》（卷二十六）中提出通过价格信息监控和货币来稳定粮价，即"愿国定市价恒以谷米为本。下令有司：在内，俾坊市逐月报米价于朝廷；在外，则闾里以日上于邑，邑以月上于府，府以季上于藩服，藩服上于户部。使上之人知钱谷之数，用是而验民食之足否，以为通融转移之法。务必使钱常不多余，谷常不至于不给，其价常平。""清代的价格记录制度承自明代，康熙时期的制度还不太规律。乾隆初年，报告制度标准化。粮价清单每十天制作一次，在提交给省会以及送往北京之前，主要由府州进行汇总。在府州的汇总中只记录了府州中主要谷物的最高和最低价格，……我们知道所有的价格都是在市镇上每十天搜集一次，单位是每升多少铜钱，并且被换算为每石多少两白银。清代档案中保存有上万份粮价清单（覆盖了从1736年至1911年每一省的数据）。"可以说，对粮食价格的监测与报告制度极具建设性，在一定程度上解决了市场的信息不对称问题，提高政府制定政策的有效性，在今天仍具有重要的理论价值和现实意义。

白居易（公元772—846年）根据唐代经济发展的条件，也在理论上对轻重论做了发展和创新：一是只把货币作为控制经济活动的制高点和杠杆，认为货币才是"权节轻重之要"，强调通过调节货币供应量的方法管理农产品价格，即通过"散钱"的方法来平抑物价。二是和刘晏一样，不把商人看作是同国家争夺轻重之势的敌人，进行"抑和困"，而是主张"和与利"；三是主张轻重政策在于"富天下""利散于天下"。《白居易集·策林十九》提出："王者平均其贵贱，调节其轻重，使百货流通，四人交利"。即粮食价格的高低与钱的轻重相关，管理农产品价格应使用货币调节的方法。

到宋代，关于逆风向的宏观经济政策已经成为政府调控经济的常态。北宋的王安石（公元1021—1086）创立了"新学学派"，对轻重论、平粜论、常平仓制度等做了与时俱进的发展和创新，创造了一系列逆市场的经济调节政策。其中"均输法"就是国营专卖法，对重要物资实行统购统销，用于反对商人垄断；"市易法"就是桑弘羊的平准法的推陈出新，即政府成为调节商品余缺的总中心，对滞销商品实行平价收购，到市场缺货时再出售；"青苗法"就是政府拿出一定钱粮在夏秋两收前给农民放贷，在财政上补助农民，防止豪强对农民的高利贷剥削。这些财政经济改革与制度设计主要解决当时商业垄断、土地兼并造成很大的贫富差距和政府财政收支矛盾缺口，具有明显的政府与豪强博弈的特征，也被后人称为大政府主义的经济管制政策。这与宋朝允许官员经商、豪强兼并、中央政府养活庞大官僚系统和军队造成的"吃饭财政"下国家财政虚弱的历史背景不可分离。但我们可以说，我国宋代就有了国家制定的反垄断法、反高利贷法、价格管制法。

周行己（公元1067—1124）对《管子》的轻重论中"币重则物轻，币轻则物重"做了新的解释，他指出"夫钱无用，而物为之用；钱本无轻重，而物为之轻重。故钱与物本无轻重。……铜钱以可运可积为贵，铁钱以不可运不可积为贱故也，以其本无轻重，而相形乃为轻重。"（《浮沚集》卷一）周行己还指出"钱之利一倍，物之贵两倍。……私铸不已则物价益贵。……出于民者常重，出于官者常轻，则国用其能不屈乎？"（《浮沚集》）这里，周行己指出货币贬值：一是引起物价上涨，并且是成倍地上涨；二是引发私人铸币，这会进一步增加货币供给，加速货币贬值，导致物价更加昂贵；三是由于官民轻重地位的不同，贬值使人民蒙受损失，政府暂时受益，但从长期、从根本上会削弱、减少国家的财政收入。在12世纪，周行已的这个认识已经十分深刻。

到了南宋，永嘉学派的著名代表人物叶适（公元1150—1223年）在《财计》中通过分析周公时代与宋代的经济发展条件变化，指出"《管子》中提出的轻重敛散之权必须由政府掌控"的观点已经不合时宜。即"夫泉府之法，敛市之不售，货之滞于民用者，以其买卖之，其赊者祭祀丧纪皆有数，而以国服为之息。若此者，真周公所为也。何者？当是时，天下号为齐民，未有特富者也。开阖、敛散、轻重之权一出于上，均之田而使之井，筑之室而使之居，衣食之具，无不毕舆。然而祭祀丧纪犹有所不足，而取于常数之外，若是者，周公不与则谁与之！将无以充其用而遂舆之也？则民一切仰上而其费无名，固赊而贷之使以日数偿，而以其所服者为息。且其市之不售，货之滞于民用者，民不足，于此而上不敛之，则为不仁。然则二者之法，非周公谁为之？盖三代固行之矣。今天下之民，不齐久矣。开阖、敛散、轻重之毕权不一出于上，而富人大贾分而有之，不知其几千百年矣。而遽夺之，可乎？夺之可也，嫉其自利而欲为国利，可乎？呜呼！居今之世，周公固不行是法矣。"

叶适的以上分析表明，没有一劳永逸的完美制度，所有市场制度都是一定时空条件约束下的产物，应该随着时空条件的变化而发展变化。

此外，南宋的董煟提出市场引导救荒论。南宋董煟在其所著的《救荒活民书》中创造性地提出：救荒政策以利用市场价格的自发作用作为指导思想，引导商人和地主企图通过市场价格以牟利的动机，达到调节供求和救荒的目的。比如，常平政策，他强调宁按市价高一、二文收购，以鼓励人们出售粮食，而决不能按不合实际的官定低价收购。关于义仓，他指出如荒歉不甚严重，米斛尚有流通，物价不甚高时，则以支钱为最省便，或钱米兼支亦可。

宋末元初的马端临（公元1254—1323年）在《文献通考》自序中对政府调控市场价格进行了历史性总结分析。他说："其市物也，亦诿曰权蓄贾居货待价之谋；及其久也，则官自效商贾之为，而指为富国之术矣。""至其极弊，则名曰和买、和籴，而强配数目，不给价直，鞭笞取足，视同常赋"。马端临的这段话说明，政府对市场价格管理政策的初衷很好，但实施一段时间后，政府、商人和农民的力量发生互动博弈，尤其是经不住官吏从中渔利，制度执行扭曲变形，成为害民的制度，且既得利益者也不愿改变这种现状。这说明不存在一劳永逸的制度，任何制度和政策都存在两面性，都是利弊相伴。随着时间推移，利弊此消彼长，官商民的利益平衡被打破是制度变迁的重要原因，制度不能达到最初设定的目标就应当进行再改革。这不是简单的交易费用理论和成本收益理论所能解释的。

直到清朝，人们还是认为："因中设市，其通商惠工，柔远能弥之规，实足为百代之良法。"比如"1759 年，乾隆二十四年，西陲底定，自辟展库车、阿克苏、乌什、和阗、叶尔羌、喀什噶尔等处，均设市集。内地运往者，绸、缎、褐毡、色布、茶封，易回部驴、马、牛、羊、翠羽、毛、革、金、银、铜、货及麦、荞、乌菱，以实边境军储。或遣官监运，或听军民贩载，其物价悉照内地价值交易。"这段史实说明，政府因军需会主动设立市场。

20 世纪后四分之一，中国政府在改革开放中不仅主动设立经济特区、经济开发区、自由贸易区等推动中国市场经济的发展，而且还主动参与世界贸易组织，实行"一带一路"倡议，推进市场经济全球化和国际市场经济秩序的发展与重构等。这段当代史也引证了"政府引导市场理论"一直是中国特色市场经济的主色调。

## 二、我国的古典市场经济理论

1. 管子的市场经济理论

《管子》中对市场经济理论进行了深入的阐释，提出了供求交换形成价格的市场理论、轻重论、逆市场风向的宏观调控理论和国际价格理论。《管子》中提出市场价格形成机制受天地（自然条件禀赋）、时空（一年四季、地理空间、年岁丰歉等）、供求关系、商贾力量和政府政令缓急调控等影响；提出市场可以解决国计民生问题，没有市场，人民就会匮乏；认为完全听凭大商贾操纵市场，实行自由放任，市场价格信号就会失灵，生产过剩和短缺就会交替发生，社会的贫富悬殊就会恶化，这会危及国家治理，所以需要国家进行调控。

关于市场的基本认识。《管子·乘马》说："市者，货之准也。……故曰，市者可以知治乱，可以知多寡，而不能为多寡。为之有道。右'务市事'……聚者有市，无市则民乏。"即市场是货物在交换中各自获得其应有价格的地方。……所以说，从市场上显露的情况可以了解国家的治乱兴衰，可以明晰社会财富的多少，而不能通过市场创造物质财富的多寡。市场是有规律地运行，掌握市场运行变化的规律来管理市场，就是符合理性（道）的治理。……并指出，方圆150里就要有市场，没有市场人民的用度就会匮乏。《管子》中已经明确地指出，市场流通领域是经济发展的一个表征，它不会创造新的价值，但离开市场人民的用度就会匮乏。在《管子·侈靡》中又提出："市也者，劝也。劝者，所以起。"即市场是一种协调生产与消费，推动经济发展的力量。在《管子·问》中进一步提出："市者天地之财具也，而万人之所和而利也。正是道也。"即市场是人类通过天地生产的财富积聚交易的地方，它使万民分工合作，是交换获利的场所，也是解决国计民生的人间正道。

关于市场经济价值论。管仲提出财富创造来源于人力和土地，其中人力是关键。《管子·八观》说："彼民非谷不食，谷非地不生，地非民不动，民非力作，毋以致财，天之所生，生于用力，用力之所生，生于劳身。"

关于市场运行论。管仲提出市场上的价格均衡没有定数，是动态变化的，但可以通过掌握不同时空物价变化的规律而制定策略。《管子·轻重乙》认为："市场上没有固定不变的均衡，均衡供求是要使物价有高有低，不经常固定在一个数字上。市场上的均衡供求不能调整划一。调整划一就静止了，静止就没有变化了，没有变化则物价没有升降差别，没有差别就会使商品流通受阻而不能利用市场了。……了解一年四季的顺序，就可以运用国家政策，使物价有十倍、百倍的升降。所以，物价不能经常固定在一个点。即不同时期均衡供求与物价没有定数。"

关于农产品价格理论。《管子》认为，农业受生产周期长、季节变化、丰歉年景的影响明显，市场自发价格机制会导致时空和价格的错配，形成生产或过剩或短缺，需要国家介入调控。《管子·国蓄》指出："岁适美，则市粜无予，而狗彘食人食。岁适凶，则市粜釜十繦，而道有饿民。……然则岂壤力固不足而食固不赡也哉？夫往岁之粜贱，狗彘食人食，故来岁之民不足也，物适贱，则半力而无予，民事不偿其本；物适贵，则什倍而不可得，民失其用。然则岂财物固寡而本委不足也哉？夫利民之时失，而物利之不平也。"

关于"看不见的手"理论，即经济利益引导经济发展的理论。《管子·禁藏》中已经对此作了精辟的总结分析，即"夫凡人之情，见利莫能勿就，见害莫能勿避。其商人通贾，倍道兼行，夜以继日，千里而不远者，利在前也。渔人之入海，海深万仞，就波逆流，乘慰百利，宿夜不出者，利在水也。故利之所在，虽千仞之山，无所不上；深渊之下，无所不入焉。固善者势利之在，而民自美安，不推而往，不引而来，不烦不扰，而民自富。如鸟之覆卵，无形无声，而唯见其成。"对"看不见的手"，政府该如何治理呢？《管子·禁藏》提出："故凡治乱之情，皆道上始。故善者圉之以害，牵之以利。能利害者，财多而过寡矣。……夫为国之本，得天之时而为经，得人之心而为纪。法令为维纲，吏为网罟，什伍以为行列，赏诛为文武。"

《管子》提出市场可以解决国计民生问题，没有市场，人民就会匮乏；认为完全听凭大商贾操纵市场，实行自由放任，市场价格信号就会失灵，生产过剩和短缺就会交替发生，社会的贫富悬殊就会恶化，这会危及国家治理，所以需要国家进行调控。这个认识和观念到汉武帝时，通过算缗告缗，均输平准，盐铁专营等关键生产行业的国营化，给固化了。从此，中国的市场经济在统一时期基本处于政府管制之下。

《管子》中提出的"轻重论"以及农产品价格理论、供求理论、市场理论、逆风向的市场调节理论，不仅在经济学理论上具有开创性的世界意义，而且被后人继承、完善、发展、实践，成为历久弥新的经济学基本理论，闪烁着人类智慧的光芒。

2. 司马迁的市场经济理论

司马迁也对市场这只"看不见的手"进行了精辟的总结抽象，提出"水之趋下说"和"善因论"。他在《货值列传》中指出："（丝竹木石等世间万物）皆中国人民所喜好，谣俗被服饮食奉生送死之具也。故待农而食之，虞而出之，工而成之，商而通之。此宁有政教发徵期会哉？人各任其能，竭其力，以得所欲。故物贱之徵贵，贵之徵贱，各劝其业，乐其事，若水之趋下，日夜无休时，不召而自来，不求而民出之。岂非道之所符，而自然之验邪？"司马迁的政策主张是："善者因之，其次利道（导）之，其次教诲之，其次整齐之，最下者与之争。"

司马迁的"水之趋下说"被一些经济学者认为是亚当·斯密"看不见的手"理论的直接渊源。

3. 宋代经济学家的市场经济理论

到了北宋，我国出现了学术发展的第二次高峰，关于市场经济的理论也获得了新的认识和发展。宋代工商业首次超过农业成为国家税收的主体,水力机械革命,焦炭炼铁革命,造船,指南针和海上商业革命,雕版印刷与文化革命,纸币发明导致货币革命等促进工商业经济和城市大发展,出现了第一批合股公司和职业经理人阶层;纸币大面积使用,铜钱是世界货币。因此,市场经济理论、商业理论、货币理论、财政理论、经济思想与经济伦理学都有了极大的发展。李觏、苏洵、苏轼、苏辙和陈亮、叶适为代表的事功学派(后者即永嘉学派,倡导言利,鼓吹道义是建立在追求功利的前提之上)偏重功利。张载、程颢、程颐和朱熹、陆九渊为代表的理学学派(对过分追求功利的伦理进行系统性反思,主张研究功利不能涵盖的10%的人类关系,提出存天理的主张)偏重性理。两派的理论争论,推动了人类对欲望、功利、理性和道德的认识。

比如,李觏通过分析市场上供给与需求的季节变化、供求力量的不对称,说明价格变化对农民都是不利的,这就大大扩展了范蠡和李悝的认识。在其所著的《富国策》中提出"谷贱伤农,贵亦伤农,贱则利末,贵亦利末"的新认识。他分析说:"古人有言曰:'谷甚贱则伤农,贵则伤末。'谓农常粜而末常籴也,此一切之论也。愚以为贱则伤农,贵亦伤农,贱则利末,贵亦利末。盖农不常粜,有时而籴也;末不常籴,有时而粜也。以一岁之中论之,大抵敛时多贱,而种时多贵矣。夫农老于作,剧于病也,爱其谷,甚于生也。不得已而粜者,则有由焉。小则具服器,大则营婚丧。公有赋役之令,私有称贷之责(通'债')。故一谷始熟,腰镰未解,而日输入市焉。粜者既多,其价不得不贱,贱则贾人乘势而罔之,轻其币而大其量,不然则不售矣。故曰敛时多贱,贱则伤农而利末也。农人仓廪既不盈,窦窖既不实,多或数月,少或旬时,而用度竭矣。土将生而或无种也,末将执而或无食也,于是乎日取于市焉。籴者既多,其价不得不贵,贵则贾人乘势而闭之,重其币而小其量,不然则不予矣。故曰种时多贵,贵亦伤农而利末也。"

李觏的这个观点和分析,扩展了人们对粮食市场结构与价格关系的认识,引入了市场上粮农和商人之间的权力不对称分析,超越了简单的供求数量分析,说明决定价格的是隐藏在市场背后的经济实力和权力格局,而非表层的即时供求,这是重要的理论创新。

李觏还在《富国策》中对平粜论的政策利弊进行了系统分析,提出了解决的对策建议。他指出:"盖平籴之法行,农人秋籴不甚贱,春籴不甚贵,大贾蓄家不得豪夺之矣。而官之出息常什一二,民既不困,国且有利,兹古圣贤之用心也。然其所未至,则有三焉:数少也,道远也,吏奸也。一郡之籴不数千万,其余畢入贾人。至春当籴,寡出之则不足于饥也,多出之则可计日而尽也。于是贾人深藏而待其尽,尽则权归于贾人矣,是数少之弊也。仓储之建,皆在郡治,县之远者,或数百里,其贫民多籴则无资,少籴则非可,朝行而暮归也,故终弗得而食之矣,是道远之弊也。今若广置本泉,增其籴数,则蓄贾无所专利矣;仓储之建,各于其县,则远民可得矣;申命州部,必使廉能,则奸吏无以侵刻矣。如此,利国便人,事可经久,是谓通轻重之权,不可不察。"

比如,王安石(公元1021—1086年)的"新学学派",不仅提倡思想解放,把新陈代谢视为自然规律,强调人应效法自然,自觉地除旧布新,实行变法,而且创立"为政富民说",在北宋中后期取得官方学术地位,"独行于世者六十年",在当时影响极大。他在《洪范传》中指出:"凡正人之道,既富之然后善。……为政于天下者,在乎富之善之。"针对反对派讳言财利,言利则背孔孟的观点。王安石指出:"狗彘食人食则检之,野有饿殍则发之,是所谓政事。政事所以理财,理财乃所谓义也。一部《周礼》,理财居其半。"《周礼》是儒家经典。在训释《周礼》"以土均之法"条中,他说:"民职、地贡、财赋,则有政矣。然远近多寡之不均,先后缓急之不齐,非政之善。于是乎以均齐天下之政。"王安石主张积极理财,提出"因天下之力以生天下之财,取天下之财以供天下之费,自古治世,未尝以理财不足为公患敚,患在治财无其道尔。"(《宋史·王安石传》)他认为只要政策得当,政府增加财政收入的同时,也可以发展民间经济。他已经能区分个人财富的增长和社会财富的增长不同,认为个人财富取之于他人也能达到,而社会财富只有通过扩大生产才能实现;社会财富的分配只是一方增多而另一方减少的,不可能增加社会财富的总量。这在我国古代经济学上是十分罕见的。

再比如,叶适为代表的永嘉学派,倡导言利,鼓吹道义是建立在追求功利的前提之上。叶适对物质利益的认识已经完全不同于春秋战国时期。叶适对理性的认识也达到了很高的学术境界,他反对唯心论,主张在物质利益基础上认识人的理性。他反对陆派"吾心即理",认为"道在器中""离器无道"。他提出"理在事物""去物非理"的学说,主张理要"验于事,考于器";论事而违实是不可以的，即实事求是，要"有的放矢"。叶适批评董仲舒的"仁人正谊不谋利，明道不计功"的观点："此语初看极好，细看疏阔。古人以利与人而不自居其功，故道义光明。后世儒者行仲舒之论，既无功利，则道义者乃无用之虚语尔。"

## 三、结语

本文通过对我国古典市场经济理论的寻根探源的研究，发现中国市场经济理论与实践的演进不同于当前流行的两种认识，发现了一些中国人原创的市场经济理论认识，证明我国古典市场经济理论随着我国经济发展阶段的不同都有与时俱进的学术成果和理论发展。比如，我国有系统的政府引导市场理论。这个理论基于人类不能完全受自然摆布、市场左右，而是按照一定的价值观和发展目标，必须进行必要的人为调节。我国政府引导市场理论有一个突出的特征，即预防与治疗并重的思想认识。对于可能的经济波动与天灾人祸乃至危机，政府应该提前进行预防，储备必要的应对手段和技术，防止波动、灾难造成系统性、整体性伤害。比如，关于"看不见的手"的市场经济理论最早的文献出现在《管子》一书中，后来司马迁又提出"水之趋下说"。再比如，从范蠡、李悝的"谷贱伤农，谷贵伤民"到李觏的"谷贱伤农，谷贵亦伤农"，反映了我国古典经济学家对市场经济的深刻认识，这个认识应该说目前现代微观经济学中还没有看见。还比如，范蠡的基于市场供求的价格区间管理理论，刘晏对轻重论创造性的发展和基于全国价格信息网提高政府调控有效性的理论，等等。这些理论和认识都对建设社会主义市场经济具有重要的现实价值，需要我们在继承中与时俱进地发展和创新。

本文还发现，在认识清楚一定时空下的经济发展规律后，即使再完美的制度设计也不总是有效的，其执行也不总是符合政府与人民的初衷。比如，粮食是人类的生活必需品，粮食价格是整个社会稳定的基础，在古代能反映经济变化的晴雨表，而农业生产受制于自然，产量不会遵循市场供需规律短期发生变化。根据对农业经济的这个认识，我国古人创造了轻重论、平粜论、平籴论、均输论、平准论，政府专营论，常平论、市平论等理论和制度。起初，这些制度在有组织能力的管理者领导下都发挥了正面的积极作用，但随着时间的演进,实施一段时间后都成为人民的负担和包袱,变为负面的消极作用,甚至一些制度在一开始就被执行者扭曲变形,背离初衷,如市易法、青苗法等。这些初衷良好的制度,在政府、商人和农民的互动博弈中,往往经不住官吏从中渔利,商人从中倒腾利用,制度执行扭曲变形,成为害民的制度。这说明不存在一劳永逸的制度,市场上不同群体的利益博弈,让再完美的制度也扭曲变形,背离初衷。所以,对一种经济政策的检讨,不仅要研究制度设计的问题、管理的问题,更要研究制度与管理背后的利益群体之间的力量与手段博弈的不同形态。

没有完美的市场和市场制度,只有合意的适合发展阶段和约束条件的市场制度。从中国经济发展的历史演进看,市场是一种人类主体互惠互利交易行为的结果,其最后表现就是交易货通。正如我在2017年的论文中指出的,在中国,尤其是秦代以后的中央集权社会,中国的市场和市场经济都是政府管制和主导的市场经济;政府一直是市场建设的最重要主体。市场得以确立的基础制度设施、基本的交易工具、交易的基础设施、主要生产要素的支配权等,都由政府这个市场上最重要的主体所承担、所支配,如土地、货币、秩序、交易场所等。一方面,政府在任何一个国家都既是供给者,也是需求者,既是投资者,也是调节者,既是市场的建设者,也是市场秩序的维护者。另一方面,如果政府制定的制度和政策不恰当,也会成为市场混乱、市场失序的最大制造者。

从市场的主体政府、企业和个人的发展关系看,我国政府一直很强,企业家、资本家改革开放以来也变得很强势,但个人组成的社会力量一直不成气候、组织化程度低,缺少有效的法治保护,被迫在依附中生存。由于市场中的组织和个人在资源配置中的短期化、机会主义和自利行为导致的经济整体的无序与全局性后果;又由于现代大型企业对市场、社会、国家的重要影响,对个人和家庭有可能形成系统性的剥削和压榨。因此,如何让法治强起来,建立"强政府、强企业、强个人"的国家治理体系是未来中国市场经济发展的关键。

需要特别指出:市场不是虚幻的,不能把市场虚拟化、神话;是我们人为市场立法;不是市场在影响人、摆布人,而是人,尤其是政治家、政府官员和企业家、资本家在影响市场、操纵市场、摆布市场、控制市场、设计市场,是我们人在构造现实世界的市场结构、市场形态和价格机制。在认识市场和市场经济的过程中,人比市场本身更重要,人们组成的利益团体甚至比市场机制还重要。

**参考文献**

[1] 白居易. 白居易集 [M]. 北京:中华书局,1979.

[2] 班固撰. 汉书 [M]. 北京:中华书局,2007.

[3] 陈焕章. 孔门理财学 [M]. 韩华译,北京:商务印书馆,2015.

[4] 何炼成. 宋代思想家的价格理论评介 [J]. 河南师大学报(社会科学版),1982(4).

[5] 胡寄窗. 中国经济思想史 [M]. 上海:上海财经大学出版社,1998.

[6] 贾太宏主编. 管子通释 [M]. [西汉] 刘向汇编,北京:西苑出版社,2015.

[7] 李觏. 李觏集 [M]. 北京:中华书局,2011.

[8] 李山译注. 管子 [M]. 北京:中华书局,2009.

[9] 李学勤主编,朱汉民等著. 中国学术史·宋元卷(下)[M]. 南昌:江西教育出版社,2000.

[10] 林光彬. 农产品价格管理的中国理论与中国方案 [J]. 中央财经大学学报,2017(05).

[11] 林光彬. 重新理解市场与政府在资源配置中的作用——市场与政府到底是什么关系 [J]. 教学与研究,2017(01).

[12] 刘波,王川,邓启铜注译. 周礼 [M]. 南京:南京大学出版社,2014.

[13] 马端临. 文献通考 [M]. 杭州:浙江古籍出版社,2007.

[14] 司马光编著. 资治通鉴 [M]. 北京:中华书局,2007.

[15] 司马迁. 史记 [M]. 韩兆琦主译,北京:中华书局,2008.

[16] 田国强. 深化制度改革才能解决增长与转型两难比较 [EB/OL]. 2015.

[17] 王文素,孙翊刚,洪钢. 十通财经文献注释 [M]. 北京:中国社会科学出版社,2015.

[18] 魏根深. 中国历史研究手册(中册)[M]. 侯旭东主持翻译,北京:北京大学出版社,2016.

[19] 杨天才译注. 周易 [M]. 北京:中华书局,2016.

[20] 叶适. 叶适文集(第三册)[M]. 北京:中华书局,1961.

[21] 约翰·伊特韦尔等编. 新帕尔格雷夫经济学大辞典(第2卷)[M]. 北京:经济科学出版社,1992.

[22] 赵靖. 经济学志 [M]. 上海:上海人民出版社,2010.

# Chinese Classical Theory of Market Economics

Lin Guangbin

**Abstract**: With its market insights and abundant theories about the market economy, China has been a core navigator of the global market economy since before the 17th century. This study investigates the origins of Chinese classical theory of market economics and seeks some knowledge originating from China that describes approaches that differ from the two other prevailing theories in modern China. In particular, we review the ancient literature regarding the theories on "government leading market" (GLM) and "classical market economics" (CME) to reveal which is used by the Chinese government to develop the market economy today and where such theory originates in history. We come to four key conclusions. 1. The innovative academic achievements and theoretical development in the context of Chinese CME were implemented to keep pace with different economic development stages. 2. No perfect market or market economy exists; only those with appropriate development stages and constraints do. 3. The earliest description about "the invisible hand" appeared in *Guanzi*. 4. Ideas changed from "cheapness hurts farmers while expensiveness hurts civilians" to "cheapness hurts farmers, and expensiveness hurts them as well" to reflect Chinese classical economists' profound understanding of market economy, which is not yet seen in modern microeconomics.

**Keywords**: Market Economy; Classical Theory; Chinese Episteme; Modern Value

CLC number: F123.9    Document code: A

## Introduction: Two Modern Market Approaches

Market approaches are widely debated subjects in modern China. How is the new market finance theory better than others? The key improvement lies in its approach to market and finance, which is based on its critique of traditional approaches and its gradual formation through observation of the evolving relationship between market and finance in China and the world.

Chinese economic institutions underwent various stages, including the socialist-planned, planned commodity, and socialist marketing stages. The role of the market in the economy also changed from supplementing the plan, through guiding enterprises while being guided by the plan, to playing a fundamental part and then a decisive one in resource allocation. This process reflects a deepening understanding of the market economy among Chinese scholars, politicians, and social media. In this understanding, two different methods must be discussed. One is to virtualize the market, with the support of those who believe that the market is omnipotent in solving any economic problem and thus regard the government as the source of all problems and claim to return to Adam Smith's "Night Watchman" theory. The other one indicates that the market economy is a discourse system lacking in ancient China but not in the reform era. Upheld and promoted by Chinese economics elites, these two approaches have almost become a religious manifesto that cloaks current Chinese academia, especially requiring reflection to identify the beneficial and harmful aspects. Hence, a new understanding of the Chinese market economy has again become a focal topic, which is even crucial for the Chinese reform and development path and for the vital interests of all people.

The dichotomy in western social science research dominates the mainstream approaches to the market and market economy. It alleges a contradictory relation between the government and the market, between fairness and efficiency, and between the individual and the collective. Three perspectives match these ideas in economics. The first one is rooted in the basic idea of neo-classical economics and Keynesianism, in which the more the government gets, the less is left for the market. Moreover, under such idea, the government's role is to compensate for market failures by using "the visible hand" to assist "the invisible hand," thereby reducing excessive fluctuations and damage in the economy to facilitate sustainable economic and social development. The second perspective excludes the government from the market and only regards enterprises as the main ruling bodies, which are crucial for resource allocation. This view is mostly accepted by liberal and neo-liberal economics, such as the Anglo-Saxon school (especially the Chicago school) and the Austrian school, both of which blindly believe that the market is the cure for all economic problems. In *The New Palgrave Dictionary of Economics*, a market is defined as an area where "production and distribution are determined by independent enterprises (state-owned, private, or otherwise)". This definition clearly excludes the government from the production and distribution in the market and is definitely inconsistent with historical facts. The third perspective proposes to advance China's reform in an ideal market economy structure, that is, "China's next market reform stage should start with a benchmark or a reference." Supporters argue the following: "With the ideal economic environment as a benchmark and free market as a reference, modern economics theories strictly deduce a precondition for the market to be good to lead to effective allocation, which points to the right direction of reform in the long run. In this way, the market is prospective in theoretically directing reform and innovation to shape the economy into an ideal one." This view fails to deduce from the facts of historical evolution but rather emerges from the so-called axiomatic hypothesis; therefore, it seems to disregard the changing circumstances. Only in a utopia can this free-market theory be realized, and using it to draw blueprint and routine for China is misleading because it completely ignores the fact that after the 1930s, the global market structure successively entered monopolistic competition, oligopoly, national monopoly, and, finally, international monopoly. Such view is divorced from reality and common sense because a complete competitive market barely exists in the real world and big enterprises always compete with one another to arrive at monopoly or oligopoly. What the western world confirms is that a government tells one story while prevailing theorists and external ideologies tell another. The most typical evidence is the divergent government policies from varied theorists and ideologies since 2008.

In sum, these perspectives and views confound the right analysis scope with the wrong ones and misidentify the subject and object. Regardless of whether it is seen as the original trading venue and platform or as a mechanism, the market is not a pairing concept that corresponds to the government because it is well-known that the state, society, and market are intensive, man-made concepts overall. They are composed of, driven, and operated by agents such as individuals in corresponding periods and transpersonally with families, enterprises, and governments. In terms of analysis level, the government pairs with enterprises or families while the market pairs with the society or state. The market operates on a transaction benefit and aims for goods distribution, whereas the society operates on an ethical order and aims to realize internal harmony, with the state implementing laws by forcible organizational behavior. These three parts constitute the basic pattern of an evolving human society.

The five-thousand-year economic history of China and the socialist market economy with Chinese characteristics confirm that the dichotomous approach in western social science is at least unsuitable for China's development practice and hence should be abandoned. The current work does not intend to conduct a deep and detailed analysis of the dichotomous approach in western market research, but it does examine the origins of

Chinese classical market economics (CME) theory. We expect an approach distinct from the two described above that apply to the evolution of Chinese market economy theories and knowledge originating from China because China has been a core navigator of the global market economy before the 17th century with insights into the market and abundant theories about market economy.

China has abundant market economy theories, whose complete and scattered descriptions are available extensively in the literature. We review those sources on "government leading market" (GLM) and CME theories to reveal what the Chinese government used to develop the current market economy and where it originated in history.

## I. GLM Theory

In the Chinese classic *Book of Changes*: Post-biography of Xici, Shen-Nung not only invented the plough for farming but also "opened the market to gather people around for transactions at noon, who shall all be properly provided for before they leave, just as the diagram of *Shihe* shows." These words reveal that Shen-Nung at least created a significant form of an ancient market for fulfilling transactions and the needs for goods distribution.

According to the *Book of Documents*: *Basic Laws* (*Hongfan*), state governance includes eight aspects, with food (Shi) and goods (Huo) being the first and second aspects, respectively. The *Book of Han*: *Records of Food and Goods* suggests that a state only needs sufficient commodity supply and an efficient distribution system for goods to prosper. "To rule a state needs eight kinds of officials, the first to manage food, the second to manage goods. The former refers to grains of high quality, and the latter refers to what is used for property distribution and benefits spread such as cloth, gold, shells, and so on. These two aspects have been the foundation of people's life since Shen-Nung's era. ' Make a plough by cutting wood down and bending it, then spread the benefits of it to the world so that plenty of food will be produced. ' ' Open the market to gather people around for transactions at noon, who will all be properly provided for before they leave. ' Then, goods are well-distributed. With food and goods all managed, the state will prosper and enrich people, and then indoctrination will naturally come into being. " Both classical works reveal that the earliest market in China was the one created by the leader of the ancient "tribal state", Shen-Nung, who also regarded the process of production and market as two key conditions for a state's prosperity.

According to these classics, China was a state with a government-organized market economy under the Zhou dynasty, wherein the market was an indispensable necessity for cities. *The Rites of Zhou* states that Zhou's market was mostly set up by the government within cities. As shown in *The Rites of Zhou: Heavenly Official Zhongzai*, "To found a state, the king needs to identify the right direction, demarcate the capital (tiguo), and appoint officials to be role models for the public (Guideline). " Here "tiguo" refers to the nine crossroads used to divide the north-south and east-west directions in the capital, where the ancestral temple was located in the left, the sajik was placed in the right, the government was in the front, and the market was in the back. This book also adds, "When a capital is constructed, the queen shall be assisted to establish a market, arrange offices even at the entry as well as sales booths where goods are displayed, and worship standard measuring tools of length, capacity, and width with ancient rites. " Thus, a Neizai ought to help the sovereign establish a market; arrange offices for officials managing the market even at the market's entry; regulate the stalls selling goods; ask merchants to display gold, jade, and silk; and trade under standard measures.

In accordance with *The Rites of Zhou: Earthly Official Situ's description*, one official called Market Manager (Sishi) specialized in market management with 164 subordinates. This arrangement means that modern market-managing institutions (such as the Price Bureau, Tax Bureau, Quality and Technology Supervision Bureau, and Industry and Commerce Bureau) already existed in Zhou and functioned well with explicit assignments. For instance, Zhiren was in charge of assessing and stabilizing prices and managing sales contracts; Chanren was responsible for levying house, goods, contract, residential taxes and fines and then handing them to Quanfu; Xunshi dealt with industrial and commercial quality supervision; Jiashi performed the sorting of goods and price determination; Sibao and Siji handled the maintenance of market order; Quanfu used taxes to adjust the market supply and demand and determine the benchmark interest rate by purchasing unmarketable goods; Simen collected goods tax at customs; Siguan checked the customs certificates of cargoes imported or exported and punished smuggling; and finally, Sizhang collected commodity tax and monitored the goods and prices in the market.

*The Rites of Zhou: Earthly Officials* also contains the principles of market management: "Whatever are traded in the market, supplement the lacking, enrich the beneficial, extinguish the harmful, and reduce the extravagant." The principles include the following: supply the goods in shortage, enrich the ones that are of good quality and are convenient to people, make the harmful ones unsellable, and reduce the demand for extravagant ones. These principles remain fundamental to constructing a socialist market economy today.

In the Warring States era, GLM theory led to great achievements, as mainly shown in *Guanzi*'s aggregative market theory. According to *Guanzi*, the government followed the market's supply-demand pattern in which "huge quantity comes with low prices while a small number comes with high ones; dispersing leads to lightness while gathering leads to heaviness" and then carried out policies of "accumulating the light and decentralizing the heavy" to "profit without tax"; that is, the financial aim was for the "treasury to gain plentiful funds without levying a tax." This "light versus heavy" (LH) theory in *Guanzi* allowed the government to take advantage of its monopoly position over currency and grains. By balancing the supply-demand relation and adjusting the prices of currency, grains, and other commodities, the government could make them appreciate by purchasing when prices were low and depreciate them by selling when prices were high. Through these actions, the government arbitraged from price fluctuations, thereby stabilizing the prices while increasing the financial revenue. *Guanzi:Finance Management of a State* proposes to follow the pattern of economic operation when making money and price policies, that is, "Purchase goods to supply currency if goods' prices are lower than currency so that people shall possess currency while the government possesses goods. Even when goods' prices increase 10 times, the government still can reduce them to normal levels by selling goods at market prices until so. Such nationwide policies are determined before production and take effect after it. It's being conducted by the government without asking the public, hence their label as 'a state's statistical and financial management (gui)'." *Guanzi:A State's Savings states*, "Grains are what people live on, and currency is what they use to exchange. A wise emperor knows how to control grains by dominating the currency and then makes the most use of people's resources... by supplying the goods restored when the market is in shortage and doing the reverse when the market is in surplus. In the former situation, market prices are high because of the shortage, and so, the emperor could sell at high prices; in the latter situation, by contrast, market prices are low because of the surplus, and so, the emperor could purchase at low prices. Then, the emperor makes a huge profit, and goods' prices are stabilized through the process. The advantage of LH is purchasing at higher prices when market prices are too low and selling at lower prices when market prices are too high. The surplus and shortage of goods vary with different seasons, with which the emperor should adjust the prices for balance; otherwise, the prices wouldn't remain at a normal level. A wise emperor knows this pattern, and so, he shall try not to violate it. " *Guanzi: Solution to Terrain* points out, "An emperor is competent to rule a state so long as he balances among food, currency, and gold. " In *Guanzi*, this power should be under the government's control; otherwise, it will be exploited by rich businessmen and thereby cause an imbalance in wealth distribution and social equity. *Guanzi: Seven Ministers with Seven Kings* indicates that "urgent policies differentiate from easy ones, just as springs differentiate from autumns, or bumper-harvest years differentiate from poor-harvest ones. Policies' urgency leads to high or low prices, quality of crops leads to shortage or surplus, and the same is true of seasons. If the government doesn't cope with prices' fluctuations, merchants would make abnormal profits, and then people won't be willing to farm because of the inequity. " *Guanzi: State Governance* concludes that such outcome is caused exactly by the government's failure to adjust and balance prices, that is, "Now the treasury is empty and people are so poor that they are down to selling their children to survive. The emperor's incompetence to balance people's wealth is to blame. "

LH theory already paves the way for two theorems: that the supply-demand relation determines 1) the price and the price affecting it in turn and 2) the variance of the exchange ratio between currency and commodities, between currency and food, and between food and other goods. According to these theorems, LH theory constructs a preliminary framework toward a national price control policy; that is, by monopolizing currency and grains, market and price changes are kept under control, a two-way regulation is realized, prices are stabilized, and arbitrage is taken, all of which lead to increases in fiscal revenue. LH's idea is to correlate food prices and production with the amount of currency issued; this idea reflects the basic concept of the "quantity theory of money. " Professor Zhao Jing said, "LH's contents can be divided into three main parts: the first is the purpose of the study and policy, that is, to realize the so-called LH force (shi) or LH power (quan); the second is the means used to implement the policy, that is, the LH approach (shu); the third is several basic principles about this issue, that is, LH knowledge (xue)…, which includes LH force's and approach's theoretical basis, theorems about the variance of the exchange ratios of currency and commodities, currency and food, as well as food and other goods. " Thus, LH covers the three levels of academic achievements, economic laws, economic institutions and economic management, all of which are of fundamental significance to a theoretical system of economics.

After Guan Zhong, Fan Li and Li Kui continued to use the economic development practice for the creative theoretical improvement of GLM theory.

Fan Li (536 – 448 B. C. ) was a politician and an economist during the Spring and Autumn Period. Following the "agricultural cycle theory" of his teacher, Ji Ran, he developed a theory for managing agricultural price range, the "Pingtiao theory," which was based on the market's supply-demand relation. *Shiji:Biographies of Great Merchants* records, "The universe is regulated by a three-year cycle…, which indicates that a harvest comes every six years, a normal-level one for the next six years, and then a famine comes every twelve years. " "Agricultural cycle theory" correlates the fluctuations in agricultural output to Jupiter's movement. It uses the climatic patterns corresponding to the movement to discover agricultural periodicity and then derives a cycle theory, including short-term (three-year), medium-term (six-year), and long-term (twelve-year) cycles, which respectively equate to small, medium, and big cycles within agricultural economics. This notion embodies the idea of macroeconomics by taking a social economy phenomenon as a whole for analysis. Inspired by that development, Fan Li claimed that the government should store goods in line with the changes from the climate and war so as to control the goods.

Hu Jichuang considered it remarkable for Fan to have discovered the regular reasons behind social economic changes and analyzed them from upstream to downstream in production chains. Periodicity in agricultural fluctuations manifests a decrease in output caused by crop failure, which would lead to increase in prices. Meanwhile, an increase caused by good harvest would lead to a decrease in prices. As "Pingtiao theory" argues, "Suppose farmers sell grain to merchants. If they trade at twenty cents per peck, the farmers would bear a loss; with ninety cents per peck, the merchants would bear a loss too. If the farmers get hurt, they would leave the fields barren; if the merchants get hurt, they wouldn't participate in currency circulation. However, if the price is between thirty to eighty cents, both parties would benefit. Therefore, adjusting prices to a fair level is crucial to state governance as it guarantees sufficient tax for the government and plentiful supply for the market." As indicated, "Pingtiao theory" posits that stabilizing the price of grains at thirty to eighty cents was beneficial for agriculture and commerce and ensured an adequate grain supply in the market. In sum, "Pingtiao theory" recognizes that price fluctuations were dominated by the law of value, develops a grain price management theory based on the market's supply-demand relation, and proposes the ideas of "expensiveness hurts civilians" and "cheapness hurts farmers," which include restricting and supporting policies in micro market price management practice. This achievement is an extraordinary contribution in the world's history of economics.

Li Kui (445 –395 B. C. ), a reformer and finance expert in Wei, developed a theoretical framework of "agricultural development" (dili) after Fan Li. He extended Fan's "Pingtiao theory" into one about agricultural economic reproduction, namely, the "Pingdi theory." By focusing on ownership institutions, allocation systems, and labor productivity, Li Kui analyzed the function mechanism of price on production and consumption, as well as the negative outcomes of abnormally high or low prices, and stated that "rice with an abnormally high price hurts civilians while rice with an excessively low price hurts farmers. Hurt civilians split the state while hurt farmers make the state penniless." According to that idea, Li Kui developed the "Pingdi theory," which supports the implementation of price restriction policies, price support policies, and a flexible tax system so that "people are properly fed and then the famine ceases"; "even in years of dearth or drought, rice's price stabilizes so people would be united" or "civilians are shielded and farmers are diligent."

The differences between the "Pingtiao theory" and "Pingdi theory" are that the former is based on benefits for farmers and merchants, with a premise of profitability for merchants; whereas the latter focuses on civilians and farmers rather than merchants, which even seemingly seems slightly suppressive for commerce. Such difference is attributed to the state where Li Kui was located, was dominated by agriculture.

GLM theory advanced with the times in the Han dynasty. LH theory in *Guanzi* was practiced, developed, improved, and innovated upon in Han when Sang Hongyang's "Law of Balanced Criterion (pingzhun)" and Wang Mang's market balance policy represented another two institutional innovations in China's market price management institutions. After considerable development in Western Han's market economy, the market was gradually manipulated by powerful officials, making commodity prices fluctuate sharply. To stabilize the market and increase fiscal revenue, the government of Emperor Wudi invented the institutions of Integrated Transportation (junshu), Balanced Criterion (pingzhun), as well as monopoly in salt and iron (S&I).

In 110 B. C. , Western Han's government formally implemented the Integrated Transportation policy and specially arranged for officials called Integrated Transporters to implement it. This policy altered the goods originally purchased by the government into tribute and tax paid by merchants, which would be delivered to the capital by transportation made by engineering mechanics. For goods undesired by the central government, the Integrated Transporter would ship them to places of high price and sell them. Thus, the central treasury was enriched as the money returned, thereby leaving the merchants with less opportunities for arbitrage. Then, the government set up the Balanced Criterion system to handle goods delivered to the capital by purchasing at low market prices and selling at high ones. Theoretically, the government could stabilize the price, increase revenue, and prevent monopoly by merchants. Note that these policies emerged under the setting of Emperor Wudi's war with the Huns, which entailed considerable cost, while wealthy merchants were unwilling to give financial support; hence, the government had to create new paths to increase revenue by implementing these policies. *Shiji: Book of Balanced Criterion* indicates that "(the government) sets up the Balanced Criterion institution for receiving all the goods delivered to the capital. This section also takes charge in gathering engineering mechanics to build vehicles with expenditure from the section called Danong, whose officials monopolize the whole state's goods, following the rule of selling at high prices and purchasing at low prices" so as to "suppress all goods' prices, hence the name Balanced Criterion." This policy, in combination with the Integrated Transportation policy, succeeded in stabilizing the prices of commodities. Chapter Four, Part Two of the *Book of Han: Records of Food and Goods* reports that "the Integrated Transportation policy brings cloth of more than fifteen million meters (five million pi) for the central government, and so the state is enriched without adding more tax on the people." The policies designed by Sang Hongyang effectively enriched the treasury, supplied the border guards promptly, and stabilized prices; thus, they were inherited and innovated by successive governments. The debates of Sang Hongyang with famous counsellors about the theory and policy of governmental monopoly in S&I were sorted by Huan Kuan into *Theory of S&I*, which was the earliest thematic classic in the world's academic history of economics.

In 54 B. C. , Geng Shouchang, a financial expert and scientist during Emperor Xuandi's rule, invented the "Evet-Balance Granary (changping-cang) System. " Geng Shouchang suggested that the government set granaries in border regions to "shield farmers from low prices by increasing purchases and selling when the price is high, which is called Evet-Balance Granary. " This system successfully dealt with problems in the army's supply and price fluctuations. The emperor even conferred Geng with the title of Master in Central Plain (Guannei Hou). Similar to Sang's theory, the Evet-Balance Granary System has been inherited and innovated by successive governments until today.

In the 1st century A. D. , Wang Mang altered the "Evet-Balance Granary System" into a price management system called "market balance (shiping). " According to the *Book of Han: Records of Food and Goods*, Wang's "market balance" policy stipulated that cities set three "market balance" prices, namely, high, medium, and with comprehensive consideration of the price in the middle months of all seasons (that is, February, May, August, and November in the lunar calendar), the quality of grains and silk, and the actual status of the market. The market price of grains fluctuated freely within the range of 10% above the "market balance" prices. If it crossed the line, then the government would undersell its storage at the "market balance" prices; if it fell below the cost price, then the government would purchase grains at cost price. In this way, price stability and producers' incentives were saved. Wang's "market balance" policy was the earliest systematic institution of market price regulation in the world's history of economics. It was also inherited and developed by successive governments. For instance, "In Emperor Xuanzong's time (742 – 754 A. D. ), the government purchased grains at market price plus three cents per bucket; Emperor Xianzong ordered to purchase with additional ten cents per bucket. In Emperor Zhenzong's time (1006 A. D. ), one confirmed price regulation policy was the government purchased at market price plus three to five coins and deducted no less coins when selling. In the Jin dynasty (1161 – 1189 A. D. ), there was a law demanding the government to purchase with a 10% raised price and sell with a 10% reduced price. In 1190 A. D. , the government's sell price was reduced to a third of the market price. In 1757 A. D. , Emperor Gaozong of the Qing dynasty ordered to sell with a deduction of three silver cents. "

In the Tang dynasty, Liu Yan (715 – 780 A. D. ) creatively generalized the LH into the price regulation of "all merchandize" and held the merchants as assistants in carrying out the LH policy rather than the opposite. His move to unite the government with merchants won huge success in disaster relief, canal transportation, and the government's monopoly over S&I, with the government unifying purchase and sale while merchants delivered and retailed. The "Salt Monopoly (queyan) Law" and "Canal Transportation (caoyun) Law" by Liu Yan introduced a market mechanism to governmental monopoly, including releasing the franchise of salt and canal transportation to merchants, which further broadened the business tax's base so that the government could obtain maximum profit with minimum cost. Liu also established a national price information network along with a reporting system for regulating market price, thereby resolving information asymmetry and the lagging problem and improving policy effectiveness. *Guanzi: Finance Management of a State* proposes the concept of a state's finance management, specifically the governmental statistics of land, population, grain price, and other information, as the basis for policy design. Since Tang, the government has linked the grain price report to the operation of the "Evet-Balance Granary System. " Institutionally, Liu Yan invented an information management system (zhiyuan-guan) that involves the setting up of intelligence networks for monitoring grain price fluctuations in different places (information on climate, agricultural production, and price was reported back every 10 days and every month), selling below the market price during crop failure, or purchasing above the market price during harvest. "Liu set up local inspection sections (xunyuan) in every province (dao), built numerous post stations near these sections, then recruited runners with high prices. Thus, he could acquire detailed information from anywhere, even those extremely remote places, within four or five days." As recorded, "In 763 A. D., Liu Yan used the empire's posts to build an efficient price reporting system. Three centuries later, Shen Kuo used the same method when he was appointed as manager of the three divisions (sansi-shi) (1075-1077 A. D.) in the North-Song dynasty. As Shen wrote, the key to Liu's method was to limit intervention within the range instructed in the report based on a pre-analysis of 10-year price fluctuations; the method enabled local officials to trade before the price changed (*Brush Talks From Dream Brook*, article 192). Late in North-Song, price reporting had become customary." In the Ming dynasty, Qiu Jun (1420-1495 A. D.) proposed the stabilization of grain price by price monitoring and currency in *the Supplement of University Teaching* (Volume 26.): "…hope government hold grain price's stability as first priority. In the capital city, the market should report rice price per month. In other places, villages should report to towns per day; towns should report to local offices per month; local offices should report to provinces per season; provinces should report to the revenue ministry of the central government. In this way, the upper decision makers are able to use price information to check whether people have adequate food to eat. The key to this policy is to make sure the amount of currency issued is appropriate and grain supply is sufficient so that the price is balanced." "The price record system in the Qing dynasty followed that of the Ming dynasty, which wasn't regular in Emperor Kangxi's times. Early in Emperor Qianlong's times, this system was standardized. The lists of grain prices were made every 10 days and were mainly summarized by prefectures before being sent to provincial capitals or Beijing. Only the major grains' lowest and highest prices were recorded in prefectures' summaries… We know that all prices were collected every 10 days in towns, and they included the number of coins per liter, which was converted to weight silver per one hundred liters. Qing's archives kept thousands of grain prices' lists (covering those of every province from 1736 to 1911). " Thus, this system was constructive in terms of monitoring and reporting grain price as, to a certain extent, it solved the information asymmetry in the market and made policy design efficient. The system remains of great theoretical and practical value today.

By considering Tang's economic conditions, Bai Juyi (772-846 A. D. ) made extended and innovated LH in three aspects. First, he used not but currency as the highlight and lever to control economic activities. Seeing currency as "key to implement LH," he emphasized the management of agricultural prices by regulating the supply of currency or stabilizing price by "infusing currency. " Second, similar to Liu Yan, he did not regard merchants as enemies of LH who should be "restrained and chained" but rather viewed them as the ones to "make peace and share interests with. " Third, he argued that the key in LH laid in the "enrichment for all" or "benefits spread all over the world. " *Bai Juyi's Collections: Tactics, Article* 19 states, "A wise king would alleviate wealth gap and regulate the lightness along with heaviness so that all goods are in good supply and all parties profit. " That statement means that grain prices are related to currency, and thus, currency regulation should be used to manage agricultural prices.

In the Song dynasty, discretionary policies became the norm for the government to regulate the economy. Wang Anshi (1021-1086 A. D. ) of the Northern Song dynasty created "Jinggong's new school" and made developments and innovations on theories such as the LH, "Pingtiao theory," and "Evet-Balance Granary System" to catch up with the time and then created a series of discretionary policies. Among them, the Integrated Transportation (junshu) policy was the state-run monopoly law, which implemented unified purchase and unified sales for important materials to combat merchants' monopoly. The "market transaction method" is the innovation of Sang Hongyang's equalizing purchase method, that is, the government became the general center for regulating the surplus of goods, purchasing unsalable goods at low prices, and selling them when the market is out of stock. The "green seedling method" means that the government lends a certain amount of money to farmers before the summer and autumn harvest periods and subsidizes the farmers financially to prevent local despots' exploitation of farmers through usurious loans. These financial economic reforms and institutional designs narrowed the gap between the rich and the poor and solved the contradiction between the government's fiscal revenue and expenditure caused by commercial monopoly and land merger at that time. Such development had obvious characteristics of the game between the government and local despots and was later called the big government doctrine economic regulation policy. This policy is inseparable from the historical background of the country's fiscal weakness under the "mouth-feeding budget" caused by the permission from government officials to conduct business, local despots' mergers and acquisitions, and the central government's support of the huge bureaucratic system and the military. However, we can say that in the Song dynasty of China, the state already formulated anti-monopoly laws, usury laws, and price regulation laws.

Zhou Xingyi (1067-1124 A.D.) gave a new interpretation of a sentence abstracted from chapters on weighing and balancing the economic factors of *Guanzi*. "When the price of currency is high, prices of tens of thousands of other things will be low. And when the price of currency is low, prices of tens of thousands of other things will be high." He pointed out the following: "Money is useless, but commodities are useful; money doesn't have value, but commodities have value. Thus, originally, the value of money cannot be compared with that of commodities. Copper money is precious because it can be transported and accumulated. Iron money is cheap because it cannot be transported and accumulated. Originally, there is no difference in value between copper money and iron money, but their physical forms make them different. " (*Fuzhiji*, Volume 1) Moreover, Zhou Xingyi stated, "When everyone profits from the currency depreciation, the prices of commodities rise doubly... Private coinage cannot be forbidden, and the prices become more expensive... Commodities made by the people are more valued, and currency minted by the government is less valued; therefore, how can the state's finances be not high?" (*Fuzhiji*, Volume 1) Here, Zhou Xingyi indicated the drawbacks of currency depreciation. First, it caused inflation of prices and exponential increase of prices. Second, it triggered private coinage, which would further increase the money supply and accelerate currency depreciation, thereby resulting in higher prices. Third, due to the different levels of importance of officials and civilians, devaluation caused losses to the people, and the government temporarily benefited; however, in the long run, devaluation would fundamentally weaken and reduce the state's fiscal revenue. In the 12th century, this understanding of Zhou Xingyi was regarded as profound.

In the Southern Song dynasty, by analyzing the changes in the economic development conditions between the Zhougong era and the Song dynasty, Ye Shi (1150-1223 A. D. ), a famous representative of the Yongjia School, pointed out in the *Financial Plan* that the view proposed by *Guanzi* on whether to issue currency must be decided by the government is out of date. That is, "The law of treasury operation is to acquire goods that are unsalable but are closely related to the citizens in the market, trade these goods in other time periods, record the money credited for sacrifices and funerals, and charge interest at the rate stipulated by the state. If such is the case, then these are behaviors of a good government. Why? At this time, the world is called Qimin, in which there are no particularly rich people. Fixing a price, the right to trade, and weight and balance are decided by the emperor alone. Dividing the land equally allows the people to cultivate, building houses allows people to live, therefore goods such clothes and food are plentiful. However, people still have an unsatisfied demand for sacrifices and funerals, and the cost of these things are beyond the normal cost. If such is the case, if Zhou Gong does not meet these needs, then who will? Will it not be used for it? People admire the emperor and their fees are unnamed; thus, the government lends money to people for a few days and charges interest at the rate stipulated by the state. And when goods are unsalable, people cannot support their family. Thus, if the emperor does not purchase these goods, then the emperor is not righteous. However, if Zhougong doesn't enforce the two methods, who will? This is done within three generations. Nowadays, the world has been inequitable for a long time. Fixing a price, the right to trade, and weight and balance are not decided by the emperor alone. Instead, they are scattered among the entrepreneurs and large groups of businessmen in the market. I don't know how many thousands of years have passed. How can the government seize it? More importantly, how can we tell the different between the government playing the banner for the benefit of the country from factly for its own benefit. Alas! In the world of the present, Zhou Gong is not the law."

The above analysis of Ye Shi shows that no perfect system exists once and for all. All market systems are products under certain time and space constraints and should evolve and change with the changes of time and space conditions.

In addition, Dong Song of the Southern Song dynasty proposed a theory wherein the market guide helps solve the problem of famine. In his book *Solve the Problem of Famine and Rescue the People*, he creatively puts forward that the policy of relieving famine using the spontaneous role of market prices as a guiding ideology for businessmen and landlords with profit-making motives to reach the goal of adjusting supply and demand and relieving famine through market prices. For example, in the Evet-Balance policy, he emphasized that buying at the higher price than the market price by one or two wen is better to encourage people to sell food and that buying at a lower price that is unrealistic and official must never be done. Regarding Yi Cang, he pointed out that if the scarcity is not serious, rice and bran are still in circulation, and the price is not high, then giving money is the most convenient method, and giving both money and rice would be useful.

At the end of the Song dynasty and at the beginning of the Yuan dynasty, Ma Duanlin (1254-1323 A. D.) made historical summaries and analyses of the government's regulation of market prices, as presented in the preface of the *Comprehensive Textual Research*. He said: "Trading goods, also known as the media of hoarding goods and marking prices for sale. And as time went by, officials followed merchants' behaviors and turned it into a way to make the country richer"; "To its extreme disadvantages, it is named Hemai or Hedi, which means forced trading at a certain amount, rather than giving the price straight, enforcing the law strictly to get adequate income, which is regarded as a taxation." Ma Duan's passage shows that the government's original intention for a market price management policy is beneficial. However, after a period of implementation, the forces of the government, businessmen, and peasants play an interactive game. Moreover, such policy cannot survive as bureaucrats make profits from it and system implementation is distorted, thereby making it a system that harms the people. Also, the vested interests do not prompt any change to this situation. This situation shows that no once-and-for-all system exists. Any system and policy comprise two sides with corresponding advantages and disadvantages. With the passage of time, the advantages and disadvantages change, and the balance between officials and businessmen is broken. This circumstance is an important reason for institutional changes. If the system fails to achieve the originally set goals, then it should be reformed. This notion cannot be explained simply by transaction cost theory and cost-benefit theory.

Until the Qing dynasty, people still believed that "establishing a market in that area is good for business and construction and will appease the edge and make up for the lack of rules; thus it is a good law for hundreds of generations. " For example, " In 1759, twenty-four years after Emperor Qianlong's enthronement, the western border finally settled down, and the government set up markets in Pizhankuche, Aksu, Wushi, Heyi, Yarkant, Kashgar, etc. Shipping silk, satin, brown felt, color cloth, and tea to the mainland and bringing donkey, horse, cow, sheep, green feather, feather, leather, gold, silver, copper, goods, wheat, and Chouling enriched the military reserves at the border. Sometimes, the government dispatched officials to monitor the transportation of goods, and sometimes, goods were carried by the army or the merchants. The prices of these commodities referred to the prices of mainland transactions. " This history shows that the government set up the market on its own initiative due to military needs.

In the latter quarter of the 20th century, the Chinese government actively set up special economic zones, economic development zones, and free trade zones to promote the development of China's market economy. It also participated in the World Trade Organization and implemented the "One Belt, One Road" strategy to promote the globalization of the market economy, as well as the development and reconstruction of the economic order of the international market. This contemporary history indicates that "government-guided market theory" has always been the main color of the market economy with Chinese characteristics.

## II. China's classical market economy theory

### 1. Market economic theory of Guan Zi

*Guanzi* gave an in-depth explanation of the market economy theory and put forward the market theory of price determined by supply and demand exchange, the theory of weighing and balancing economic factors, the theory of macroeconomic regulation with discretionary policies, and the theory of international price. *Guanzi* proposed that the market price formation mechanism is affected by the heavens and the earth (natural conditions endowment), time and space (four seasons, geography, harvest, or famine), supply and demand, business forces, and government policies. *Guanzi* posited that the market can promote the development of the national economy and improve people's living quality; furthermore, without the market, basic goods will be scarce. *Guanzi* believed that if the influential merchants manipulate the market and implement the policy of laissez-faire, then the market price signal will fail, overproduction and shortage will alternate, and the disparity between the rich and the poor will worsen. Such condition will jeopardize state governance, and thus, the state must regulate the market.

Basic understanding of the market. According to *Guanzi: A team of horses*: "The market is where the goods find their due price in exchange... Therefore, from the situation revealed by the market, we can know whether the country is at a turbulence, and we can clarify the amount of social wealth, but we cannot create the material wealth through the market. We need to master the regular operation. The chapter Wushishi also said that in gathering people in a market, people will be short of daily necessities without the market." The market is where goods find their due price in the exchange process. Therefore, from the situation revealed by the market, we can identify whether the country is at a turbulence, and we can clarify the amount of social wealth. However, we cannot create material wealth through the market. The market operates regularly, and mastering the laws of market operation changes to manage the market is in line with rational (dao) governance. *Guanzi* also pointed out that a market must be present within a radius of 150 li and that people will be short of daily necessities without the market. *Guanzi* clearly explained that the market circulation field is a representation of economic development and will not create new value, but people will be short of daily necessities without a market. *Guanzi: Extravagance* proposes, "The market is an inspirational force to encourage production. Productive industry thrives because of market." That is, the market is a force that coordinates production and consumption and promotes economic development. As suggested in *Guanzi: Asking about Position*: "The market is the place where human beings gather and trade through the wealth produced by natural resources. It enables the division of labor and cooperation among the people, it is a place for exchange to make profits, and it is also the right way to promote the development of the national economy and improve people's living quality." The market is the place where human beings gather and trade through the wealth produced by natural resources. It enables the division of labor and cooperation among the people, it is a place for exchange to make profits, and it is the right way to promote the development of the national economy and improve people's living quality.

The theory about market economy value. Guan Zhong proposed that wealth creation comes from labor and the land, with labor being the key. According to *Guanzi: Eight Observations*: "The people cannot have food without cultivation, crops cannot grow without land, the land cannot be cultivated without the people, and the people cannot get wealth without their labor. The production of wealth is from labor, and the production of labor is from the body."

The theory about market operation. Guan Zhong proposed that no fixed price equilibrium exists in the market, which is dynamic, but strategies can be formulated by mastering the laws of price changes in different time and space conditions. *Guanzi: Weighing and balancing economic factors B* shows: "There is no fixed equilibrium in the market. When supply and demand reach equilibrium, prices are not always fixed, and different goods have different prices. The equilibrium of supply and demand in the market cannot be adjusted. Any adjustment means that the price is stati, and static means that there are no differences in the changes of prices. The absence of any difference means that the circulation of goods will be blocked and we cannot take advantage of the market... Understanding the order of the seasons, we can use national policies to make prices higher or lower by tenfold or even a hundredfold. Therefore, the price cannot be fixed at one point. That is, the equilibrium of supply and demand and the prices are not fixed in different periods. "

On the theory of agricultural prices. *Guanzi* believed that agriculture is affected significantly by its long production cycle, seasonal changes, and the period of harvest for the year. The spontaneous price mechanism of the market will lead to a mismatch in time, space, and price, thereby resulting in overproduction or shortage. Thus, the market needs state intervention. *Guanzi: State Reserves* points out: " During a bumper harvest, the farmers can't sell the food, and even the pigs and dogs eat food that people eat. During famine, it takes ten series of metal currency to buy a pot of food, and there are hungry people in the streets... Is this caused by poor soil and insufficient food? This is because the price of food is too low in the past years, pigs and dogs are eating food for people, and the food for the following year is not sufficient. When the price of commodities fall, they will not be sold at half the cost price, and the production cannot be completed. If price of commodities rise, it will be 10 times higher than the normal price, and people's demand cannot be satisfied. Is this the reason behind the limited production and storage? As the government cannot seize the opportunity to adjust people's wealth and profits, the price of commodities and properties fluctuates. "

The theory of the "invisible hand" explains that economic interests guide economic development. *Guanzi: Jin Cang* presents an insightful summary analysis of this concept: " Pursuing interests and avoiding harm are human nature. Merchants do business, traveling on the road day and night. They are not afraid of the long journey because they make profits in terms of distance. A fisherman goes fishing on the sea, which is deep. The fisherman sails against the current, takes an adventure, sails hundreds of miles, and stays up late at night because of the profit it gains from being on the sea. Therefore, even if mountains are extremely high, people climb them so that they can make profits; even if the sea is deep, people still go as they can make profits there. Therefore, good governance grasps the sources of interest, and as a result, people will naturally admire and accept it, go forward without pushing, and follow it without guidance. The government will not disturb and bother the people, and the people will be rich. This case is like a bird hatching an egg. You don't see its shape and smell it, but the bird will break out of the nest." How should the government govern the "invisible hand"? *Guanzi*:*Jin Cang* puts forward: "The root solutions of containing chaos are formulated by the emperor. Therefore, those who are good at governing the country must use 'harm' to restrain people, use 'profit' to guide people, and grasp people's interests; then, the wealth will increase, and the faults will decrease."

*Guanzi* proposed that the market can promote the development of the national economy and improve people's living quality; without the market, basic goods will be scarce. As mentioned, *Guanzi* also suggested that if influential merchants manipulate the market and implement the policy of laissez-faire, the market price signal will fail, overproduction and shortage will alternate, and the disparity between the rich and the poor will worsen. Such condition will jeopardize state governance, and thus, the state needs to regulate the market. During the reign of the Emperor Wu of Han, this understanding and concept were solidified through property taxes, the average transfer method, equalizing purchases, and monopoly of S&I to conduct state-run businesses in key production industries. Since then, China's market economy has been under government control under stable conditions.

The theory of the weighing and balancing of economic factors, the theory of agricultural product price, the theory of supply and demand, the theory of market regulation through discretionary policies, and the market theory put forward by *Guanzi* not only have groundbreaking significance in economic theory around the world but were also inherited, improved, developed, and practiced by descendants. These theories become the long-standing basic theory of economics, shining a light on human wisdom.

## 2. Sima Qian's Market Economy Theory

Sima Qian also made an incisive summary of the "invisible hand" of the market and posited the "the theory of water's downward tendency" and the theory of "let nature take its course." He pointed out the following in the *Biography of Outstanding Merchants*: "These are all things (musical instruments, woods, stones, and other things in the world) that Chinese people like and use in folk customs, such as for wearing, eating, health, and death. Therefore, people rely on peasants to cultivate and obtain food, on miners to mine in the mountains, fishermen to catch fish, on artisans to make and obtain equipment, and on merchants to trade and circulate goods. Therefore, low-priced goods can be sold at high prices, and high-priced goods can be purchased at low prices. People work hard to run their own businesses and are willing to do their own work. This is just like water flowing from a high place to a low place day and night. People will come automatically without being called and will produce goods without command. Isn't this the proof of natural development in line with the law?" According to Sima Qian's policy, "The best management is to let nature take its course, the second is to guide people with profits, and the third is to teach them morality; meanwhile, the worst management method is to fight for one's interest against that of the people."

Sima Qian's theory of "water's downward tendency" is considered by some economists as the direct origin of Adam Smith's "invisible hand" theory.

## 3. The Market Economy Theory of the Economists in the Song Dynasty

In the Northern Song dynasty, the second peak of academic development occurred in China, and the theory about the market economy gained a new understanding and underwent development. During the Song dynasty, industry and commerce surpassed agriculture to become the main body of state taxation for the first time; hydraulic machinery revolution, coke ironmaking revolution, the revolution of shipbuilding, compass and maritime commerce, engraving printing, cultural revolution, and the banknote invention led to the currency revolution and other revolutions that promoted the industrial and commercial economy and urban development. Furthermore, the first group of joint-stock companies and professional managers emerged, banknotes became widely used, and copper coins became the world currency. Therefore, market economic theory, business theory, monetary theory, fiscal theory, economic thoughts, and economic ethics all underwent substantial expansion. Li Gou, Su Xun, Su Shi, Su Zhe, Chen Liang, and Ye Shi are the representatives of the Shigong School, which stressed utilitarianism. The Shigong School later was called the Yongjia School, which advocated profit, and suggested that morality is based on the premise of pursuing utilitarianism. Zhang Zai, Cheng Hao, Cheng Yi, Zhu Xi, and Lu Jiuyuan are the representatives of the Science School, which focused on rationality. The Science School had a systematic reflection of the ethics of an excessive pursuit of utility, advocated that utilitarianism cannot cover 10% of human relations, and put forward the idea of maintaining pure goodness. The theoretical debate between the two factions promoted human understanding of desire, utility, reason, and morality.

For example, by analyzing the asymmetry of supply and demand as well as their seasonal changes in the market, Li Gou proved that price changes are unfavorable to farmers, greatly expanding the understanding of

Fan Li and Li Kui. In the book *Policies to Make the Country Prosperous*, he proposed this new understanding: "When the price of grain is low, the interests of farmers are damaged, but businessmen can make profits from this condition. When the price of grains is high, the interests of farmers are also damaged, and businessmen can make profits. " He posited that: "The ancients once said that when the price of grains is low, the interests of farmers are damaged. When the price of grains is high, the interests of businessmen are damaged. It is basic common sense that farmers usually sell grains and that merchants usually purchase grains. But in my opinion, when the price of grains is low, the interests of farmers are damaged, but businessmen can still make profits. When the price of grains is high, the interests of farmers are damaged, but businessmen can also make profits. Farmers don't always sell out, and sometimes, they buy in. Merchants don't always buy in, and sometimes, they sell out. Therefore, during the year, when merchants buy grains, the grains are cheap. When farmers sow, grains are expensive. Farmers suffer from farming and diseases, and farmers cherish grain more than they cherish their own life. There are several reasons that farmers have to sell grains, from selling them for clothes and tools to selling them for weddings and funerals. Farmers need to pay taxes to the government and repay loans to the private sector. Therefore, once the grains mature, before farmers rip their sickle off their belt, grains have flood into the market, and. When the amount of grain supply increases, its price will decrease. Merchants will take advantage of the condition, making the currency depreciate and the demand to expand further; otherwise, farmers cannot sell them out. Therefore, when merchants buy grains, the price of grains drops, the interests of farmers are damaged, and businessmen can make profits. There are not enough grains in farmers' houseware sometimes for several months and several days, and consequently, peasants' grain stocks are exhausted. Farmers have no seeds in the season of sowing; they pick up farm implements without food to eat. As a result, farmers buy grains from the market every day. The rising demand for grains leads to price increases. And merchants take advantage of it, making the currency appreciate and causing the supply to reduce further; otherwise, merchants refuse to sell grains out. Therefore, when farmers have seeds, the price of grains rises, the interests of farmers are damaged, and businessmen can make profits."

This view and analysis of Li Wei expands people's understanding of the relationship between grain market structure and price, introduces the analysis of the asymmetrical power between grain farmers and merchants in the market, and surpasses the simple quantity analysis of supply and demand. The result indicates that price is determined by the economic strength and power structure hidden behind the market and not by the immediate supply and demand. This feature is an important theoretical innovation.

In *Policies to Make the Country Prosperous*, Li Wei also systematically analyzed the advantages and disadvantages of "equalizing purchases policy" and proposed countermeasures. He pointed out the following: "The equalizing purchases policy made it possible for farmers to sell grains at a price that is not cheap in the fall and buy grains at a price that is not expensive in the spring and prevented merchants aiming to stockpile grains from squeezing interests from farmers. The interest rate set by the government is usually one tenth or two tenths, and so, the peasants will not be poor, and the country will be profitable. This idea is the thought of the ancient sages. But this ideal state cannot be reached for three reasons: the small amount, the vast distance, and the treacherous officials. The amount of grains sold by a county is small. The remaining grains are sold by merchants. When spring arrives, grains should be sold. If the government sells a small quantity of grains, then hungry people will be dissatisfied. If the government sells a large quantity of grains, then grains will be sold out in a few days. Therefore, merchants store grains until the food is sold out. If such is the situation, merchants will have the right to decide the market.

This case is the drawback of a small quantity of grains. The county has the responsibility to establish a granary. People far from the county are sometimes hundreds of miles away from the county. Therefore, as poor people come to the county town in the morning and go back at night, it's impossible for them to buy large quantities of grains for poverty, and it's not necessary for them to buy in small quantities. This case is the drawback of vast distance. Nowadays, if the government can build more granaries and increase the quantity of grains it buys, then stockpiling merchants will not be profitable; if granaries are established in each county, then granaries can be available for people in remote areas; if the state issues laws and emphasizes order, then officials will be honest and clean, and treacherous bureaucracy cannot erode the country. If such is the case, it will benefit the country and help the people, and this policy can be implemented for a long time. This process is weighing and balancing economic factors and must be adopted."

For instance, the "Jinggong's New School" founded by Wang Anshi (1021 - 1086 A. D.) advocated ideological emancipation, regarded metabolism as a natural law, and emphasized that people should imitate nature as well as consciously abolish what is old and establish in its place a new order of things and implement reforms. Jinggong's New School also created "the theory of enriching people by governing" and obtained an official academic status in the middle and late period of the Northern Song dynasty by "being the mainstream theory in the world for sixty years," thereby exerting great influence at the time. In the *biography of Hong Fan*, he pointed out, "The way to rule the people is to let the people become rich and then educate the people. People who govern the people should care about enriching people and educating the people. " In response to the opposition to avoid talking about properties and interests (as discussing interests is against the views of Confucius and Mencius), Wang Anshi pointed out the following: "If dogs and pigs eat food that people eat, the government should stop them. If people are starving to death on the road, the government should distribute food to the poor. This case is a political matter. Political affairs involve financial management, and financial management is the most important political affair, that is, righteousness. In the *Rites of Zhou*, the content of financial management accounts for half." *Rites of Zhou* is a Confucian classic. In explaining "the law of averaging land" in *Rites of Zhou*, he said: "Politics comes from taxes on the people, land, and property. If the amounts of taxation in different regions are different and the government imposes taxes without considering time and urgency, then it is not a good rule. Therefore, a fair rule should be implemented." Wang Anshi advocated active financial management and proposed the following: "With the strength of the whole world, we will seek the wealth in the world and use the acquired property to supply the world. Since the ancient times, insufficient financial resources have never become a common concern when it comes to the management of the country. The concern is that the method of managing finances is not correct." (*The History of Song Dynasty: The Biography of Wang Anshi*) He believed that as long as the policies are correct, the government can increase fiscal revenue while developing the private economy. He was able to distinguish the differences between the growth of personal wealth and the growth of social wealth. He deemed that the increase of personal wealth can be achieved by appropriating others' wealth and that the increase of social wealth can only be attained by expanding production; furthermore, the distribution of social wealth involves the increase of only one side while the other side decreases. Thus, increasing the total amount of social wealth is impossible. This concept is rare in ancient Chinese economics.

In another example, the Yongjia School, represented by Ye Shi, advocated for profit and recommended that morality is based on the premise of pursuing utilitarianism. Ye Shi's understanding of material interests completely differs from those in the Spring and Autumn Period and the Warring

States Period. Ye Shi's insights into the principle also reached a high academic level. He opposed idealism and advocated for the comprehension of the principle on the basis of material interests. He opposed Lu's School's "My heart is right" and thought that "the Tao is in the device," "there is no Tao without devices." He proposed the doctrine of "the principle comes from things" and "there is no principle without things." He also advocated that "principle can be tested by things and devices" and that arguing the principle that is against facts is impossible, that is, to seek truth from facts and to "Do things with a clear purpose and target." Ye Shi criticized Dong Zhongshu's view that "Those who are justified do not care about their own gains and losses, and those who understand the truth do not care about their fame." Ye Shi thought: "This sentence looks correct at first glance, but it lacks adequate evidence after careful reading. The ancients gave the benefits to others without boasting about their merits. Therefore, this is regarded as morality. The paradox of Confucian descendants, such as Dong Zhongshu, is that if we cannot build up establishment, it is unnecessary and unuseful to talk about morality."

## III. Conclusion

Through the research on the roots of China's CME theory, this study finds that the evolution of China's market economy theory and practice differs from the two popular cognitions at present. It also discovers some original Chinese market economy theories and proves that China's CME theory has academic achievements and theoretical developments that keep pace with the times as China's economic development stage changes. For example, China has a systematic theory for governance to guide market theory. This theory is based on the fact that human beings cannot be completely manipulated by nature and the market but by certain values and development goals, and thus, necessary human adjustments must be made.

The Chinese government's guiding market theory has a prominent feature, that is, prevention is better than cure. For possible economic fluctuations, natural or man-made disasters, and even crises, the government should prevent them in advance and reserve necessary countermeasures and techniques to prevent systemic and holistic damage caused by fluctuations and disasters. For instance, the earliest literature on the theory of the "invisible hand" market economy appeared in the book *Guanzi*. Later, Sima Qian proposed the theory of "water's downward tendency." Fan Yi and Li Wei's "When the price of grains is low, the interests of farmers are damaged. When the price of grains is high, the interests of people are damaged" and Li Wei's "When the price of grains is low, the interests of farmers are damaged. When the price of grains is high, the interests of farmers are damaged" reflect Chinese classical economists' profound understanding of market economy. This understanding has not been seen in modern microeconomics. Other examples include Fan Wei's theory of price interval management based on market supply and demand and Liu Yan's innovative development of the theories of weighing and balancing economic factors and of improving the effectiveness of government regulations based on the national price information network. These theories and knowledge have important practical value for building a socialist market economy, and we must inherit, develop, and innovate them to keep up with the times.

  This study also finds that even after understanding the laws of economic development under certain time and space conditions, even a perfect system design is not always effective or in line with the original intention of the government and the people. For example, food is a necessity for human beings. The price of food is the fundamental aspect of the stability of the whole society. In ancient times, food price was a barometer of economic changes, agricultural production was subject to nature, and production did not follow the law of market supply and demand to change in a short term. According to this understanding of the agricultural economy, the ancient Chinese created theories and systems, such as the theories of weighing and balancing economic factors, of equalizing purchases, of equalizing selling, of the average transfer, and of government monopoly; as well as the Changping theory, the theory of Pingzhun, and the theory of Shiping. At first, these systems played a positive role under the leadership of organized managers. However, after a period of implementation, they became a burden for the people and had negative effects. Some systems, such as the market transaction and green seedling methods, were even distorted by the performers at the beginning, and they were divorced from their original intentions. These well-intentioned systems transformed into ones that harmed the people in the interactive game between the government, merchants, and peasants as the bureaucrats profited from them and the merchants took advantage. This situation shows the absence of a once-and-for-all system as the interest game of different groups in the market also distorts the perfect system and makes it deviate from its original intention. Therefore, the review of economic policies should not only examine the problems of system design and management but also investigate the different game forms of power and means between the interest groups behind the system and management.

No perfect market and no perfect market system exist, and only a desirable market system suitable for the current development stage and constraints does. The historical evolution of China's economic development shows that the market is the result of humans' trading behavior, and its final performance is the transaction of goods. In China, especially in the centralized society after the Qin dynasty, the market and market economy are government-controlled and dominant market economies. That is, the government has always been the most important body for market construction. The basic institutional facilities, basic trading tools, trading infrastructure, and control over major production factors (such as land, currency, order, and trading venues) decided by the market are all borne and dominated by the most important entity, the government. On the one hand, the government is a supplier and a demander, an investor, a regulator, a market builder, and a market order maintainer in any country. On the other hand, if the government's system and policies are inappropriate, then it will become the biggest producer of market chaos and market disorder.

From the perspective of the development relationship of the main government, enterprises, and individuals in the market, the Chinese government has always been strong. Entrepreneurs and capitalists have also become formidable since the reform and opening up. However, the social forces from individuals have been weak and disorganized and have been lacking effective protection by rules and laws, thereby they survive by means of attachment. The short-term behaviors, opportunism, and self-interests of organizations and individuals in the market lead to the disorder of the economy and overall consequences. Moreover, given the important influence of modern large enterprises on the market, society, and the state, individuals and families may suffer from systematic exploitation and crushing by them. Therefore, how to strengthen the rule of law and establish a national governance system of "strong government, strong enterprise, and strong individual" is the key to the future development of China's market economy.

Note that the market is not illusory, and we cannot virtualize and mythologize the market. It is for the people to formulate market legislation. It is not the market that affects and arranges people, but people themselves, especially politicians, government officials, entrepreneurs, and capitalists who influence, manipulate, arrange, control, and design the market. It is the people who construct the market structure, market form, and price mechanism in the real world. In understanding the market and the market economy, people are more important than the market itself, and the interest groups formed by the people are more important than the so-called market mechanism.

## References

[1] Bai Juyi. *Bai Juyi's Collections*[M]. Beijing: Zhonghua Book Company, 1979.

[2] Ban Gu. *Book of Han*[M]. Beijing: Zhonghua Book Company, 2007.

[3] Chen Huanzhang. *The Economic Principles of Confucius and His School*[M]. Translated by Han Hua, Beijing: The Commercial Press, 2015.

[4] He Liancheng. Review of Ideologists's Price Theories in Ming & Qing[J]. *Social Science Journal*, 1982(05).

[5] Hu Jichuang. *Chinese History of Economic Thoughts*[M]. Shanghai: Shanghai University of Finance & Economics Press, 1998.

[6] Jia Taihong, Liu Xiang (the West-Han Dynasty). *General Explanation of Guanzi*[M]. Beijing: Xiyuan Press, 2015.

[7] Li Gou. *Li Gou's Collections*[M]. Punctuated and collated by Wang Guoxuan, Beijing: Zhonghua Book Company, 2011.

[8] Li Shan. *Guanzi*[M]. Translated and annotated edition. Beijing: Zhonghua Book Company, 2009.

[9] Edited by Li Xueqin, written by Zhu Hanmin et al. *Chinese Academic History: Song & Yuan Volume (Part 2.)* [M]. Nanchang: Jiangxi Education Publishing House, 2000.

[10] Lin Guangbin. Chinese Theory and Chinese Scheme of Agricultural Price Management [J]. *Journal of Central University of Finance and Economics*, Issue 5, 2017.

[11] Lin Guangbin. A new Understanding of the Role of market and government in resource Allocation—What is the relationship between market and government[J]. *Teaching and Research*, Issue 1, 2017.

[12] Liu Bo, Wang Chuan, Deng Qitong. *The Rites of Zhou* [M]. Translated and annotated edition. Nanjing: Nanjing University Press, 2014.

[13] Ma Duanlin. *Book of General Literature*[M]. Hangzhou: Zhejiang ancient books publishing house, 2007.

[14] Sima Guang. *Comprehensive Mirror for Aid in Government*[M]. Beijing: Zhonghua Book Company, 2007.

[15] Sima Qian, Han Zhaoqi (translated). *Shiji*[M]. Beijing: Zhonghua Book Company, 2008.

[16] Tian Guoqiang. Only Deepening Institutional Reform Can Solve the Dilemma between Growth and Transition[EB/OL]. 2015.

[17] Wang Wensu, Sun Yigang, Hong Gang. *Ten Notes to Financial and Economic Litera-*

ture[M]. Beijing:China Social Sciences Press,2015.

[18] Endymion Wilkinson. *Chinese History:A New Manual* (*Vol.2*)[M]. Translated by Hou Xudong. Beijing:Peking University Press,2016.

[19] Yang Tiancai. *Book of Changes*[M]. Translated and annotated edition. Beijing:Zhonghua Book Company,2016.

[20] Ye Shi. *Ye Shi's Collections* (*Vol.3*)[M]. Beijing:Zhonghua Book Company,1st edition in 1961,reprint in 2013.

[21] John Eatwell,et al. *The New Palgrave Dictionary of Economics*(*Vol.2*)[M]. Beijing:Economic Science Press,1992.

[22] Zhao Jing. *History of Economics*[M]. Shanghai:Shanghai People's Publishing House,2010.

# 《管子》中的商贸立国方略及其在后世帝国的命运

刘守刚

**摘 要**：在中华国家向帝国转型之际，《管子》一书特别反映了以管仲为代表的一派学者对于商贸立国方略的思考，如以掌控资源作为商贸立国的条件、以商贸为手段来治理国家并调控国内经济与社会、以商贸为手段赢得对外战争的胜利等。从中华帝国后来的发展历史来看，管仲学派商贸立国原则总体而言始终为商鞅的重农抑商原则所压制，只是在汉武帝改革与王安石变法等短暂时期占据上风，构成某种"重商"的变异。到了晚清乃至民国时期，商贸立国方略才真正发展为现代重商主义并成为国家治理的主导原则。

**关键词**：《管子》 商贸立国 重农抑商 财政思想

[中图分类号] F810.2 　　[文献标志码] B

在春秋战国时期，中华国家从以人口为支撑点的城邦转向以土地为支撑点的帝国[1]，并就此奠定了2000多年帝国制度构建、帝国国家治理的基础。对于当时的各诸侯国而言，如何改变旧有的制度并构建出新的成功制度，以便在短期内迅速提升国力、赢得国家间的生存竞争，进而获得统一天下的机会，是摆在那个时代君主与政治家面前最重要的难题。

在这样的时代背景下，以管仲为代表的思想家们登上历史舞台。他们通过对时代问题与历史经验的透彻把握与深入思考，提出了自己的治国理论，并积

---

[作者简介]：刘守刚，上海财经大学教授，主要研究方向为财政思想史、财政史、财政政治学。
① 刘守刚编著：中国财政史十六讲[M]．上海：复旦大学出版社，2017．

极参与到国家制度改革与实际治理活动中去,从而为后世留下了宝贵的思想财富。《管子》① 一书,特别反映了以管仲为代表的一派学者对于帝国国家治理的思考。众所周知,后世中华帝国的制度原则与治国方略是经由秦统一天下而奠定的,而秦制的基础又是由商鞅变法决定的。商鞅变法及《商君书》中推崇的治国方略是重农抑商。与《商君书》形成鲜明对比并持续影响后世的是《管子》一书推崇运用商贸手段治理国家。作为国家治理方略,重农抑商后来成为根本原则与正统标志,但管仲等人倡导的商贸立国方略也始终隐伏在帝国国家治理之中,并在特殊时期变异为主导性原则,直至在晚清开始的中国国家转型活动中成为现代重商主义的先导。

《管子》一书是一部伟大的作品,对于这本书以及它的作者,目前还有许多疑问。迄今为止,学术界通行的见解是,它并非一人之作,也非一时之书。从今天的眼光看,它反映了中华帝国构建与国家治理的另一种可能道路。今天的我们已无法知道,历史是否有可能让齐国通过商贸手段统一天下,并构建起体现管仲学派想法的另样中华帝国。

本文基于《管子》一书内容,概括其中包含的商贸立国战略构想,然后说明这些构想在后世帝国发展中的命运。

## 一、以掌控资源作为商贸立国的条件

管仲以及管仲学派活动的时期,依然是农业经济占优而非机器工业生产的时代。因此,以商贸手段立国的前提,是国家(或君主)手中必须掌握基于粮食与自然资源而形成的商品。在《管子》一书中,可以用商贸手段来操作并进而实现对内治理、对外争霸甚至统一天下的资源,主要有四项:粮食、货币、盐铁与市场渠道。当然,掌握这些资源,不仅可用于商贸操作,实现国家治理("货多事治,则所求于天下者寡矣,为之有道",《乘马》),而且可以实现"利出一孔"以便吸引民众归附(对此商鞅同样提倡),"故予之在君,夺之在君,贫之在君,富之在君。故民之戴上如日月,亲君若父母"(《国蓄》)。不过,管仲学派主张的靠商业手段来实现利出一孔,比起商鞅靠强制手段,明显

---

① 本文凡引用《管子》的文字,皆来自谢浩范、朱迎平译注:《管子全译》,贵州人民出版社1996年版。引文出处只标注《管子》一书的篇名,不再一一列明页码。

要缓和得多，这也是商贸立国战略不同于重农抑商政策的一个突出表现。

首先，在春秋战国时代，粮食对于国内治理和对外争霸的重要性是不言而喻的。对此，《商君书》中多处进行讨论。《管子》也强调，"彼守国者，守谷而已矣"（《山至数》）。粮食对于百姓而言，尤为重要，"五谷食米，民之司命也"（《国蓄》）。因此，治国的关键在于积粟，"是以先王知众民、强兵、广地、富国之必生于粟"（《牧民》），"不生粟之国亡，粟生而死者霸，粟生而不死者王"（《治国》）。粮食多，民众的道德水平就会因此提高（"仓廪实，则知礼节；衣食足，则知荣辱"，《牧民》），军事力量也因此增强（"甲兵之本，必先于田宅"，《侈靡》）。粮食多，可以用来吸引外国民众投奔，它也是各种财富归集乃至开疆拓土的关键（"粟也者，民之所归也；粟也者，财之所归也；粟也者，地之所归也。粟多则天下之物尽至矣"《治国》）。粮食多，还可以用来调控市场、抑制兼并（"凡谷者，万物之主也"，"故人君御谷物之秩相胜，而操事于其不平之间"，《国蓄》）。那么国家怎样才能有效地掌握更多的粮食？《管子》建议，先要尽可能生产更多的粮食，办法至少有以下几项：一是君主施政要从民所欲让民众有积极性（"故从其四欲，则远者自亲"《牧民》），使民以时以免耽误农时（"彼王者不夺农时，故五谷丰登"，《臣乘马》）；二是要禁末作文巧，以增加劳动力（"末作文巧禁则民无所游食，民无所游食则必农"，《治国》）；三是要设法防止高利贷侵害农民利益（"夫以一民养四主，故逃徙者刑而上不能止者，粟少而民无积也"《治国》）；四是要设法让士、农、商、工四民负担均衡（"是以民作一而得均。民作一则田垦，奸巧不生。田垦则粟多"，《治国》）；五要重视土地（"地者，万物之本原，诸生之根菀也"，《水地篇》），要按不同土地类别做好国土规划（"有山处之国，有氾下多水之国，有山地分之国，有水洪之国，有漏壤之国"，《山至数》），分别加以管理。在粮食生产的基础上，国家不是依赖横征暴敛而是巧用谷、币、货物的关系来进行市场操作，以便把更多的谷物掌握在手中，这一点下文再讨论。一旦君主掌握了粮食资源，就可以将其用于国家治理并立于不败之地，"彼人君守其本委谨，而男女诸君吾子无不服籍者也"（《国蓄》）。

其次，国家必须掌握货币资源。在那个时代，货币显然还是商品货币。正如《国蓄》篇所列举的，主要有三种货币，"以珠玉为上币，以黄金为中币，以刀布为下币"。《管子》特别强调，国家一定要掌握这些货币资源，才能达到治理国家的目的,"三币握之则非有补于暖也,食之则非有补于饱也,先王以守财物,以御民事,而平天下也"(《国蓄》)。运用货币治国,最为重要的是利用货币、谷物与货物之间的关系进行经济社会的调控,"人君操谷、币、金衡,而天下可定也"(《山至数》),"黄金刀币,民之通施也。故善者执其通施以御其司命,故民力可得而尽也"(《国蓄》)。特别是在《轻重》诸篇中,管仲学派多次提到了"人君铸钱立币",即君主必须掌握货币的发行权。

再次,国家要掌握盐铁等资源。与其他诸侯国相比,齐国的耕地资源并不丰富,但因所处的半岛地形而拥有着广阔的海岸和滩涂,这意味着齐国可以充分发展海洋经济,尤其是开发鱼盐资源,这是其他诸侯国无可比拟的优势。事实上,海洋资源早在姜子牙时代即已得到开发,政府从中大获其利,这一获利方法也因此常被后世称为"太公之术"。在《海王》篇中,管仲学派将"官山海、正盐策"作为特别的措施提出,主张齐国要对盐业、铁矿等消费弹性低的资源商品实行统一管理,以发展相应的产业。既然家家户户、男女老少都要吃盐用铁,国家就通过垄断并加价出售来获取财政利益,"百倍归于上,人无以避此者"(《海王》)。除了盐铁等自然资源外,《管子》还主张对其他自然资源也实行国家垄断,"故为人君而不能谨守其山林、菹泽、草莱,不可以立为天下王"(《轻重甲》)。当然,从真实的历史看,盐铁这样的资源在齐国多大程度上实现了专卖实属有疑问,有学者因此认为《海王》篇为汉代学者的著作。需要指出的是,管仲学派此处提倡的"官山海",未必是汉代桑弘羊主张的全面垄断盐铁资源的政策,因为《管子》中反复提出要跟商人合作而不应实施全面垄断,"故善者不如与民,量其重,计其赢。民得其十,君得其三"(《轻重乙》)。

最后,国家必须掌握市场渠道。渠道也是资源。在齐国这样因处于四通八达的交通所在而商品经济一直比较发达的国家,市场的重要性不言而喻("市者,天地之财具也。而万人之所和而利也,正是道也",《问》)。国家掌握市场渠道,自然不能靠强制性力量,而要依靠公共服务,比如《轻重乙》建议为商贾立客舍。管仲在齐国主要靠设立市场、减轻关税、提供优质服务、鼓励外贸四大政策来达到"天下商贾齐归若流水"的目的。《问》中对国家掌握市场渠道的建议是,"征于关者,勿征于市;征于市者,勿征于关。虚车勿索,徒负勿入,以来远人,十六道同身"。另外,管仲还通过设立 6 个工商乡(另外还设 15 个士农乡）来优待工商，比如说不服兵役。这样可以让他们集中精力发展工商业，并有利于他们教导子女、互相切磋技艺、交流经验与信息等（《小匡》）。

## 二、以商贸为手段来治理国家并调控国内经济与社会

此处说的商贸手段，在《管子》一书中被称为"轻重术"。运用轻重术，自然离不开市场；商贸手段只有在市场存在的前提下，才能用于国家治理。因此，《管子》一书对市场作用的重视，在中国古代经典著作中是罕见的。它认为货物价格应由市场自由买卖决定（"市者，货之准也"《乘马》），国家可以从市场获取国家治乱的信息（"市者，可以知治乱，可以知多寡，而不能为多寡。为之有道"，《乘马》），并坚决主张政府不能固定市场价格，衡数（即供求平衡关系）"不可调（调，固定），调则澄（澄，静止），澄则常（常，固定），常则高下不二（高下不二，没有涨跌），高下不二则万物不可得而使固（使固，利用）"（《轻重乙》）。

以商贸为手段来治理国家、调控经济与社会，首先体现为国家要尽可能地运用商贸手段来掌握粮食。在前述建议国家要采取措施增加粮食产量的基础上，《管子》倡导用谷、币、货物三者之间关系，通过市场买卖来尽量积储粮食，并通过提高粮价来激发相关主体的积极性，"君有山，山有金，以立币，以币准谷而授禄，故国谷斯在上。谷贾什倍，农夫夜寝蚤起，不待见使；五谷什倍，士半禄而死君，农夫夜寝蚤起，力作而无止"（《山至数》）。管仲学派还设想利用粮价季节变化，在收获季节低价购买囤粮并在青黄不接时高价出售，以达到民众依赖国家粮储、大夫无法操控的目的，这样"出实财，散仁义，万物轻"（《山至数》）。在《山至数》中，管仲学派还具体设想国家用货币贷款形式来增加财政收入并获取民众手中的粮食：第一年在青黄不接、粮价高企时给贫民发放货币形式的贷款，到秋收粮价下跌时要求按货币数字归还粮食并支付利息；第二年在青黄不接时再将粮食贷给百姓，并在秋收时要求按市价将粮食折为货币归还国家（还粮食也可以）并支付利息，这样国库就会增加粮食仓储或增加收入。君主有了粮食，才有能力实施有效的国家治理。

以商贸为手段来治理国家、调控经济与社会，其次体现为可用此手段获取

财政收入供国家之用。财政收入是运行国家不可或缺的手段，因此管仲学派并不赞成轻税政策。在他们看来，"彼轻赋税则仓廪虚，肥（肥，通'俾'，薄）籍敛则械器不奉（奉，供应）。械器不奉，而诸侯之皮币（币，此处指帛）不衣；仓廪虚则偩（偩，通'士'）贱无禄"（《山至数》）。不过，管仲学派更不支持为了增加财政收入而对农民索取重田赋、对商贾征收高关税，甚至对房屋、树木、六畜征税，他们尤其反对的是临时加税。在他们看来，最好的财政征收手段是"见予之形，不见夺之理"（《国蓄》）。若能这样做的话，"是人君非发号令收啬（啬，敛取）而户籍也，彼人君守其本（本，指粮食生产）委（委，指粮食储备）谨，而男女诸君吾子无不服籍者也"（《国蓄》）。《管子》中为此提出来的方法有：一是通过"官山海"等措施，对盐、铁、林木资源实行某种形式的专卖措施，以商品加价方式在自愿买卖掩盖下实现财政征收；二是运用货币等手段，通过贷款、钱货关系等形式获取增值；三是利用市场性差价和其他因信息不对称而导致的巨额价差来进行买卖，获取盈利。这样几种获取财政收入的机会，《管子》都将其称为"轻重之术"。在书中，管仲学派尤其推崇第三种方式，即利用"物多则贱，寡则贵，散则轻，聚则重"（《国蓄》）来"以重射轻，以贱泄平"，即在物价低时高价买入，物价高时低价卖出。由于货币数量完全垄断于国家手中，于是利用钱、谷、货等关系，国家就可以操控商品价格、调节商品流通，即"人君知其然，故视国之羡不足而御其财物。谷贱则以币予食，布帛贱则以币予衣。视物之轻重而御之以准，故贵贱可调而君得其利"（《国蓄》）。

  以商贸为手段来治理国家、调控经济与社会，还体现在调节贫富阶层的收入与财富上。显然，古今同理的是，贫富差距过大会造成社会势力失衡，并进而影响到国家的稳定。"民人之食，人有若干步亩之数，然而有饿馁于衢间者何也？谷有所藏也。今君铸钱立币，民通移，人有百十之数，然而民有卖子者何也？财有所并也。故为人君不能散积聚，调高下，分并财，君虽强本趣耕、发草立币而无止，民犹若不足也"（《轻重甲》）。《国蓄》篇说明，社会财富分配不均是现实的客观存在，并列举了几个原因：农时的季节性；年岁的丰歉和财政征收的缓急；民智不齐；少数人蓄意操控、百般盘剥等。对于这样的差距，如果"人君不能调"，那么"民有相百倍之生也"（《国蓄》）。如何调节这样的贫富差距呢？《管子》虽然认为需要由国君进行筹划并利用法制手段加以纠正,"法令之不行,万民之不治,贫富之不齐也"(《国蓄》),但主要的方法应该是运用商贸手段,"故凡不能调民利者,不可以为大治;不察于始终,不可以为至矣"(《揆度》)。比如,国家通过调剂物资、确保粮食的供应等,来干预市场的运行,以防止巨贾商家豪夺百姓并保障民众的正常生活生产。还有,国家将手中掌握的粮食、物资或者货币,在农忙或青黄不接之时贷放、赊售或租借给贫困农民,实现以丰补歉、调剂民食。国家也可以利用建设公共工程等手段来实现以工代赈,甚至主张扩大公共支出达到侈靡的境地来救济贫民,内容反映在《侈靡》篇中。

以商贸手段治国,还体现在《管子》对商人这一社会阶层的重视上,这在中国古代学者的作品中是少有的。在国家治理及争霸于天下的过程中,为了富国强兵,管仲鼓励百姓将各种农副产品"鬻之四方",大力发展商业,高度肯定市场对于农业生产的积极促进作用,"市者,天地之财具也,而万人之所和而利也"(《侈靡》),"市也者,劝也,劝者,所以起本事"(《侈靡》)。与此同时,他还极力抬高商人的社会地位,采取了与商鞅重农抑商极不相同的策略。《管子》将商人与士、农、工一道称为国家柱石,"士农工商四民者,国之石民也"(《小匡》),并高度肯定商人在买卖活动中的智慧以及对于经济的积极作用,"今夫商群萃而州处,观凶饥,审国变,察其四时而监其乡之货,以知其市之贾。负任担荷,服牛辂马,以周四方。料多少,计贵贱,以其所有,易其所无,买贱鬻贵。是以羽旄不求而至,竹箭有余于国,奇怪时来,珍异物聚"(《小匡》)。

## 三、以商贸为手段赢得对外战争的胜利

在诸侯林立的现实世界,如何才能实现争霸乃至统一天下,完成帝国内在的使命?商鞅的想法简单直接,那就是要有足够多的粮食及有积极性的战士。《管子》重视粮食,也重视战争("国富者兵强,兵强者战胜,战胜者地广",《治国》)。但是《管子》认为,仅靠粮食无法争霸,争霸乃至统一天下也未必需要战争手段,而可以采用商贸手段来达到目的。在《地数》中,管仲学派认为,在诸国林立的环境中,仅仅粮食多是危险的,"夫本富而财物众,不能守,则税于天下。五谷兴丰,巨钱(巨钱,当为'吾贱')而天下贵,则税于天

下，然则吾民常为天下虏矣。夫善用本者，若以身（身，疑为'舟'）济于大海，观风之所起，天下高则高，天下下则下，天下高我下，则财利税于天下矣。"就是说，管仲学派主张的是，应该更多使用商贸手段、发动贸易战，来实现对外争霸乃至统一天下。

《管子·轻重》诸篇中记载了许多精彩的"贸易战"。后世学者普遍认为，这些贸易战大多应该属于纯粹的设想而非历史的真实。虽然帝国时期传统的学者对这些设想大多评价不高，甚至认为粗鄙不堪，但站在熟悉贸易战的今人立场来看，我们不得不叹服其中存在的天才与智慧。

纵观这些事例，管仲以商贸手段来赢得对外争胜，至少可分为两类。

一类以《轻重丁》中记载的"石璧谋""菁茅谋"为代表。这类计谋利用齐国的霸主地位能接近周天子，再利用周天子尚存的礼节性权威为齐国谋取巨额利润。比如著名的"石璧谋"，管仲先命齐国能工巧匠制造一批不同规格的石璧，再让周天子下令让齐王率天下诸侯朝拜周王室宗庙，前提是要以周王室的"彤弓"和齐国的"石璧"为入场券。于是天下诸侯纷纷携带各国财货珍宝来齐国换取石璧，齐国很快就填补了葵丘会盟后产生的财政亏空。"菁茅谋"也采取了类似的手段，只不过是让诸侯参加周天子封禅仪式时，必须花重金换取周王室贡品"菁茅"用作祭祀垫席，使得周天子在几天之内赚了大笔财富，"七年不求贺献"。这样做，不但帮助了周天子，也提高了齐国的霸主地位，从而解决齐桓公的问题（"天子之养不足，号令赋于天下则不信诸侯，为此有道乎"《轻重丁》）。

另一类是齐国凭借雄厚的财力，从敌国大量买入特定商品，破坏其经济生产周期，从而用经济手段控制敌国。《轻重戊》中记载的"衡山谋"就是此类战略的典型。首先，管仲建议齐王"贵买衡山之械器而卖之"，蓄意引发周边各国对衡山国兵器的抢购热潮，使得衡山之民"释其本，修械器之巧"。所谓"本"，正是指农业。随后，齐国以高于赵国国内粮食收购价的价格，前往赵国收购粮食，使得包括衡山国在内的许多国家纷纷向齐国卖粮，如此持续数月后，齐国突然宣布闭关，停止与周边国家的一切经贸往来。此时的衡山国，农业生产周期已经被兵器生产所打乱，国内存粮又多被卖至齐国，国力被消耗殆尽。面对即将被齐鲁两国瓜分的局势，衡山国"内自量无械器以应二敌，即奉国而归齐矣"。在《轻重甲》中的设想是，以四夷所产宝物（吴越的珠象、朝鲜的皮货、昆仑之虚的璆琳琅玕、禺氏的白璧)为货币,抬高它们的价值,这些国家的人与商品,就会远道而来。于是,通过这样的经济手段,达到了征服或吸引敌国的目的:"故物无主,事无接,远近无以相因,则四夷不得而朝矣"。在《轻重戊》中,还提出了一个以粟制敌的谋略。就是说,用巧妙的手段(高价收购敌国"鲁梁"的纺织品绨),扰乱敌国农业生产(鲁梁君主让百姓放弃粮食生产而专门织造绨),使之粮食匮乏,不得不依赖我方,从而达到降服敌国的目的。《轻重乙》还设想,齐国反复运用盐粮价格关系,让自己国家愈富而各国愈贫。《轻重戊》中则设想了齐国利用治柴征服莒、利用田鹿征服楚、利用狐皮征服代等事例,这些都属于用商贸手段达到争胜于天下的例子。

## 四、商贸立国原则的后世发展

管仲学派倡导的商贸立国原则,在后世帝国治理中作为正统"重农抑商"原则的对立面,事实上包含了两个方面的含义:一是用商业手段处理国家与民众的关系,包括用货币财政代替实物财政、运用利益诱导(自愿交易)等手段完成国家治理任务;二是重视商业活动,包括私商经营活动与官商经营活动(含手工业在内)。在帝国农业经济时代,"重农"或者说重视粮食生产、抬高农民的法律地位,在理念上对各家各派学者而言其实都没有异议,当然在现实中真实状况如何那是另一回事。管仲学派倡导的用商业原则处理国家与民众的关系,虽然在实践中历代王朝都在使用,但在理念上一直有儒家学者从重农抑商原则高度加以反对。这些人更加反对政府对私商或官商经营活动的重视,视为不可原谅的"重商"行为。不过,在帝国一些特殊时期,治国者会更多吸取管仲学派商贸立国的主张,变得更加"重商",这样的变化不妨称为"重商变异"。

根据国家对商业活动态度的不同,帝国2000多年在处理私商与官商经营活动时至少有以下三种表现:(1)既抑私商也抑官商,就是说全面压制工商业活动,既贬低私商的社会地位,也排斥国家用官营商业从工商业获取财政收入;(2)抑私商扬官商,就是说抑制私人从事工商业活动,但国家积极发展官营工商业以获取财政收入或达到其他目的;(3)私商与官商并重,就是说既鼓励私人从事工商业活动，国家也发展官营工商业，从而用税收形式或商业手段获取财政收入并达到其他目的。第一种表现实际上是全面抑商的状态，从理论上来说最符合"重农抑商"的要求，也因此被后世儒家学者视为帝国最为正统的治国原则。第二种、第三种表现被正统儒家学者视为"重商"，认为违背了重农抑商原则。这两种表现是重商变异，突出体现在汉武帝改革时期与王安石变法时期。只有在晚清洋务运动之后才真正兴起了现代的重商主义，这已不属于重商变异而意味着重商转型。从逻辑上说，还存在第四种对商业活动的态度，即扬私商抑官商。不过这样的态度在现实中只存在于现代自由主义经济体中，在帝国时期乃至今日中国都未出现。大体上，由商鞅变法为秦国奠定的重农抑商原则在帝国国家制度构建与治国理财活动中始终占据上风，成为主导后世帝国2000多年的正统原则。管仲学派提倡的商贸立国方略虽然处于被压制状态，但始终隐伏在帝国制度运行之中，在特殊时期（重商变异和重商转型）成为主导性原则。

## （一）汉武帝改革时期的重商变异

在汉初，按照重农抑商原则建构了帝国制度。它的薄赋敛的收入政策应对着国家无事（尤其是对外采取消极忍让的军事策略）的支出安排，在治国理财方面完全符合了"重农"的要求，特别是其中的"文景之治"更是被后世学者推崇。

不过，汉初虽然重农，也在法律上采取了"贱商"举措（"高祖乃令贾人不得衣丝乘车，重租税以困辱之"《史记·平准书》），但在现实中却无法做到真正的抑商，这体现在以下两个方面：（1）由于汉初民生凋敝，管理能力薄弱，政府不得不允许民间（主要是贵族、官僚、大地主与大商人）开发铜、铁、盐等自然资源，甚至允许民间势力铸造货币，由此，民间商人及拥有特权的豪强大量积聚财富；（2）由于田赋低导致国用不足，汉初不得不发展出人头税（算赋、口赋、更赋等）作为主要收入形式（人口往往集中居住，比较容易计算数字，征税时也可受到当时户籍制度的支持），这样的财政收入形式史称"轻租重赋"，于是民众为缴纳人头税而需出售粮食或其他实物方能获得货币，政府获得人头税后需要在市场上采购物资，导致商业活动畸形繁荣。

汉兴70多年后，随着雄才大略的汉武帝掌握政权，汉帝国开始显露出对外扩张的本能。在财政上就体现为军事支出大幅提升,在不长时间内将前几代的积蓄全部消耗殆尽。再加上自然灾害的频繁发生与国家赈灾支出的增长,财政上遭遇到收支的危机。此时,需要财政方面的改革,以扩大财政收入的来源。另外,汉武帝还需要运用财政手段抑制国内豪强势力的成长,以恢复政治秩序和社会势力的平衡。于是汉武帝发动财政改革,以扩大财政收入、抑制国内豪强势力,运用的就是后世学者诟病不已的"重商"政策。

汉武帝采用的"重商"政策,既体现为大量运用货币手段与利益原则来实现国家治理,更体现在抑制私商、发展官商的做法上。这又有以下几个方面:第一,运用货币改革手段,集权中央,夺取豪强富商的财富,特别是在公元前113年由桑弘羊主持让中央政府彻底垄断货币发行权。第二,以算缗告缗,即征收财产税配合鼓励告密手段,来增加财政收入,削弱豪强富商的财力。第三,调整财政管理方式,实行盐铁官营专卖,夺取豪强富商的财富,即在公元前110年由桑弘羊大力贯彻执行盐铁专卖。第四,其他商业手段的运用,比如实施均输法与平准法,还有入钱谷赎罪和卖官鬻爵。

## (二)王安石变法中的重商变异

在宋代立国之初,由于延续了五代十国以来国家生存竞争的格局并在社会经济商业化发展的大趋势下,虽然重农抑商作为治国原则的地位并未动摇,但政府却将一定程度的"重商"作为国策。这种重商表现在以下几个方面:(1)取消了许多对商人在政治、经济和社会生活上的歧视政策;(2)经济领域广泛地向私人开放;(3)社会管理也向有利于商业活动的方向发展,完全废除了定时定点的坊市交易制度,城市经济生活完全开放;(4)政府制定了系统的商税征收条例,建立起覆盖城乡各地的商税征收网络,商税和工商业收益成为重要的财政收入来源。因此,宋代来自工商业的财政收入,在财政中占据比较重要的地位,数量多数时候超过来自田亩的两税。而且与汉武帝改革时重官商抑私商政策不同,宋代商业活动的主体是私商,来自工商业的收入主要是私商广泛参与其中的暴利性资源商品的禁榷收入[1],以及向一般商品征收的商税。

---

[1] 汪圣铎将宋代针对暴利性资源商品获取的财政收入统称为"禁榷收入",即"官府将直接专卖、由专卖派生出来的官商合营分利、对某些商品在严峻法律和严密措施保证下征收高额产销税的制度混合使用",在这其中私商广泛参与(参阅:汪圣铎著. 两宋财政史 [M]. 北京:中华书局,1995.)。

在宋神宗皇帝即位前后，财政上发生严重的收支危机。如何才能解决财用危机并进而实现善治？王安石坚决反对单纯地从民众身上敛财，因为这种做法就像"阖门而与其子市，而门之外莫入焉，虽尽得子之财，犹不富也"（《与马运判书》）。他继承了管仲学派主张的商贸立国方略，赞成"民不加赋而国用饶"，但反对（至少在理念上不赞成）汉武帝改革中发展垄断性官商来获取财政收入的做法。他提出"理财"的概念，即运用动态生财的办法，通过一种帕累托改进（在不伤害甚至增进一方效用的前提下，改进另一方的效用）的方法，以不伤害民众为前提，创造出更多的财政收入。就是说，他认为财政收入是可以大幅增长的，其基础是生产的发展，"盖因天下之力以生天下之财，取天下之财以供天下之费。自古治世，未尝以不足为天下之公患也，患在治财无其道耳"（《上仁宗皇帝言事书》），"方今之所以穷空，不独费出之无节，又失所以生财之道故也"（《与马运判书》）。他指出，"富其家者资之国，富其国者资之天下，欲富天下，则资之天地"（《与马运判书》）。显然，这是一种"动态"取财的思想。

从现代财政的眼光看，能够动态生财无非有以下几个途径，而王安石变法正好体现。

第一条途径是发展生产、创造经济增值，"农田水利法"正好体现。王安石试图通过大力兴修农田水利、鼓励提高农业技术，以此来发展生产，实现官、民双方的利益增加。

第二条途径是通过自愿交易行为来增加官民双方的效用，"免役法"和"保马法"的目的就是如此。"免役法"允许那些苦于差役的人出钱免役，官府则花钱雇役，免役的人效用提高，政府也因收大于支而获得增收。"保马法"是官府资助民间养马，以代替原来耗资巨大、效果极差的官方牧场，这样既节约政府开支又增加养马户的收入。

第三条途径是通过市场深化而获取财政收入，"青苗法""市易法"就想这样。在宋代经济发展过程中，出现了对资本借贷的要求，而国家通过两税法和税商措施，征收了大量的钱粮，放在库房中并不能创造经济增值。于是，王安石通过"青苗法"将官府手中的钱粮按低于民间高利贷的利率贷给民众，既可以帮助民众度过青黄不接的春荒，又让官府获得利息收入。"市易法"规定，设立机构向商人提供低息贷款，或者贷款给官营商号去收购商旅卖不出去的货物，以待机转卖，这是把官府库房中的钱粮资源转化为资本性商品。

第四条途径是通过加强财政管理来扩大财政收入，"方田均税法"就想这样。"方田"是清丈田亩，整理土地账册；"均税"是落实"履亩而税"。这样既能增加财政收入，又能减少普通民众的负担。

可见，王安石重视利用商业手段来增加财政收入，而就商业活动中主体（私商与官商）来说，至少在变法初期，王安石并不赞成以官商垄断方法来经营商业。不过，在变法过程中，由于国营商业机构天生的低效率，它要能产生盈利就只能依赖于垄断特权。因此，王安石采用商业经营手段来增加国家财富，到最后都变成了国家垄断，如在茶、盐、酒、矿冶等领域都是如此，执行"市易法"的市易务也渐渐成为具有垄断地位的官方商业机构，并带来了文学贤良在"盐铁会议"上批评过的国营商业的一切弊病，如"榷货卖冰致民卖雪不售，卖梳朴则梳朴贵，卖脂麻则脂麻贵"（《续资治通鉴长编》卷236）。

### （三）晚清兴起的重商转型

明代初期，鉴于宋、元王朝的教训，帝国政府重申两税作为国家正宗财政收入的地位，从而以土地为支撑点，在全国重新建立一个简约的田赋制度。与此同时，明政府区分不同的民众群体，重建起亲身服役的差役体系。这样，明政府以田土和人丁为基础，重建了一个以获取粮食和劳役等实物性收入为主的财政体系。相形之下，来自于工商业的财政收入为数极少，运用工商业获取财政收入的做法被视为横征暴敛，从而真正贯彻了重农抑商的治国原则。虽然明代中期开始赋役折银，财政运行大量运用货币化手段，但直至清代中期，来自两税（田赋）的财政收入仍占正式财政收入的75%左右，而取自工商业的财政收入只具有补充性的作用。可是到了晚清，随着外敌入侵与内部叛乱，军费、赔款、债务利息等支出迅速增加。在巨大的支出现实面前，清政府不得不放弃原有的财政原则，努力为不断增长的支出寻找收入支持。于是，管仲学派倡导的商贸立国方略再次浮现并成为主导性原则，而且与汉武帝时期、王安石变法不同的是，在此时一方面工业的重要性超过了纯粹的商业，另一方面私商逐渐代替了官商成为主要经济活动的主体和财政收入来源。

在汉武帝时期与王安石变法时表现出来的重商变异，在清末发展为现代的重商主义。这又有两个方面：一方面是朝廷经济政策转向肯定和扶持工商业活动的发展，它体现了国家职能向现代的转变，另一方面体现为私营工商业的壮大及其逐步现代化。就是说，实践中的重商主义表现在，政府以发展工商业为政策出发点，民间以创办工商业企业为经济活动的重点。

政府发展工商业政策，又包括机构组织设置、法律法规制定、行业政策调整等多个方面。在机构组织设置方面，与帝国时期没有专门的行政机构来管理工商业活动、不将促进工商业发展作为自己的职能相反，清廷正式设立商部后改组为农工商部，并在各地遍设商务局或农工商局，以推动工商实业的发展、沟通官商关系、联络工商从业者、调查商情、保护工商业者利益，它还倡导在各省省城、各大商埠设立商人自己的组织即商务总会，以此为主体来沟通商商关系，突破传统的行会体制壁垒，以集体合作的力量参与外贸竞争。在工商业法律法规制订方面，为提供必要的市场规则与权利保障以促进工商业的发展，清廷制定了《商人通例》《公司律》《公司注册试办章程》《商标注册试办章程》《破产律》等法律。在工商业行业政策调整方面，从清初严格地限制对外贸易，转变为鼓励对外贸易发展，如推动货品改良和出口增加、鼓励工商业者参加国际商品博览会以改进生产并扩大出口，还积极寻找对策来改进茶叶和生丝的生产以恢复传统的优势地位等，另外还积极主动地自开商埠，促进商业贸易的发展。

民间创办工商业企业，除了商人天生的求利动机促动及前述政府政策许可外，还受到外国商业活动的冲击和本国洋务运动等力量的推动。1840年之后，随着五口通商，外国工业产品大量输入。于是商业与商人有了跟以往不同的特征：商业交易的对象从传统农副产品、手工业产品转向机械工业制造品（即"洋货"），商业活动也更加深入到内地城市和乡村；商人中出现新式商人，他们大多由买办商人（受雇于外国洋行、为外国商人服务）转化而来，这些买办商人通过自立商号、创办工业企业，而成为近代工商活动的创办者，他们的商业活动与地位也随之逐渐提高。对于民间创办工商业特别有推动作用的是洋务运动中的"官督商办"政策（在政府监督下，以招商形式引进商人资本创办工业企业）。官督商办政策接续了帝国的某些传统（如王安石变法中的官民合作），又有极强的开创性，为转向重商主义奠定了如下基础：在官方层面上正式肯定了私商和私人资本的地位；充当了重商经济政策的试验田；部分解决了创办近代工业企业的资金与物质基础问题。以至于到19世纪90年代后期,像上海的华新纺织新局这样的由民间资本投资的企业,政府已不再要求实行正式的官方督办。到20世纪前10年,由商人和士绅倡导者创办的现代工业公司大量涌现,使用机器、私人投资、私人管理,已成为这些公司的普遍特征。与此同时,政府也以立法和实际行动来鼓励民间商人和实业家投资创办企业,从而真正实现了现代的重商主义。

## 五、小结

从中华帝国发展历史来看,管仲学派商贸立国原则总体而言始终为商鞅的重农抑商原则所压制,只是在汉武帝改革与王安石变法等短暂时期占据上风,构成某种"重商"的变异。到了晚清乃至民国时期,商贸立国才真正成为现代的重商主义。

从管仲学派的商贸立国方略到晚清时期的重商主义的发展,反映了以下几个方面的时代意义。

第一,它标志着中华国家的经济基础开始从农耕国转为工商国。在农耕经济条件下,管仲的商贸立国原则不可能成为国家治理的主导原则,而只能在前述汉武帝改革与王安石变法时期一时占据上风。晚清政府推行重商主义经济政策,使得工商业活动在地位上不断得以提升,其重要性远远超过了农业,并进而奠定了现代国家的基础,为构建起以资本法则与个人法则为主导的社会政治制度提供了可能条件。

第二,它标志着中国传统社会结构开始出现变化。在"重农抑商"原则的影响下,工商业从业者的地位绝大多数时候都比较低,处于士农工商之末,居于社会结构的底层,其权利和利益谈不上受到多少保护。虽然《管子》中将商人与工匠视为与士、农平行的国之柱石,但在现实中不可能实现。晚清重商主义兴起后,原有的等级结构开始动摇,"士商平等"在观念上开始慢慢确立。工商业从业者纷纷兴实业、扩商权、通商情、开商智,引导着时代潮流,从而为社会各阶层所瞩目。虽然就整体而言,这一现代的社会力量还比较小,但却是引领中国国家转型的重要力量。

第三,它标志着中国工商业经济结构内在格局的一种变化,即从官方垄断工商业向私营工商业经济发展。虽然汉武帝改革与王安石变法时期出现重商变异，但在理念上或实践中却变成官方垄断工商业经济。晚清重商主义的兴起，是在洋务运动的经验和教训基础上进行的，其中一个重要的方面就是政府发现私营工商业的效率远远高于国营工商业，为此从经济政策上对私营工商业给予大力扶持。这是真正现代意义上的重商主义。

# Strategy of Basing National Development on Trade in *Guanzi* and its Fate in the Empire

Liu Shougang

Abstract: During a period of the transformation of Chinese states into an empire, the book *Guanzi* (*Writings of Master Guan*) reflected Guan Zhong's school of thought where national development strategies hinge on trade. These include taking control of resources as a condition for basing national development on trade, using trade to govern and regulate the domestic economy and society, and using trade to win external wars. Accordingly, from the later developments in the history of the Chinese empire, Guan Zhong's school of thought was largely overshadowed by Shang Yang's principle of valuing agriculture and suppressing commerce, except for prevailing for a while when Emperor Wu of Han pushed reforms, and Wang Anshi introduced new policies. During such periods, the country experienced changes in "valuing commerce." It was not until the late Qing Dynasty and the period of the Republic of China that Guan Zhong's strategy developed into modern-day mercantilism and the leading principle of governance.

Keywords: *Guanzi* (*Writings of Master Guan*); Basing national development on trade; Valuing agriculture and suppressing commerce; Fiscal thought

CLC number: F810.2  Document code: B

During the spring and autumn and the Warring States periods, Chinese states (city-states based on their respective populations) were transitioning into an empire underpinned by the land area,① laying the foundation for constructing an imperial system and governing an imperial state for the next 2000 years and beyond. For the vassal states at the time, the rulers and politicians faced the vital issue of how to construct a new system to rapidly boost the power of the states, curb the competition between states, and grasp the opportunity of unifying and leading the country.

In that period, a group of thinkers represented by Guan Zhong emerged. With a thorough grasp and deep thinking of the issues and history of the times, they proposed theories of governance. Further, they actively participated in the reform of the states' systems and practical governance, leaving a valuable wealth of ideas for future generations. The book, *Gaunzi*,② especially reflected Gaun Zhong's school of thought on the governance of an imperial state. It is widely known that the institutional principles and governance strategies of the Chinese Empire in later generations were established when the Qin state unified China. Moreover, the foundation of Qin's system was determined by the Shang Yang reforms. The governance strategy advocated by the Shang Yang reforms and *Shangjun Shu* (*The Book of Lord Shang*) was valuing agriculture and suppressing commerce. In stark contrast to *Shangjun Shu*, *Guanzi* advocated using commerce to govern, which has continued to influence generations. As a governance strategy, valuing agriculture and suppressing commerce has become a fundamental principle and symbol of orthodoxy. However, the strategy of basing national development on trade, as per Guan Zhong and others, had long existed implicitly in the governance of the empires. It became the dominant principle in special periods and herald of modern-time

---

① Liu Shougang. *Lectures on history of public finance in China* [M]. Shanghai: Fudan University Press, 2017.

② All texts of *Guanzi* cited in this article are from the translated and annotated edition by Xie Haofan and Zhu Yingping: *Guan Zi Annotated*, Guizhou People's Press, 1996 edition. In the citations, only the chapter names in *Guanzi* are cited, and the page numbers are not listed.

mercantilism in the national transformation actions of China since the late Qing Dynasty.

*Guanzi* is a widely noted work; nonetheless, there remain many questions about the book and its author. The prevailing view among scholars today is that it was not the work of one person, nor was it completed in a short period. From a modern perspective, the work reveals an alternate path for building and governing Chinese empires. However, whether China could be unified by the Qi state through commerce or construct a different Chinese empire that embodied the ideas of Guan Zhong's school of thought cannot be known.

Therefore, this study examines the content of *Guanzi* and summarizes the ideas of basing national development on trade, tracing the fate of these ideas in the development of later empires.

## I. Resource control as a condition for basing national development on trade

Guan Zhong and the Guan Zhong school were active in a period when the agricultural economy prevailed over industrial production by machines. Therefore, the premise of basing the country's development on trade was that the state (or ruler) must control food and natural resource commodities. In *Guanzi*, four major types of resources—food, currency, salt and iron, and market channels—could be operated via trade for internal governance, external hegemony, and national unity. Of course, the advantages of mastering these resources were not limited to trade operations and implementing state governance ("When the resources are abundant, and the agricultural issues are well managed, there is no need to ask for others' help. There is a pattern when we put it into practice," *Chengma* [*Economic Calculation and Planning*]). It could also realize the "centralization of economic interests controlled by the state" such that people would follow and obey the ruler (Shang Yang also advocated such an idea); "therefore the ruler can determine what to give and what to take and who to be rich and who to be poor. In this way, people will be loyal to the ruler like how they adore the sun and the moon and be close to the ruler like how they treat their parents" (*Guoxu* [*Savings of a State*]). However, the "centralization of economic interests controlled by the state" via commerce, advocated by the Guan Zhong school, was milder than the coercive means used by Shang Yang, which highlights the difference between basing national development on trade and valuing agriculture and suppressing commerce.

First, in the spring and autumn and the Warring States Period, the importance of food for domestic governance and fighting for external hegemony was self-evident. *Shangjun Shu* discusses the issue repeatedly. *Guanzi* also emphasizes that "those who govern the state only need to manage the food" (*Shanzhishu* [*The Best Methods for Insuring Fiscal Control*]). Food is particularly important for the common people: "The five grains, including rice, are vital to the lives of people" (*Guoxu*). Therefore, the key to governing a state lies in food reserves; "the glorified kings of the previous generations knew that food is the foundation for a large population, strong army, vast territory, and wealthy state" (*Mumin*, [*Herding the People*]). "A state that does not produce food will perish, a state that produces food but consumes all can only seek hegemony, and a state that can produce an inexhaustible supply of food can build an empire" (*Zhiguo*, [*Governing a State*]). With abundant food, the morale of the people will rise ("with full granaries, people know the etiquette; with sufficient food and clothing, people can distinguish between honor and disgrace," *Mumin*); the military strength can also be likewise increased ("The source of armed soldiers fundamentally lies in fields and houses," *Chimi* [*Extravagance*]). With sufficient food, people will be induced to migrate from other states, which is also key to collecting various sources of wealth and territorial expansion ("Food can attract people to come; Food can attract wealth; Food can also lead to territorial expansion. When food is abundant, the goods from the whole country will gather here", *Zhiguo*). The abundance of food can also be used to regulate the market and avoid wealth concentration ("Grains are the master of all things", "therefore, a ruler [must] manage the alternating rises and falls of the prices of grains and materials and control the situation [accordingly]," *Guoxu*). Thus, how can a state effectively store more food? *Guanzi* suggested that the first thing to do is to produce as much food as possible. For instance, the ruler must implement policies per the desires of the people to motivate them ("Therefore, fulfilling their four desires, the alienated people will become close," *Mumin*) and draft the people to services at a suitable time. Thus, farming works are not affected ("the rulers who built an empire never drafted people into service during the time for farming for the state to have good harvests," *Chen Chengma*, [*Implementation of Economic Calculation and Planning*]). Moreover, the ruler must ban the lower-end production and trade of luxury goods to increase the labor force ("When the lower-end production and trade of luxury goods are banned, people cannot wander for a living. When the people cannot wander for a living, they must be engaged in agricultural works," *Zhiguo*). Further, the ruler must plan to prevent usury from damaging the interests of farmers ("A farmer must provide for four lenders; therefore, the case when those who escape from taxes are punished and the ruler can still not stop them from fleeing is caused by the lack of food and people having no storage," *Zhiguo*). Furthermore, the ruler must make plans to share the burden between scholars, farmers, merchants, and artisans ("Thus, farmers can focus on farming, and their income can be equal to other vocations. When the farmers focus on farming, fields can be reclaimed, and devious acts will not occur. When fields are reclaimed, crops will increase," *Zhiguo*). Additionally, the ruler must value the importance of land ("Land is the origin of all things and the root of all living things," *Shui Di* [*Water and Land*]) and plan the use of the state's land per different land types ("There are mountainous areas, low-lying water-logged areas, areas half-covered by mountains and half with plains, areas that always suffer from overflow, and areas with soil leakage," *Shanzhishu*), and manage separately. Regarding food production, a state should not demand excessive taxes and levies but conduct market operations while controlling the relationship between grains, currencies, and goods to hold more grains, as later discussed. Once rulers control food resources, they could use them to govern the state and become invincible. "The ruler only needs to closely control the production and reserve of food for all men and women, adults, and children to pay the taxes" (*Guoxu*).

Second, the state must control monetary resources. At the time, currencies were commodity money. The *Guoxu* chapter lists three major types of currencies: "pearls and jade are the superior currencies, gold is the middle currency, and knives and spades are the inferior currencies." *Guanzi* especially emphasizes that a state must control these monetary resources to govern. "For the three kinds of currencies, holding them does not make you feel warm, and eating them does not make you full. The glorified kings of the previous generations use them to control wealth and materials to manage the people's consumption and adequately govern the nation" (*Guoxu*). The essence of using currencies to govern a country is to utilize the relationship between currencies, grains, and gold to adjust the economy and society ("When the ruler can control the balance between food, currencies, and gold, the economic order of the whole country can be stable", *Shanzhishu*). Gold and knife money is the people's means of trade. Therefore, a proficient ruler must master the flow of currencies and control the things crucial to people's lives such that human resources can be used to the greatest extent (*Guoxu*). In the chapters of *Qing Zhong* (*Light and Heavy Theory*), the Guan Zhong school repeatedly mentions that "money is minted and issued by the ruler"—the monarch must grasp the right of issuing currency.

Third, the state should control resources, such as salt and iron. Relative to other vassal states, the Qi state was not rich in arable land resources. However, as it was located on a peninsula, it had coasts and tidal flats that covered vast areas. Hence, Qi could fully develop the marine economy, especially fish and salt resources, giving the state an unparalleled advantage over other vassal states. Indeed, marine resources were developed as early as the Jiang Ziya era, from which the government benefited significantly. This method to generate profit is called the "Great Grand Duke's technique" in later generations. In the chapter *Hai Wang (Building an Empire with Ocean Resources)*, the Guan Zhong school proposed the specialized measures of "state-run mountainous and ocean resources" and "deliberate policy on salt taxes." It urged the Qi state to implement a unified resource commodity management with low consumption elasticity, such as salt and iron ore, to develop corresponding industries. Given that salt and iron are ubiquitous needs, the state could obtain financial benefits by monopolizing the commodities and selling them at higher prices. "Even if the ruler gains a hundred times the benefits, people have no way to avoid it" (*Hai Wang*). Beyond salt and iron, *Guanzi* also advocated for the state to monopolize other natural resources: "If a ruler cannot control his mountain forests, mires, and grasslands, he cannot become the emperor of the whole country" (*Qing Zhong I*). From the perspective of real history, the extent to which resources such as salt and iron had been monopolized by Qi is inconclusive. Therefore, some scholars posit that the chapter *Hai Wang* was written by scholars in the Han Dynasty. Notably, "state-run mountainous and ocean resources" proposed by the Guan Zhong school are not necessarily equal to the policy of the absolute monopoly of salt and iron resources advocated by Sang Hongyang in the Han Dynasty. This is because *Guanzi* repeatedly proposed to cooperate with merchants and disapproved of absolute monopoly: "A better way is to let the people do the business while calculating the asset values and the benefits. The people shall take 70% of the benefits, and the ruler shall take 30% of it" (*Qing Zhong* Ⅱ).

Finally, the state must control the market channels. Channels are also resources. In a state like Qi, the commodity economy had always been relatively developed, given an extensive network of transportation and the importance of its market ("The market gathers the wealth of the whole country, where tens of thousands of people come into contact and gain benefits, and this is reasonable," *Wen* [*Questions*]). The state could naturally not control the market channels by force but rely on public services; for example, *Qing Zhong* Ⅱ suggested building guest houses for merchants. In Qi, Guan Zhong mainly relied on four policies—setting up markets, reducing tariffs, providing high-quality services, and encouraging external trade—to attract "the merchants from different states of the country to Qi like the flow of water." In the chapter *Wen*, the suggestion for a state to control market channels was that "the taxes levied on passing the border should not be levied on the market, and the taxes levied on the market should not be levied on passing the border. Vehicles with no goods should be exempted from taxes, and people delivering goods on foot should also be exempted to attract people from far away. This should be applied to all sixteen regions." Moreover, Guan Zhong set up six artisan and merchant regions (there were 15 scholar and farmer regions), which gave preferential treatments like exemption from military service to artisans and merchants. The purpose was to allow them to concentrate on developing production and commerce and help them teach their children, study skills from each other, and exchange experiences and information (*Xiao Kuang* [*The Last Chapter of Correcting and Supporting the Ruler*]).

## Ⅱ. State governance and domestic economy and societal regulation via trade

The means of trade regards "light and heavy techniques" in *Guanzi*, the concept of which was not inseparable from the market. Thus, it could only be used to govern a state on the premise of the market's existence. Therefore, among Chinese classics, *Guanzi*'s emphasis on the role of the market is rare. It posits that the price of goods should be determined by the free trade in the market ("Market is the indication of the supply and demand of commodities" *Chengma*), and the state can gain information on whether it was prosperous or chaotic from the market ("Through the market, we can know whether the society is prosperous or chaotic and whether the materials are abundant or lacking. However, we cannot affect the quantity of materials through it. There is a pattern when putting it into practice," *Chengma*). The book firmly disapproves of fixed market prices set by the government, mentioning that the balance between supply and demand "cannot be fixed; if it is fixed, it becomes constant; when it is constant, it becomes rigid; when it is rigid, there will be no ups and downs; when there are no ups and downs, all commodities cannot be controlled and used by us" (*Qing Zhong II*).

First, governing the state and regulating the economy and society via trade should translate into a state's control of food accordingly where possible. Given the suggestions that the state should take measures to increase food production, *Guanzi* advocates storing food as much as possible through market trade using the relationship between grain, currency, and goods and motivating the people responsible for each business by increasing the prices of food. "When the ruler has mountains with metals in them, money can be minted. When money can be exchanged for food and distributed as salaries across the state, then all food is in the hand of the state, and the prices can increase ten-fold. Farmers will stay up late and wake up early, increasing production ten-fold willingly. When the value of the five grains is increased ten-fold, the fighters will be loyal to the ruler even if they only receive half of the salary relative to the past. Farmers will stay up late and wake up early, farming non-stop with the greatest effort"

(*Shanzhishu*). The Guan Zhong school envisions taking advantage of the seasonal price changes of food. It suggests buying food at low prices during harvest season and selling at higher prices during the season in which food reserve is exhausted and new crops are yet to mature. Thus, the people would rely on the state's food reserves, and the local leaders cannot control the situation. Hence, the state "provides food and material and gains the recognition of being benevolent while lowering the prices of all goods" (*Shanzhishu*). In *Shanzhishu*, the Guan Zhong school also suggests specific means for the state to use monetary loans to increase fiscal revenue and obtain food from the people. In the first year, when food reserve is exhausted, new crops are yet to mature, and food prices are high, offer monetary loans to the poor. When the prices decrease during the harvest season in autumn, ask them to repay the debt with food per the amount of money borrowed and pay the interest. In the second year, during the time of food deficiency, lend food to the people, and ask them to repay the amount of food per the current prices during the harvest season in autumn (or repay by food) and pay the interest. Thus, the state can increase the food reserve or income. When the ruler has food, he can govern the state effectively.

Second, governing the state and regulating the economy and society via trade should translate into obtaining fiscal revenue for the state's use. Fiscal revenue is an indispensable means of running a state; thus, the Guan Zhong school disapproved of low-taxation policies: "When the taxation is low, the food reserve of the state will be small. Low taxation also leads to an insufficient supply of weapons and tools. When the weapons and tools are insufficient, the furs and silks of vassals cannot be exported. When the food reserve of the state is small, the fighters fall to the lowest ranks and gain no salaries (*Shanzhishu*)." However, the Guan Zhong school did not support levying heavy land taxes on farmers, high tariffs on merchants, or even taxes on houses, trees, and six domestic animals to increase fiscal revenue. They were opposed to temporary tax increases, positing that the best way to collect taxes is "to devise impressive acts benefiting the people and conceal the details when taking away their benefits" (*Guoxu*). Accordingly, "the ruler must not order the collection of taxes door to door but must closely control the production and reserve of food for everyone to pay the taxes" (*Guoxu*). The methods proposed by *Guanzi* for this purpose are as follows. Adopt policies such as "state-run mountainous and ocean resources" to monopolize the selling of salt, iron, and forest resources in a certain form and realize taxation collection by increasing the prices under the cover of voluntary trade. Moreover, use monetary and other means to obtain added value via loans and money-good relationships. Further, trade and generate profits using the market price differences and other huge price differences from information asymmetry. The means to obtain fiscal revenue are the "light and heavy techniques" by *Guanzi*. In the book, the Guan Zhong school advocates for the third method: "buying goods at higher prices when the market prices are low and then selling them at lower prices when the market prices are high," given that "goods are cheap in abundance and expensive when scarce; the prices fall when sold in large quantities and increase when hoarded." As money is completely monopolized by the state via the relationships between money, grains, and goods, the state can control commodity prices and adjust the circulation of commodities——"the ruler understands this, so he will control the money and materials in the state per the supply of materials in the domestic market. When the food is cheap, he uses the money he issues to buy food, and when clothing and silks are cheap, he uses the money he issues to buy cloth and silks. Subsequently, he observes the ups and downs of commodity prices and controls them with the equalization technique. Thus, the commodity prices can be adjusted, and the ruler can benefit" (*Guoxu*).

Third, governing the state and regulating the economy and society via trade should translate into adjusting the income and wealth of the rich and the poor. One principle that applies to ancient and modern times is that a significant disparity between rich and poor causes an imbalance in societal forces, affecting the stability of the state. "The food of each person is supposed to be secured by a certain area of the field. Therefore, why are there still people suffering from hunger and cold in the streets and alleys? It is because food is being hoarded by some people. Now, my ruler, you mint the money and people use it to trade, and each person is supposed to have hundreds and thousands of money. Why are some people still selling their children? It is because the money is saved up by some people. Hence, if the ruler cannot distribute the hoarded food, adjust the prices, and disperse the accumulated wealth, even if he strengthens the agriculture, supervises the production, and endlessly reclaims wasteland and mints money, the people will still be poor" (*Qing Zhong I*). The *Guoxu* chapter explains that the uneven distribution of wealth in society is an actual and objective reality, listing several reasons: the changes in different farming seasons, the number of harvests in the year, the tightness of taxation collection, differences in the intelligence of people, and the deliberate manipulation and exploitation by the minority of people. If "the ruler cannot adjust" such differences, then "the rich will earn a hundred times more profits by exploiting the weaknesses of people" (*Guoxu*). How can the state adjust this disparity between rich and poor? Although *Guanzi* posits that the ruler of a state must make plans and adjust the disparity with laws, "the failure in implementing the law and governing the people are the reasons for the disparity between rich and poor in the society" (*Guoxu*). However, the primary method should be the means of trade: "Therefore, any state that cannot adjust the wealth of people cannot achieve prosperity; without the insight in commerce from the beginning to end, the management cannot be at its best" (*Kuidu* [*Estimations*]). For example, the state can intervene in market operations by adjusting materials and ensuring the supply of food to prevent powerful merchants from exploiting the people, thereby protecting people's normal life and production. Moreover, food, materials, or money held by the state were used to lend, sell, or rent to poor farmers during the agricultural season or the season when food reserve is exhausted and when new crops are yet to mature. The purpose was to "store up in fat years to make up for lean ones" and adjust the amount of food consumed by people. The state can also use public work construction to create jobs instead of engaging in direct alms-giving. Further, public spending can be expanded to the point of extravagance to relieve the poor (the extravagent techniques are mentioned in *Chimi*).

Governing the country via trade is also reflected in *Guanzi*'s emphasis on merchants as a social class, which is rare in Chinese scholarly works. In governing the state and fighting for hegemony across the country, Guan Zhong encouraged people to sell their agricultural and sideline products "everywhere across the country," vigorously develop commerce, and strongly acknowledge the positive role of the market in promoting agricultural production. The aim was to enrich the country and strengthen the army. "The market gathers the wealth of the whole country, where tens of thousands of people come in to contact and gain benefits" (*Chimi*), and it can "encourage production such that the business can be developed" (*Chimi*). Meanwhile, Guan Zhong vigorously attempted to raise the social status of merchants, unlike Shang Yang, who values agriculture and suppresses commerce. Merchants were considered a pillar of a state like scholars, farmers, and artisans by *Guanzi*. "The four types of people—scholars, farmers, artisans, and merchants—are the pillars of a state" (*Xiao Kuang*). The book also strongly acknowledges the wisdom of merchants in trade activities and their positive role in the economy. "Let the merchants live in a concentrated area to observe the omens of bad years and hunger, analyze the changes in the state, watch the situations of the four seasons, and closely monitor the goods of their townships so that they can predict the market prices. They carry the cargoes, drive cattle and horses, and travel everywhere. They predict the quantity of materials needed, estimate the prices of goods, use what they have to exchange for what they do not, buy at low prices, and sell at high prices. Therefore, treasures like pheasant feathers and yak tails flow in without searching. Products like bamboo arrows are abundant in the state. Weird products usually flow in, while precious objects amass" (*Xiao Kuang*).

## III. Using trade as a means to win external wars

In the real world with many vassal lords, how can a state fight for hegemony or even unify the country, completing the inner mission of an empire? The idea of Shang Yang was straightforward—there should be sufficient food and soldiers with enthusiasm. *Guanzi* attached considerable importance to food and wars ("When a state is wealthy, the army can be strong. A strong army wins wars, and a state that wins wars will have a larger territory," *Zhiguo*). However, *Guanzi* posits that food alone was inadequate for fighting for hegemony. While wars might not be essential in fighting for hegemony or even unifying the country, the means of trade might also be used to achieve the same purpose. In the chapter *Dishu* [*Fiscal Management based on Geography*], the Guan Zhong school notes that in a world full of vassal lords, reliance on abundant food is dangerous. "When a state is wealthy, and the money and materials are abundant, but without good management, the wealth will be robbed by other states in the country. When there are good crops, although we have low prices and other states have high prices, the crops will also be robbed by other states in the country. Thus, the people of our states will become the prey of other states in the country. Those proficient at governing a state should manage it like sailing a ship on the sea. They would watch the origins of the winds; when the prices in other states are high, our prices should also be high. If the prices in other states are low, our prices should also be low. If the prices in other states are high while only our prices are low, the wealth of our state will be robbed by other states in the country." The Guan Zhong school advocates that a state should use more means of trade and wage more trade wars to fight for hegemony and unify the country.

The chapters of *Qing Zhong* of *Guanzi* document many fascinating stories of trade wars. Scholars of later generations generally believe that most trade wars were fictional. Although scholars with traditional thoughts in the imperial period had a low opinion of such fiction, even considering them as coarse, people today who are familiar with trade wars have to be amazed at the genius and wisdom within the imaginary cases.

Considering these cases, Guan Zhong's use of trade to win external competition can be divided into at least two categories.

The first category is represented by the "stone disc plot" and "silver grass plot" in *Qing Zhong IV*. Such plots used Qi's hegemony to get close to the King of Zhou and used the King's remaining ceremonial power to make huge profits for Qi. For example, regarding the famous "stone disc plot," Guan Zhong first ordered Qi's skilled craftspeople to manufacture a batch of stone disks of different standards. Subsequently, Guan Zhong asked the King of Zhou to make an order requesting the ruler of Qi to induce other vassal lords in the country to worship at the ancestral temple of the Zhou royal family, carrying "vermilion bows" of the Zhou royal family and "stone disks" of Qi before they could join the ceremony. Therefore, the vassal lords across the country brought valuables and treasures of their states to Qi to exchange for stone disks, and Qi quickly made up for the fiscal deficit from the Kuiqiu political conference. The "silver grass plot" employs a similar trick. The difference was that when the vassal lords join the Feng-Shen (praying to the heaven) ceremony of the King of Zhou, they must spend a significant amount of money in exchange for the Zhou royal family's tribute, the "silver grass," to use as the mat in the sacrifice ceremony. The King of Zhou earned abundant money within a few days; thus, he "did not ask for tributes in the following seven years." The plot helped the King of Zhou while raising the level of Qi as a hegemony. It solved the question raised by Duke Huan of Qi: "The King of Zhou is short of money, and the vassal lords refuse to pay whenever he asks for contributions. Are there any methods to solve this problem?" (*Qing Zhong IV*).

Another category of Guan Zhong's strategy involves Qi using its strong financial resources to buy specific commodities from the enemy states in large quantities, thereby disrupting its economic cycle of production and controlling the enemy states with economic means. The "Hengshan plot" in *Qing Zhong V* is a typical example of such strategies. First, Guan Zhong suggested that the ruler of Qi must "buy the Hengshan state's weapons at high prices and sell them," deliberately causing a manic rush to buy Hengshan's weapons by other states such that Hengshan's people "abandoned the essential work and devoted to developing the techniques of making weapons." The "essential work" refers to agriculture. Subsequently, Qi bought food from the Zhao state at prices higher than Zhao's domestic food purchase price; thus, many states, including Hengshan, sold food to Qi. After several months, Qi suddenly announced to close its borders and stop all trading with neighboring states. At this time in Hengshan, the production cycle of agriculture had been disrupted by the production of weapons, while much of the state's food reserve had been sold to Qi, exhausting the power of the state. About to be carved up by the states of Qi and Lu, "Hengshan estimated its power and believed it had no forces to face two enemies; thus, it finally surrendered to Qi." The idea in *Qing Zhong I* is that Qi could use the treasures produced by four foreign countries (pearls and ivory from Wu and Yue states, furs from Joseon, high-quality jades and stones from Kunlun, white jade disks from Yuzhi) as currencies to raise their values for the people and goods of those states to reach Qi from afar. Thus, with such economical means, the purpose of conquering or attracting enemy states was achieved: "Therefore, if no one manages the treasures and deals with the economic issues in different regions, then the states from far and near cannot benefit each other, and the four foreign countries will no longer come to pay respect. " *Qing Zhong V* also proposes a strategy to conquer an enemy by manipulating the food market—using ingenious means (purchasing ti, a type of silk, from the enemy state "Luliang" at a high price) to disrupt the agricultural production of the enemy state (the ruler of Luliang ordered his people to give up food production and focus on weaving ti). Hence, the enemy state would suffer food shortages and must rely on Qi's supply to subjugate the enemy. *Qing Zhong II* also imagines that Qi could repeatedly use the relationship between the prices of salt and food to become richer while other states became poorer. *Qing Zhong V* imagined Qi using its firewood production, deer, and fox furs to conquer the Ju, Chu, and Dai states, respectively. These are the cases of using means of trade to win other states in the country.

## IV. Advancements of basing national development on trade in later generations

The principle of basing national development on trade advocated by the Guan Zhong school, which had become the opposite of the orthodox principle of "valuing agriculture and suppressing commerce" in empire governance in later generations, comprises two aspects. First, it comprises using commercial means to address the state-people relationship, including substituting monetary finance for physical finance, using revenues to induce (voluntary trade) favorable behavior to fulfill the tasks of state governance. Second, it comprises emphasizing commerce activities, including private and government merchant activities (including handicrafts). In the era of an imperial agricultural economy, "valuing agriculture," which also means valuing food production and raising the legal status of farmers, had not induced objections from scholars of different schools at the ideological level. However, the actual situation could be different. The Guan Zhong school of thought advocated for the use of commercial principles to address the state-people relationship. Despite being used in practice by successive dynasties, Confucian scholars had always opposed it from the perspective of the principle of valuing agriculture and suppressing commerce. They were even more opposed to the government's emphasis on private or government merchant activities, regarding them as an unforgivable behavior of "valuing commerce." Nevertheless, in certain periods when China was an empire, the rulers of the country employed more ideas from the Guan Zhong school of thought and "valued commerce" more, which can be described as "mutations of valuing commerce."

Per the different attitudes of the country toward commercial activities, throughout the two thousand years when China was an empire, there were at least three types of practices to address private and government merchant activities. First, the activities of private and government merchants were both suppressed—industrial and commercial activities were suppressed wholesale. The social status of private merchants degraded, while the state was prevented from obtaining fiscal revenues from industrial and commercial activities through government merchant activities. Second, suppressing private merchants and supporting government merchants. People were discouraged from engaging in private industrial and commercial activities, while the state actively developed government-run industry and commerce to obtain fiscal revenues or fulfill other purposes. Third, equal emphasis was placed on private and government merchants. While encouraging people to engage in private industrial and commercial activities, the state also developed government-run industry and commerce to obtain fiscal revenues and fulfill other purposes in the form of taxation or commercial means. The first type is a comprehensive suppression of commerce, which, in theory, best meets the requirements of "valuing agriculture and suppressing commerce. " Therefore, it was regarded by later Confucian scholars as the most orthodox governance principle of the empire. The second and third types of practices were regarded by orthodox Confucian scholars as "valuing commerce" and were considered to be violations of the principle. The two practices were mutations of valuing commerce and were prominently reflected when Emperor Wu of Han implemented reforms, and Wang Anshi introduced new policies. Only until the Self-Strengthening Movement during the late Qing Dynasty did a transformation to modern mercantilism fully emerge beyond the scope of mutations of valuing commerce. Logically, there could be a fourth type of attitude toward commercial activities to support private merchants and suppress government merchants. However, in reality, such an attitude exists only in modern liberal economies but never in imperial times nor in today's China. The principle of valuing agriculture and suppressing commerce established by Shang Yang reforms for the Qin state had long prevailed in the construction of the imperial state system and the financial activities regarding the governance of the empire. It had become the orthodox principle that had dominated subsequent imperial governments for more than 2,000 years. Although the strategy of basing national development on trade advocated by the Guan Zhong school had long been suppressed, it had long existed implicitly in the operation of the imperial system. Further, it had become the dominant principle in special periods (mutations of valuing commerce and transformation to mercantilism).

## 1. Mutations of valuing commerce when Emperor Wu of Han implemented reforms

In the early Han Dynasty, the imperial system was constructed per the principle of valuing agriculture and suppressing commerce. The low-taxation policy of the principle shaped the expenditures of the country during peaceful times (especially when the country adopted a passive and tolerant military strategy). Regarding the financial management in governance of the country, it fully meets the requirements of "valuing agriculture," while the period of the "Rule of Wen and Jing" that adopted the policy has been praised by later scholars.

However, the government in the early Han Dynasty emphasized agriculture and adopted a legal measure of "degrading merchants" (Emperor Gaozu banned merchants from wearing silks or riding in cars and increased their rents and taxes to induce economic distress and humiliation, *the Treatise of the Balanced Standard, Shi Ji [Records of the Grand Historian]*). Nevertheless, the suppression of merchants was not practiced in reality. It is reflected in the following two aspects. First, as the people lived in destitution, while the management ability was weak during the early Han Dynasty, the government had no choice but to allow the people (mainly nobles, bureaucrats, big large landowners, and powerful merchants) to develop natural resources such as copper, iron, and salt or even allow private forces to mint money. Hence, private merchants and tycoons with privileges accumulated wealth. Second, given the low land tax and the lack of state funds, the government in the early Han Dynasty had to develop the poll taxes (adult, children, and military taxes) as the main source of income (the population tended to live in clusters, and the number of people was easier to calculate. The household registration system at that time could also support the collection of taxes). Such means of collecting fiscal revenue are the "light rents and heavy duties." Thus, the people had to sell food and other materials in exchange for money to pay the poll taxes, while the government had to buy materials in the market after collecting the poll taxes, creating an abnormally prosperous commercial atmosphere.

More than 70 years after the establishment of the Han Dynasty, Emperor Wu of Han, a man with considerable talent and bold strategies, assumed power, and the Han Empire began to show its instinct to expand externally. Regarding finance, military spending increased drastically, and the savings of previous generations were exhausted within a short period. Coupled with the frequent occurrence of natural disasters and the subsequent increase in the state's expenditures on disaster relief, the government encountered a deficit crisis. At this point, to increase the sources of fiscal revenues, fiscal reforms were necessary. Moreover, Emperor Wu of Han also needed to use financial means to stop the tycoons in the country for expanding their power and restoring the political order and balance of forces in society. Therefore, Emperor Wu of Han launched fiscal reforms to expand fiscal revenue and curb the power of tycoons. He used the "valuing commerce" policy, which was criticized by later scholars.

The policy reflected the extensive use of monetary means and the principle of interests to govern the country while suppressing private merchants and developing government merchants. It also comprised the following aspects. First, it employs currency reform to centralize power and seize the wealth of powerful tycoons, especially the policy implemented by Sang Hongyang in 113 BC, which allowed the central government to monopolize the right to issue currency completely. Second, it employs the methods of Suan Min and Gao Min—which involved levying property tax and encouraging whistle-blowing of tax evasion—to increase fiscal revenue and reduce the financial strength of powerful tycoons. Third, it adjusts the ways of financial management, monopolizing the sale of salt and iron to seize the wealth of tycoons, as vigorously implemented by Sang Hongyang in 110 BC. Fourth, it employs other commercial means, such as the methods of balanced delivery burden and controlling prices, atonement for crimes with money and grains, and the sale of official positions and titles.

## 2. Mutations of valuing commerce during Wang Anshi's reforms

At the beginning of the Song Dynasty, there was a continued pattern of struggling to survive since the Five Dynasties and Ten Kingdoms period and the general trend of commercialization of the society and economy. Therefore, although the status of "valuing agriculture and suppressing commerce" as a principle of governing the country had not been threatened, the government employed "valuing commerce" as a national policy to a certain extent. The emphasis on commerce was reflected as follows: (1) abandoning many discriminatory policies against merchants in political, economic, and social life; (2) widely opening the economic field to private merchants; (3) developing societal management in a direction beneficial to commercial activities, completely abolishing the fixed-point and fixed-time trading system of markets, and fully opening up the economic life in cities; (4) formulating systematic regulations for the collection of business taxes and establishing a collection network of business taxes covering urban and rural areas. Business taxes and the income from manufacturing and commerce became important sources of fiscal revenue. Therefore, in the Song Dynasty, the fiscal revenue from manufacturing and commerce occupied a relatively large proportion of the national finance, and the amount usually exceeded those from grain and material taxes, collected twice a year (two-time tax). Moreover, unlike the policy of Emperor Wu of Han, which supported government merchants and suppressed private merchants, private merchants were the principals of commercial activities in the Song Dynasty. The income from manufacturing and commerce was mainly from the Jin Que income (monopoly system)[①] from trading resource commodities that generated huge profits, where private merchants were widely involved. Furthermore, the business tax levied on general commodities was a major source of income.

When Emperor Shenzong of Song ascended the throne, the government

---

[①] The fiscal revenue from levying taxes on resource commodities that generate huge profits in the Song Dynasty is called the "Jin Que income" by Wang Shengduo. It refers to "the mixed application of systems by the government, where the systems included direct monopoly of sale, joint venture and sharing of profits by the government and merchants derived from the monopoly of sale, and levying heavy production and sale taxes on certain commodities with the support of strict laws and strict measures," in which private merchants were widely involved (Wang Shengduo: *Financial History of the Song Dynasty*, Zhonghua Book Company, 1995 edition, p. 243).

faced a serious deficit crisis. How could the income crisis be solved to achieve good governance? Wang Anshi firmly opposed simply collecting money from the people, as this kind of practice was like "closing the door and doing business with one's son, where none of the wealth outside the door can get inside. Although the money of the son is fully obtained, the wealth does not increase" (*A letter to Yunpan* [*transportation officer*] *Ma*). He inherited the strategy of basing national development on trade advocated by the Guan Zhong school and agreed that "the country can have sufficient income without levying more taxes on the people." However, he opposed (at least at the ideological level) the reform method of Emperor Wu of Han, which developed monopoly government merchants to obtain fiscal revenues. He proposed the concept of "wealth management" to use dynamic wealth generation and Pareto improvement (improving the utility of one party without harming or even increasing the utility of the other party) to generate more revenue on the premise of not harming the people. He believed fiscal revenue could be dramatically increased based on production development. "As the country forces are used to generate wealth for the whole country, such wealth is used to cover country expenses. Regarding the governance of the country since ancient times, insufficient wealth has never become a problem that affects the whole country; rather, the problem is caused by wealth mismanagement (*A Letter Speaking out Matters to Emperor Renzong*)." "The financial problems of the state are caused by uncontrolled spending and losing the ways to generate wealth" (*A letter to Yunpan Ma*). He notes the following: "the wealth of a family is based on that of the state, and the wealth of the state is based on that of the people. To generate wealth for the whole people, we must develop its nature" (*A letter to Yunpan Ma*). Obviously, this is an idea about the "dynamic" generation of money.

From the perspective of modern finance, there are a few ways to generate wealth dynamically, and Wang Anshi's reform had practiced the methods.

The first way is to develop production and create added value, as embodied in the *Farmland Irrigation Law*. Wang Anshi tried to develop production by vigorously developing farmland water irrigation and encouraging the advancement of agricultural technology to increase the benefits for officials and the people.

The second way is to increase the utility of officials and the people through voluntary trade, as per the "Policy of Service Exemption" and the "Horse Policy." The "Policy of Service Exemption" allows those reluctant to participate in mandatory services to pay in exchange for exemption, while officials used the money to hire workers. The utility of the people exempted increased, while the profit of the government increased, as the income was higher than the expenditure. According to the "Horse Policy," officials subsidized horse breeding by the people to replace government-run ranches that cost heaps of money and generated extremely poor results, reducing government expenses while increasing the income of horse breeders.

The third way is to obtain fiscal revenue by deepening the market as per the "Green Crops Policy" and the "Market Exchange Policy." In the Song Dynasty's economic development, requirements were imposed on capital borrowing. With Two-Time tax and business tax measures, the state collected huge amounts of money and food but could not generate wealth if kept in the treasury. Therefore, Wang Anshi adopted the "Green Crops Policy" that lends government money and food to the people at an interest rate lower than that of private-run usury. The implementation of the policy earned interests for the officials while helping the people survive the spring famine when food reserve is exhausted and new crops are yet to mature. The "Market Exchange Policy" stipulated the establishment of institutions to provide low-interest loans to merchants or loans to government-run businesses for purchasing goods that could not be sold by traveling merchants.

The goods would be stored until it was suitable to sell. Thus, money and food resources in the government treasury became capital commodities.

The fourth way is to increase fiscal revenue by strengthening fiscal management as per the "Land Survey and Equitable Tax Policy." "Land Survey" means surveying the land situation and organizing its accounts carefully. "Equitable Tax" means collecting tax per unit acre. Beyond increasing fiscal revenue, it also reduced the burden on ordinary people.

Wang Anshi emphasizes using commercial means to increase fiscal revenue. Regarding the principals (private and government merchants) of commercial activities, Wang Anshi did not agree with operating businesses with the monopoly of government and private merchants, at least in the early days of the reform. However, during the reform process, the state-run commercial institutions relied on monopoly privileges to generate profits because of their inherent inefficiency. Therefore, Wang Anshi used means of business operation to increase the state's wealth, which eventually became state monopolies, and this happened in the fields of tea, salt, wine, mining, and metallurgy. The Office of Market Exchange, responsible for the Market Exchange Policy, also gradually turned into an official commercial organization with a monopoly position, as all ills of state-run businesses criticized by scholars emerged. For example, "the office that has monopolized the market sells ice so that the ordinary people cannot sell their ice. When the office sells combs and sesame, they become expensive." (*Extended Continuation to Zizhi Tongjian*, Volume 236).

## 3. Transformation to mercantilism emerged in the late Qing Dynasty

In the early Ming Dynasty, given the lessons learned in the Song and Yuan dynasties, the imperial government reaffirmed the status of the Two-Time tax as the authoritative fiscal revenue of the state and reestablished a simple land tax system across the country with land as the anchor. Meanwhile, the Ming government divided people into different groups and rebuilt a system of compulsory services that required people to serve themselves. Thus, the Ming government rebuilt a financial system focusing on the acquisition of food, labor, and other in-kind income based on land and people. However, the fiscal revenue from manufacturing and commerce was scanty. Obtaining fiscal revenue by levying taxes on manufacturing and commerce was considered as extorting excessive taxes, thereby truly implementing the governance principle of valuing agriculture and suppressing commerce. Although silver taxation started to be applied in the mid-Ming Dynasty, and many monetary means were used in finance, until the mid-Qing Dynasty, the fiscal revenue from the Two-Time tax (land tax) still accounted for 75% of the official fiscal revenue. The fiscal revenue from manufacturing and commerce was only complementary. Nevertheless, in the late Qing Dynasty, given the invasion of foreign enemies and internal rebellions, the expenditures in military spending, indemnities, and debt interests increased rapidly. Given the reality of huge expenditures, the Qing government abandoned its original fiscal principles and sought revenue to cover the ever-increasing expenditures. Hence, the strategy of basing national development on trade as per the Guan Zhong school emerged again and became the dominant principle. What was different from the era of Emperor Wu of Han and Wang Anshi reforms was that the importance of manufacturing at the time had exceeded pure commerce. Private merchants had gradually replaced government merchants as the principal of major economic activities and source of fiscal revenue.

The valuing commerce mutations in the era of Emperor Wu of Han and Wang Anshi reforms developed into modern mercantilism in the late Qing Dynasty. It comprises two aspects. First, the government's economic policy affirmed and supported the development of manufacturing and commercial activities, which reflected the transformation of the state's functions to modernity. Moreover, it was reflected in the expansion of private manufacturing and commerce and their gradual modernization. Mercantilism in practice was manifested in that the government considered the development of manufacturing and commerce as the policy starting point. The private sector considered the establishment of manufacturing and commercial enterprises as the focus of economic activities.

The government's efforts in developing manufacturing and commercial policies included various aspects, such as establishing institutions and organizations, formulating laws and regulations, and adjusting industry policies. Regarding the establishment of institutions and organizations, there had been no specialized administrative agency to manage manufacturing and commercial activities in the imperial era. The governments did not consider the promotion of manufacturing and commercial development as their functions. However, the Qing court formally established the Ministry of Commerce, which was reorganized into the Ministry of Agriculture, Manufacturing and Commerce. Bureaus of Commerce or Bureaus of Agriculture, Manufacturing, and Commerce were established everywhere across the country. The objectives were to develop manufacturing and commerce, facilitate communication between officials and businesspersons, contact manufacturing and commercial personnel, investigate business conditions, and protect the interests of manufacturing and commercial operators. Moreover, it advocated for businesspersons to establish their own organizations, namely commerce associations, in provincial capitals and major commercial ports. The aim was to promote the relationship between businesspersons through the associations, break through the barriers of the traditional guild system, and participate in foreign trade competition through the power of cooperation. Regarding the formulation of laws and regulations for manufacturing and commercial activities to set out necessary market rules and provide rights protection to promote the development of manufacturing and commerce, the Qing court formulated laws including the following: *General Regulations for Merchants*, *Company Law*, *Trial*

*Regulations for Company Registration*, *Trial Regulations for Trademark Registration*, and *Bankruptcy Regulations*. Regarding the adjustment of industry policies for manufacturing and commercial activities, from the strict restriction of foreign trade in the early Qing Dynasty, the government encouraged the development of foreign trade. The measures included promoting the improvement of goods and increasing exports and encouraging manufacturing and commercial operators to participate in international commodity fairs to improve production and expand exports. It also actively sought measures to improve the production of tea and raw silks to restore the traditional dominant position of the country in the industry while proactively opening commercial ports to promote the development of commercial trade.

When the people set up manufacturing and commercial enterprises privately, beyond being induced by the natural motive of businesspersons to seek profit and affected by the permission of the government via the abovementioned policies, they were also affected by forces such as the impact of foreign business activities and the domestic Self-Strengthening Movement. After 1840, when the five treaty ports were opened, foreign industrial products were imported in large quantities. Thus, commerce and businesspersons started to have new characteristics. The targets of trade changed from traditional agricultural and sideline and handicraft products to machine-manufactured products (i. e., foreign goods). Further, the commercial activities operated deeper into inland cities and villages. New types of businesspersons also appeared, most of whom were compradors (merchants hired by foreign firms and serving foreign businesspersons) in the past. They set up manufacturing enterprises by establishing their own companies and became founders of modern manufacturing and commercial activities. Their commercial activities and statuses had also gradually advanced. What had particularly promoted the private sector to set up manufacturing and commercial enterprises was the policy of "government supervision and merchant operation" (under the supervision of the government, capitals of businesspersons were introduced to establish manufacturing enterprises in the form of investment promotion) implemented during the Self-Strengthening Movement. The policy of "government supervision and merchant operation" continued some of the empire's traditions (such as the cooperation between officials and the people in Wang Anshi reforms) while being extremely groundbreaking, laying the following foundations for the transformation to mercantilism. At the official level, the status of private business and capital was formally recognized; it served as a test field for mercantilist economic policies and partially solved the problems of the capital and material basis in establishing modern manufacturing enterprises. Hence, by the late 1890s, for enterprises invested by private capital, such as the New Bureau of Huaxin Textiles of Shanghai, the government no longer requested formal official supervision. By the first decade of the 20th century, modern manufacturing companies founded by pioneers among businesspersons and the gentry mushroomed. The common features of these companies include using machines and being invested and managed by the private sector. Meanwhile, with legislation and actions, the government also encouraged non-governmental businesspersons and industrialists to invest and set up enterprises, truly realizing modern mercantilism.

## V. Conclusion

Judging from the developments in the history of the Chinese empire, the Guan Zhong school's principle of basing national development on trade had always been suppressed by Shang Yang's principle of valuing agriculture and suppressing commerce, except for prevailing during a short period when Emperor Wu of Han pushed reforms, and Wang Anshi introduced new policies. During such periods, the country experienced "valuing commerce" mutations. In the late Qing Dynasty and the period of the Republic of China, Guan Zhong's school of thought transformed into modern mercantilism.

From the evolution from the strategy of basing national development on trade to mercantilism in the late Qing Dynasty, the significance of the times is reflected in the following aspects.

First, it marks the transformation of China's economic foundation from an agricultural country to a commercial and manufacturing country. Retrained by the conditions of an agrarian economy, Guan Zhong's school of thought could not become the dominant principle of the governance of the country. It could only prevail temporarily during the period of Emperor Wu of Han's reform and Wang Anshi's reform. The late Qing Dynasty government implemented mercantilist economic policies; thus, the status of manufacturing and commercial activities improved continuously, surpassing that of agriculture. Hence, the foundation of a modern country was laid, as it provided the conditions that allow the construction of social and political systems led by capitalism and individualism.

Second, it marks the beginning of changes in the traditional Chinese social structure. Under the influence of the principle of "valuing agriculture and suppressing commerce," the status of manufacturing and commercial operators had been relatively low most of the time. They held the lowest rank among scholars, farmers, artisans, and merchants, living at the bottom of the social hierarchy, and their rights and interests were hardly protected. Although *Guanzi* regards merchants and artisans as the pillars of the country, similar to scholars and farmers, this view was never realized in reality. After the rise of mercantilism in the late Qing Dynasty, the original hierarchical structure become unstable, and the concept of "equality of scholars and businesspersons" began to be gradually established. The manufacturing and commercial operators were devoted to developing the industries, expanding the business rights, strengthening the communication between businesspersons, and advancing their knowledge in commerce, thereby leading the trend of the times and attracting attention from all walks of life. Although this modern social force remained relatively weak, it was an important power that led to the transformation of China as a country.

Third, it marks a change in the internal pattern of China's manufacturing and commercial economic structure—the development from an economy with the government monopolizing the manufacturing and commercial sectors to an economy dominated by private manufacturing and commercial activities. Although there had been mutations in valuing commerce during the period of Emperor Wu of Han's reforms and Wang Anshi's reforms, at ideological and practical levels, the government finally monopolized the manufacturing and commercial economy. The rise of mercantilism in the late Qing Dynasty was conducted based on the experience and lessons from the Self-Strengthening Movement. One important aspect was that the government discovered that the efficiency of private-run manufacturing and commerce was much higher than that of state-run manufacturing and commerce. Thus, it provided strong support to private-run manufacturing and commerce through economic policies. This is mercantilism in the true modern sense.